Education and the Culture of Consumption

For nearly 200 years the organisational form of the school has changed little. Bureaucracy has been its enduring form. The school has prepared the worker for the factory of mass production. It has created the 'mass consumer' to be content with accepting what is on offer, not what is wanted. However, a 'revised' educational code appears to be emerging. This code centres upon the concept of 'personalisation', which operates at two levels: first, as a new mode of public service delivery; and second, as a new 'grammar' for the school, with new flexibilities of structure and pedagogical process. Personalisation has its intellectual roots in marketing theory, not in educational theory, and is the facilitator of 'education for consumption'. It allows for the 'market' to suffuse even more the fabric of education, albeit under the democratic-sounding call of freedom of choice.

Education and the Culture of Consumption raises many questions about personalisation which policy-makers seem prone to avoid:

- Why, now, are we concerned about personalisation?
- What are its theoretical foundations?
- What are its pedagogical, curricular and organisational consequences?
- What are the consequences for social justice of personalisation?
- Does personalisation diminish the socialising function of the school, or does it simply mean that the only thing we share is that we have the right to personalised service?

All this leads the author to consider an important question for education: does personalisation mark a new regulatory code for education, one which corresponds with both the new work-order of production and with the makeover-prone tendencies of consumers?

The book will be of great interest to postgraduate students and academics studying in the fields of education policy and the social foundations of education, and will also be relevant to students studying public policy, especially health care and social care, and public management.

David Hartley is Honorary Senior Research Fellow at the Department of Education, University of Oxford, UK.

Education and the Culture of Consumption

Personalisation and the social order

David Hartley

Routledge
Taylor & Francis Group

LONDON AND NEW YORK

First published 2012
by Routledge
2 Park Square, Milton Park, Abingdon, Oxon OX14 4RN

Simultaneously published in the USA and Canada
by Routledge
711 Third Avenue, New York, NY 10017

Routledge is an imprint of the Taylor & Francis Group, an informa business

British Library Cataloguing in Publication Data
A catalogue record for this book is available from the British Library

Library of Congress Cataloging in Publication Data
Hartley, David, 1945-
    Education and the culture of consumption : personalisation and the
    social order / David Hartley.
        p. cm.
    ISBN 978-0-415-59882-8 (hardback) — ISBN 978-0-415-59883-5
    (paperback) — ISBN 978-0-203-81768-1 (e-book)   1. Education—
    Economic aspects.   2. Education—Marketing.   3. Individualized
    instruction.   4. Consumption (Economics)   I. Title.
    LC65.H38 2012
    338.4737—dc23

ISBN: 978-0-415-59882-8 (hbk)
ISBN: 978-0-415-59883-5 (pbk)
ISBN: 978-0-203-81768-1 (ebk)

Typeset in Galliard
by RefineCatch Ltd, Bungay, Suffolk

MIX
Paper from
responsible sources
FSC
www.fsc.org   FSC® C004839

Printed and bound in Great Britain by the MPG Books Group

For Bion Solsona-Tenedor

Contents

1   Introduction

The municipal rubbish-dump near to where I live is open on a Sunday, a day when one might be forgiven for thinking that business would surely not be too brisk. But normally it is, with a long queue of cars waiting to enter the site, especially in the afternoon. It is a drive-through arrangement and the road within the site forms a long horse-shoe shape. Tangential to this road are small bays in which cars can be parked while the items are unloaded into large metal skips and containers. Each off-loading bay relates to a particular category of rubbish: batteries, clothing, footwear, glass, plastics, paper, cardboard, wood, metal, green waste, and so on. It is intended to be a slick operation, but it assumes that you, the 'disposer', know how to classify correctly the items which are to be thrown away, and it also helps if the sequence of the bays is known before you enter the site: 'glass', for example, comes before 'cardboard' (but not before 'paper').

Rubbish is usually associated with messiness, but at the dump there is a strong classification and demarcation of space; and there are clear procedures. Unless you have only a few items to dispose of, going to the dump requires of you a good deal of planning. You will need to arrange the order of goods in your car (if you have one) so that it matches the order in which they will be discarded at the site. In spite of this quest for good order, the possibilities for confusion and category-error are considerable. Take a book: if it is hard-backed, does it go in 'cardboard', or in 'paper'? Or a coat-hanger: if it is a plastic-coated wire-hanger, does it go in metal or plastics (which may be 'hard' or 'soft')? The staff at the dump are clearly visible, with brightly coloured vests. Each staff-member oversees about two categories of rubbish, and inspects any bag or box which is to be emptied. Anyone who has furtively mixed in some of the wrong type of waste with the correct type will be despatched, without a nice smile from the overseer, to the correct bay. On a busy day this redirected 'traffic' causes much congestion. If you were mistakenly to drive past the off-loading bay which you require then you cannot just reverse your car (as you would reverse a shopping-cart in a supermarket). Instead, it is necessary to go forward with the flow; there is nothing for it but to complete another circuit. What was meant to be a smooth operation can so easily become fraught. If it does, then you must navigate your exit as best you can. What adds to the frustration is that there are no spaces where the exhausted depositor can calm down. It is impossible to park your car and to wander about the wasteland;

it is very much a matter of drop and go. To be sure, the *flâneur* has no place here, except for those who lurk in search of 'rich pickings'.

About 15 miles from the dump is a purpose-built 'village' which contains about 130 designer-brand boutiques, together with a few cafes. All of these are arranged either side of the pedestrian-only 'street'. Most of the shops are on the ground-floor; a few span two floors. The shops resemble houses, and most have clapboard cladding around the display windows. Each shop has its own distinctive canopy. Nowhere is there polished marble, reflective glass or a visible steel beam; it is all slightly rustic. There is a vast car-park, part of which is multi-level, at a short distance from the village. As at the rubbish dump, Sunday at the 'village' is a very hectic day, unlike on a weekday when there is a certain discreet calm pervading the place. Some of the larger stores become too crowded. Their staff struggle to keep the goods on neat display, and to retain that chic and charming ambience which the brand would like to create. But this is usually a doomed endeavour; the number of shoppers far exceeds the amount of space in which they need to move freely. Often, at the entrance to the boutiques, dark-suited male attendants finger the ear-pieces of their radio-microphones as they interpret the trustworthiness of the customers who pass before them. Long queues fidget as they await their turn at the check-outs. But once the deal is done, the designer-name on the bag will mark the status of its holder: even amongst the grand designers there is a pecking-order, and the bags will reveal it.

The dump is municipal and public; the 'village' corporate and private. They are at opposite ends of the contemporary quest for personal renewal. In this sense they need each other. A quick and efficient means of disposal of goods is no less important than an agreeable ambience for their acquisition (Bauman 2005: 308). But while they need each other, the rituals surrounding the rites of passage through each are not yet similar. The dump is bureaucratic. Its spaces are clearly labelled and zoned. The metal skips at the off-loading bays are as solid as can be. There is no equivalent at the dump to the 'soft sell' of the designer boutique, where the customer seeks status-affirming packaging around the bought object; the disposer needs none. The process of dumping remains decidedly physical and macho, and at times quite dangerous. No money changes hands. There is no pleasant reception area. Taking rubbish to the dump today is like taking a car to a garage 30 years ago when it was all a little rough and ready. Some garages have since softened up their image. Separate reception areas dispense coffee and provide comfortable seating. The noise and smells are separated from the customer, who nevertheless may be able to see the activity in the workshop through a glass panel. The modes of address tend now to be more polite and scripted. Perhaps, as dumping 'becomes' recycling, and is privatised, we may expect the 'dumper experience' to improve. But not yet.

Like the rubbish which is processed bureaucratically, those who lack the means to buy into consumer culture are processed in a similar way. They literally have no credit, and so they are corralled and constrained. They have been deemed unworthy of credit; they quite literally owe nothing. Those who for whatever reason lack access to education and employment opportunities have insufficient funds to buy the branded identities which give them style and status (Bird 2011: unpaginated). The compulsion to shop (and to discard) seems particularly strong in the UK. In 2007, UNICEF published its report on children's well-being. Among the dimensions of well-being was 'relationships'. The UK ranked 21st out of 21 countries (the US ranked 20th). Moreover, the highest incidence of risk-taking behaviours (obesity, substance abuse, violence and sexual risk-taking) occurred in the UK (UNICEF Innocenti Research Centre 2007). A subsequent study commissioned by UNICEF UK (of 250 children aged between 8 and 13 in the UK, Sweden and Spain) sought to investigate further these findings. The study was qualitative, and included observations and filming in 24 families of different socio-economic makeup. The report concludes: 'Consumer culture in the UK appeared in our research to be "disposable" with households full of broken and discarded toys and a compulsion to continually upgrade and buy new' (Ipsos MORI 2011: 71). Historically, this is something new. Things of substance which lasted used to be an indication of high social standing. Nowadays, there seems to be a lesser inclination to retain them, or to regret the loss of them. A new fashion always provides a ready excuse to be rid of them (Thompson 1979; Bauman 2001: 249). Noticeably, the need to symbolise identity with branded goods was particularly strong in deprived areas, and especially in areas of 'mixed affluence'. Not so in Spain and Sweden, where toys and gadgets were maintained and retained. But, in the UK, what is paradoxical is that even when these goods are acquired, and when status is deemed to have been achieved and symbolised, the satisfaction and happiness which they are meant to confer is fleeting. Indeed, between 1988 and 2008, levels of 'despair' and 'anxiety' among adolescents rose rapidly and significantly in the US and the UK. The financial crash of 2008 gives reason to pause for thought: should these levels continue, or should we now set aside the 'ethos of greed and despair'? (Dorling 2009: 9).

Occasionally the frustration at being excluded from 'consumer culture' erupts, as in the London riots of 2011. They seemed not to have been about basic needs and political rights, but about fulfilling wants and desires. The conspicuous destruction by the looters was said to have been the counterpart of the conspicuous consumption by those who had 'bought in' to consumer culture: 'These are not hunger or bread riots. These are riots of defective and disqualified consumers' (Bauman 2011: unpaginated). Tellingly, much of the disorder occurred in high streets and shopping malls. In order to 'become someone', the rioters would have to 'brand' themselves accordingly in a flurry of designer looting. They – the 'they' being mainly male – had taken to heart Campbell's telling mantra: 'I shop, therefore I know that I am' (Campbell 2004). For them, there was no ethic; they sought only an aesthetic. They acted openly, and seemingly without fear or shame, oblivious to the legal consequences, which by most accounts were unusually harsh (Lewis *et al.* 2011). But this view that it was unmet wants, not unsatisfied needs, which drove the rioters to destruction and looting may be a stereotype in need of refinement. Elizabeth Chin's renowned anthropological study of consumption among the poor black community of New Haven, Connecticut, calls into question the common view that this 'mixture of consumer culture and poverty' is 'dangerously combustible, resulting in crazed pathological consumers who kill for sneakers and who are addicted to brands' (Chin 2001: 6). What was so alarming for the middle classes in parts of London was that these riots spilled over into the areas where they lived. Unlike the rioters in Paris in 2005, those in London lived not in the suburbs beyond the belt-way or ring-road, but in many cases they resided among, and contiguous to, the middle classes. Unlike in Paris, the police in London could not easily contain the fast-moving rioters. But in both London and Paris there was something redolent of *Le Nouveau Moyen Age*: the market pushes those who cannot afford its offerings to the margins, almost beyond the reach of the state where the writ of the local 'micromafias' runs (Minc 1993: 89).

What has all of this got to do with education? At the annual conference of the British Labour Party in 2006, Gordon Brown stated: 'We cannot leave public services as they were. We must build them around the personal aspirations of the individual.' By 2008, personalisation was said to have been the UK Labour government's 'big idea' (Wilby 2008), and it has gained currency, even if its label has changed slightly. After the defeat of the Labour government in May 2010, the Conservative-led coalition government published in July 2011 its *Open Public Services* White Paper (Her Majesty's Government 2011):

> Therefore, we will, on a customised basis, establish *a robust framework for choice in individual services* – in adult care, education, skills training, early years, other children's services, family services, health and social housing. Each framework will ensure that: funding follows the choice of the individual to their provider of choice; those choosing a service are well informed and prompted about the options available; access is fair and the poorest are advantaged; providers meet basic quality requirements enforced by appropriate inspectors or regulators; and if an individual does not receive their right to choose, then there is a means of redress.
>
> (Her Majesty's Government 2011: 14; emphasis in original)

This book provides a critical analysis of the emergence of marketisation and personalisation in education, especially of personalisation. Marketisation is not the same as privatisation, for it remains the case that compulsory schooling is largely funded by the state. But the range of 'providers' has become more diverse, so as to include both the private and the voluntary sectors. It is within this 'market', or 'quasi-market' (Le Grand 1991), that parents have been encouraged to choose – or rather to express a preference for – a 'provider'. As for personalisation, it is a term borrowed from marketing theory, and it marks a further step towards the 'marketisation' of the public services in the sense that it sits easily with the notion that the customer (not the professional) knows best. Whereas marketisation enables the parent to choose a structure (namely a school), personalisation seeks to 'employ' the pupil in the co-production of what is to be learned, and how. And whereas the marketisation is explicit, personalisation is more implicit. In the United States, personalised education is predicted to be 'The next big thing'

(Gardner 2009). In England, it had been deemed so in 2005 (Department for Education and Skills 2005). Given its currency, personalisation has attracted remarkably little critical analysis insofar as education is concerned. (Much of the literature has centred upon the possibilities of digital technologies to enhance 'personalised learning'.)

The book begins by setting out briefly how and why contemporary education finds itself facing a profound discontinuity. For much of the modern period (say, from about 1750 to 1960), there had been something of a '*goodness of fit*' among education, economy and society. This period of modernity has been referred to as 'solid' (Bauman 2000) or as 'first' (Beck and Grande 2010). Its emphasis has been very much on the presumed causal relationship between mass education (or, more precisely, schooling) and mass production under Fordist managerial regimes, especially in manufacturing and low-skill clerical work.

But this phase of modernity gradually began to reveal signs of tension within it – what the sociologist Daniel Bell referred to as the '*cultural contradictions of capitalism*'. Specifically, there has gradually occurred a tension between, on the one hand, an economy wherein a highly rational, standardised, instrumental and technical mind-set prevails; and, on the other hand, within the culture, a gradual undermining of the bourgeois or Protestant ethic that had initially been the 'spirit' in which industrial capitalism grew. In its stead has emerged a more hedonistic, not to say even narcissistic quest – one not given to deferred gratification, nor to the interests of the social. Shops – quite literally – provide the 'outlets' for this personalised quest to construct an identity. This orientation has become more pronounced especially since the emergence of the service and culture industries. And what has further facilitated this latter has been the shift from personal to personalised computing; from the PC to the smart-phone. In short, there has been a noticeable shift in the emphasis placed upon consumption; its salience has risen, largely as a result of the so-called service economy and the emergence of new digital technologies.

Schools have necessarily been part of this cultural change, but their forms and functions are not yet of a piece with it. Chapter 2 explores the emerging uneasy relationship between schooling and production during the period of 'solid' modernity. Chapter 3 dwells upon what appears to be the point – the financial crisis of 2008 – when the tensions within first modernity could no longer be contained. To be sure, even before 2008, the consumerist mind-set had established a strong foothold in the public services. Both Prime Minister Thatcher and President Reagan had set them on the path to the market. The Third Way refinements by President Clinton and Prime Minister Blair did little to alter that direction. Since 1980, state bureaucracies have endured the criticism that they were self-serving and inefficient; markets, on the other hand, were deemed to be better able to serve the client or user, and would find their own level without the need for too much government regulation.

By 2008, the market had made considerable inroads into education. Chapter 4 explores the uneasy co-existence of bureaucracy and markets in schooling, particularly in relation to charter schools (in the US), academies (in England) and free schools (in the US, England and in Sweden). All of these tended to be indicative of what had been the 'quasi-market' and the 'new public management'. The term 'consumer' has been part of educational discourse since the school-choice legislation in the early 1980s but, notwithstanding its affinity to the notion of a (free) market, there has always been a high level of regulation by the government. This is because, in order for a market to operate, parents (now defined as 'consumers') required objective and comparable information about the various 'providers' (namely schools) in order to make a 'rational' choice among them. In England, all this had been set in train by the Conservative governments between 1979 and 1997, but thereafter the Labour government continued it, though with more Third Way heed being paid to 'equity' than hitherto. And whereas the Conservative government had sought to restructure education along the lines of a quasi-market, the Labour government, in addition, set about a more *dirigiste* re-culturing of education: that is, it intervened with national pedagogical prescriptions for the teaching of numeracy and literacy. Indeed, national standards in literacy and numeracy did initially improve, thereafter to level out. But the prescribed pedagogy was highly didactic, and arguably ill-suited to preparing children for life as both producers and consumers in a 'new' economy. If anything, it was more of a piece with an age of mass production and mass consumption.

Until about 2005, the notion of consumerism and education had centred largely on the issue of school choice – it had been about marketisation. In addition to the research and scholarship on school choice, there have been important contributions on the presence of advertising, sponsorship and sub-contracting in the publicly funded school system. All this goes well beyond what had hitherto been the extent of commercial companies' involvement in publicly funded schools. It is now not just about stationery, technology and furniture; it is about the outsourcing of management, assessment, school inspection, consultancy and staff development and training. Nor are these local providers; they can be multi-nationals in search of a global reach and economies of scale (Ball and Youdell 2007). But there are emerging signs of an even more pervasive presence of consumerism in education, and they are beginning to circulate at the levels of both policy and practice. Put simply, there are indications of an emerging personalisation of learning. In other words, whereas until recently we have come to regard the *parent* as an active consumer of schools (as in school choice), now – and in addition, and complementary to it – there are indications that the *pupil* or student is to be regarded as a co-consumer and co-producer of what, where and how she or he learns (that is, personalised learning). In this latter respect, there is a temptation to say that personalised learning is no more than the nostalgic revival of child-centred or progressive education (Hartley 2009). But the similarity in nomenclature does not explain why, now, personalisation and customisation loom on the horizon. The convergence of 'personal' digital technologies, together with new modes of production and consumption (loosely referred to as 'prosumption'), may now allow for the emergence of personalised learning to mark a further stage in the consumerisation of education.

All this prompts a range of considerations about personalisation and its historical and contemporary contexts. On the historical, it needs to be stressed that during the modern period up to about 1960 the relationship between education and the economy was largely a matter confined to the realm of production (the subject of Chapter 2). Thereafter, as the culture and service industries take priority in economic activity, so does the emphasis paid to consumption. This is especially so from the mid-1980s when economic neo-liberalism takes root in the United States and in the United Kingdom, only to result in the 'double bubbles' of 1990 and 2008 (the subject of Chapter 3). Inherent within neo-liberalism are strong tensions: between prudence and pleasure; between individual and collective; between the nation-state and the global; and between credit and debt. In 2008, the tensions became all too visible: for decades, individuals had bought things which they did not need, with money which they did not have, in order to impress people whom they did not know. The flaunting and accumulation of wealth had become its own justification. Gradually, the prices of property and equities became disconnected from their real values. Few economists saw the folly in this, and some who did were ridiculed for daring to speak out.

Chapter 4 explores the path taken by education towards the market, and it considers in particular charter schools, free schools and academies. Paradoxically, in wending its way to the market, education encountered an intensification of bureaucracy, something which might not have been expected in a policy which champions unfettered free choice. But all of this marks only a first stage in the marketisation of education, for it is but about the consumer's preference for, and choice of, structures (that is, schools). And here the consumer is the parent, not the pupil. The next stage (Chapters 5 and Chapter 6) is to position the pupil as a consumer of personalised learning. But, before dealing more fully with the details of personalised learning (Chapter 7), it is necessary to make a short *excursus* into the new forms of production and consumption which are beginning to emerge in the wider economy. In part, these new forms are enabled by the convergence of digital technologies, for not only do they facilitate new kinds of personalised production, but also they enable the greater personalisation of consumption, especially of services. In short, they begin to set aside mass production and mass consumption. But more than that, they bear witness to a conflation of production and consumption into what is termed 'prosumption', or as 'co-production' and 'co-configuration'. Personalisation in education, in short, reveals a deeper penetration of the market into schooling. Whereas school choice had been the beginning of this process, personalisation now beckons. In all of this, however, is a paradox (which is explored in Chapter 8). The paradox is that personalisation prompts collaboration: that is to say, as the pupil seeks to co-construct with professionals its learning needs and desires, the professionals may be required to collaborate in order to meet them effectively. So a process which begins with the needs and wants of the *individual* may portend a *collective* endeavour on the part of others in order to provide them.

The disciplinary orientation of the book is sociological. Chapter 9 considers how personalisation might be regarded from the standpoint of different paradigms in sociology. The book is not about endorsing, or providing a recipe for, the implementation of personalisation. It seeks to understand the emergence of personalisation as part of the increasing consumerisation of schooling and society. (By 'school', I refer to the period of compulsory schooling, and not to the stages beyond it.) It bears noting, too, that personalisation or customisation has emerged contemporaneously to economic neo-liberalism and to the convergence of digital technologies. It resonates with both. Even so, the perturbations prompted by the 2008 economic crisis may have the effect of reining in what had been the rampant run of market-managed solutions to educational problems. At the time of writing, there are not many signs of this.

2 Modernity, production and education

There sits on public view in University College London a rather portly man wearing breeches and a wide-brimmed hat. He stares straight ahead. Jeremy Bentham, who died in June 1832, stipulated in his will that his effigy was to be placed on public view (Marmoy 1958). Why he made this request is unclear, but nevertheless his legacy is writ large in nearly all of our buildings which house pupils, patients, soldiers and inmates. It was Bentham who set out the principles of the *Panopticon* (Bentham 1995; original 1787). The full title of the book (which comprises a series of letters on his 'inspection principle') states:

> Panopticon; or the inspection-house: containing the idea of a new principle of construction applicable to any sort of establishment, in which persons of any description are to be kept under inspection; and in particular to penitentiary-houses, prisons, houses of industry, work-houses, poor-houses, lazarettos, manufactories, hospitals, mad-houses, and schools: with a plan of management adapted to the principle.

The idea behind it was that control need not always be coercive and constant; it was sufficient only that those to be controlled thought that they might – at any time – be overseen and overheard; and the same was true for the controllers. That being so, they were all the more likely to be self-regulating. Here emerged a world of highly demarcated spaces wherein one knew not only one's place in the social hierarchy but also one's expected actions within it at any given time and place. This is a society of enclosures – the family, the school, the barracks, the factory, the prison (the archetypal closed environment), the hospital – each with its rules and regulations (Deleuze 1992: 3).

The period of modernity which began with the Enlightenment is not an easy concept to define. Before about 1750, there had existed a coherent world-view – a unity – which was ordered largely on religious lines. Gradually thereafter we began to have 'faith in science', which sounds somewhat contradictory, given that the point of the scientific endeavour is to question authority, or to set aside blind faith. The world was to be discovered, scientifically; it was to be theorised and understood, so that interventions or treatments could be made or given.

Life could thereby be improved. Thus it was that progress would come to pass. And whereas before there had been little sense of the individual, thereafter we began the long journey which has come to be known as the project of the self. No longer was the self to be a given; it was to be a never-ending production. In 1987, Bell published 'The World and the United States in 2013'. Although the title suggests otherwise, this was not an attempt to predict the future. Instead, it purported to 'identify significant structural changes in world society and in the United States so as to provide a framework for analysis' (Bell 1987: 1). Bell's analysis had begun in the 1960s and his 1987 paper informed the revised version (Bell and Graubard 1997). For Bell, there are three levels or realms of social analysis: the *structural* level (that is, the technological and economic institutions, now capitalism); the *political* (that is, the political forces and relationships both within and among nations; in the West broadly liberalism at the time of his writing); and the *cultural* (that is, 'ideologies and passions, the religious identifications and philosophical ideals that give meaning to people's beliefs'); again, at the time of his writing, it was broadly the Protestant work ethic, and the bureaucratic mind-set of instrumental rationality, of which Bentham's *Panopticon* is typical (Bell 1987: 1).

Modernity and capitalism: the economic realm

The modern period comprised three technological revolutions. The first technological revolution made three technological advances: from 1771, the great surge in canal transportation in England; from 1829, advances in steam technology, mining and railways in England; and from 1875, the development of steel and heavy engineering in the UK, the US and Germany (Perez 2009a: 782). The second technological revolution was marked by the application of electricity: to the telegraph, to the telephone, and to lighting. Electricity allowed for the use of elevators, and therefore enabled the construction of skyscrapers. Later – the third advance – developments in chemistry informed the production of plastics and synthetic materials (Bell 1987: 11). These technological innovations themselves required a compatible social infrastructure or 'social technology'. That is to say, each required the structuring (or imposition) of new dispositions towards authority, time and space. Insofar as space was concerned, none was more crucial than that of the factory. Factories required workers as well as machines. The efficiency and effectiveness of the former was more difficult to assure than that of the latter. The historian of management theory, Pollard, sums up the central concern faced by the factory owner: workers had to be 'acclimatized'. They had to become accepting of the 'cash stimulus', and to respond to it obediently. That is, they needed to change from working in order to subsist towards working on behalf of profit-seekers. They had to accept that they existed only for their labour power; their status as persons was of no consequence (Pollard 1963: 254).

Factory-owners exerted both external and internal power over the workers. Take the 'extra-mural powers' (Pollard 1963: 270). They owned houses (indeed whole villages), and as landlords they could evict at will. They had influence over the laws regarding drinking, over schooling and over the courts (Deleuze 1992: 5). As for the intra-mural or organisational arrangements for controlling the workers, that was altogether problematic, if not a dilemma. The dilemma was thus: given all of these controls over the lives of the workers, who should be blamed if they remained 'immoral, idle and rebellious'? But worse: if indeed the workers were to be taught the virtues of their employer, then what would stop them from becoming entrepreneurs themselves; and if so, who then would comprise the workforce? (Pollard 1963: 271). To be sure, the social technologies which would be compatible with the industrial technologies were far more difficult to decide upon and to implement. The obvious 'soft' technology was the panoptical architecture. Spatial arrangements could literally be 'over-seen' (hence 'supervisor'); factory walls were high, with little sunlight penetrating; the sights and sounds of nature were kept at bay; ventilation was poor, and the air stank of gas (from gas-lighting) and of the smell of grease; spaces were clearly delineated, and no movement beyond was permitted. There was a place for everything and everyone, and all had to be in place.

Not only was space regulated, so also was time (Thompson 1967). Production had to be synchronised. Before the industrial revolution, time had simply 'passed'; it had ebbed and flowed with the tides and the seasons, with night and day. Time was cyclical, not linear, its measurement imprecise. Few people had watches, and so they had to rely upon the church bells or on the sun-dial. In the industrial revolution, time 'became' money; it was to be 'spent' assiduously (not 'wasted') on the owner's behalf; it was recorded meticulously on time-sheets. The 'shift' from rural time to industrial time was problematic, to say the least. There did not exist a clean break between the two. For example, factory workers might move from the cities to the rural areas during the summer in order to work in agriculture, only to return after the harvest to the cities (Paterson 1988).

There is little doubt that an introduction to the factory was something of a temporal culture-shock. Below are some extracts from *Chapters in the Life of a Dundee Factory Boy: an Autobiography*:

> When I went to the spinning mill I was about seven years of age. I had to get out of bed every morning at five o'clock, commence work at half-past five, drop at nine for breakfast, begin again at half-past nine, work until two, which was the dinner hour, start again at half-past two, and continue until half-past seven at night. Such were the nominal hours; but in reality there were no regular hours, masters and managers did with us as they liked. The clocks at the factories were often put forward in the morning and back at night, and instead of being instruments for the measurement of time, they were used as *cloaks* for cheatery and oppression.
>
> (Myles 1850: 12–13)

What was especially insidious about this time-management was that the workers did not themselves have clocks at home, but not waking up 'on time' could literally cost them dearly:

[T]o be behind the hours was not only to lose *double* wages for the lost time, but to run the risk of being instantly discharged [. . .] We had no clock in the house, and my mother used to rise at all hours of the night, and sit until she heard the Cowgate clock strike an hour. Often she has sat from a little past three until five, when she would waken me and return to her bed.

(ibid.: 28–9; emphasis in the original)

Children were to be tamed and timed.

Whereas time and space could be measured in standard units, there was no such agreement on what we would today call managerial 'good practice'. Management lacked a theoretical basis; it was somewhat whimsical, turning on the personality of the owners and the managers themselves. It was not a discipline whose knowledge was codified; it was not yet a 'science'; there were no textbooks; there was no 'organisational learning'. Assimilating the once-independent workers into the routines of factory life came slowly. It required a fundamental change in their mind-set. Mass elementary schooling sought to provide this (Pollard 1963: 270–1). A gradual orientation towards standardisation and systems occurred. At first, this systematisation was applied to technical procedures, but thereafter – in the late 1880s – an engineering mind-set was applied to processes which were organisational and social. Even today, we refer to these processes as 'mechanisms'. The assumption was held that human-beings could be regarded and treated *as if* they were non-human. They were to be manipulated. Their behaviour could be 'engineered' – itemised, recorded, coordinated and monitored. The machine is the enduring metaphor of this 'solid' modern period.

So begins our obsession with the 'system', with cold calculation, with Weberian 'disenchantment', with life within the 'iron cage' of bureaucratic rationality, with the prevalence of reason over emotion. Not only were systems thought to be efficient and effective, they were deemed also to be fair and democratic; and moral. The impersonal prevails over the pastoral, but by so doing nepotism and favouritism are thereby reduced. Authority derives from expertise, not from social connections, or from ascribed characteristics (Shenhav 1995: 564).

In the twentieth century, large-scale assembly-line production sites for cars moved the mode of control further from the 'overseer' and into the very moving 'line' itself. The worker had to keep up with the flow. Control was built in to the very technology. The innovation was made in 1913 at Henry Ford's plant at 91 Manchester Avenue, Highland Park, Michigan. Fordism, as it came to be known, appeared to be a refinement of the ideas of F. W. Taylor's *Principles of Scientific Management*, first published in 1911 (Taylor 2005). Taylorism had been, in Bell's phrase, a kind of 'social physics' (Bell 2000: 233). Fordism was all about size, specification and efficiency:

The 'Fordist factory', that most coveted and avidly pursued model of engineered rationality in times of heavy modernity, was the site of face-to-face meeting, but also a 'till death us do part' type of marriage vow between capital and labour.

(Bauman 2000: 176)

Ford surely believed in Benjamin Franklin's adage that 'time is money', but also that 'money talks'. In order to retain his workers and to dissuade them from 'soldiering', or leaving, in January 1914 he introduced a pay-rate of five dollars per day, an amount considered then to be very generous. The full payment was conditional upon the outcome of a scrutiny of the personal lives and habits of the workers by the company's Sociological Department. Apart from the company's intrusion into the private lives of its workers, there was a further price to be paid for this wage-rise, as explained by the wife of one of Ford's workers. She wrote to him:

> The chain system you have is a *slave driver! My God!*, Mr. Ford. My husband has come home and thrown himself and woht eat his supper – so done out! Can't it be remedied? . . . That $5 a day is a blessing – a bigger one than you know but *oh* they earn it.
>
> (Hounshell 1985: 259; emphasis in the original)

Bauman's imagery does not always depict accurately the mode of management within modernity. A rather heavy-handed approach does not always elicit compliance. Management 'styles' appear to draw upon a range of 'appeals': the calculative (that is, compliance is 'paid for' as wages); the coercive (compliance arises out of fear and harassment); and the normative (non-compliance is said to be not normal, not conventional; even immoral) (Etzioni 1975). It is a question of 'manufacturing consent' (Burawoy 1988), arriving at the most effective mix of these. Again, one can take an historical perspective, and ask what kind of rhetorics of regulation have prevailed throughout the modern period up to about 2000.

The history of management theory may provide some clues. Abrahamson (1997) has provided a two-fold categorisation of these management appeals, or – in his terminology – management rhetorics. These are, first, 'rational rhetorics'; and second, 'normative rhetorics'. The rational rhetoric comprises references to standardisation, hierarchy, audit, appraisal, efficiency, time-on-task, best practice and efficiency. Management theories such as Taylor's scientific management, management by objectives and business process re-engineering are typical. Normative rhetorics make psychological appeals to the worker in the hope and expectation that this will be sufficient to motivate them into being more productive. Human relations management theory, industrial psychology, quality circles, organisational culture and organisational learning are typical. That said, normative rhetorics do not replace rational rhetorics; they merely 'soften' them, make them palatable (Courpasson 2000).

Abrahamson does more than just classify the types of control; he seeks to know why they emerge and fade at different times. It appears that during the solid modern period up to about 1960 these rational and normative rhetorics correlated with changes in the economic cycle. That is to say, rational control rhetorics tended to emerge towards the end of each economic down-swing, and they intensified during the early part of the subsequent expansionary up-swing (Abrahamson 1997: 523). Thus it was in the phase of monopoly capitalism between 1890 and the mid-1920s. From 1890 to 1905, the economic cycle had been in a down-swing phase, and thereafter (after 1911) it began its rapid up-turn, a rise enabled by new technologies, notably the car assembly-line. Then the 'rational' rhetorics of Taylorism and Fordism prevailed, with no 'normative' appeals to workers. Thereafter, in the early and mid-1920s, it became apparent that these rational management rhetorics no longer elicited productivity gains: the motivation of workers waned; production was on a plateau, no longer climbing; disillusionment had set in. Human relations management theory was applied in order to re-motivate workers: it sought to ease the rigours of Fordism and bureaucracy. In short, normative rhetorics 'will tend to emerge shortly before the end of long wave up-swings'. As an up-swing falters, managers may deploy normative rhetorics in order to stem the economic slowdown (Abrahamson 1997: 502, 523).

Take another example: the period before and after the peak in the economic cycle which occurred during the 1973 oil-crisis. For much of the 1940s, 1950s and 1960s a rational rhetoric had been deployed during the up-swing of the economic cycle which followed the Great Depression. It is revealed in systems rationalisation, and in management by objectives. As in the 1920s, during the late 1950s and 1960s workers began to tire of bureaucratic rationality, and thereafter – up until the 1973 fiscal crisis – normative rhetorics are once again re-asserted (Abrahamson and Eisenman 2008: 736), and these more normative rhetorics continued in the first part of the down-swing. As this down-swing neared the end of its decline about 1995 there emerged once again (as in the 1890s and in the 1940s) a series of rational management 'mechanisms': total quality management, benchmarking, audits, appraisals, core competencies and business process re-engineering. Organisations were to focus on their core business. This rational rhetoric was back in vogue, and it prevailed until after 2000. Its presence was felt particularly in education policy, especially in England and other neo-liberal regimes, where the metaphors of accountancy and industrial production supplanted those of equality of opportunity and liberal humanism (Hartley 2010).

Modernity: the cultural realm

Cultures are expressed symbolically. The age of solid modernity, or first modernity, was one of fixed spatial arrangements and boundaries. It was not easy to become 'lost', because the whole point was to render us as predictable, to know our place, both socially and spatially. The latter is revealed in street-patterns, especially in the cities of North America. They are arranged as a grid. The streets are numbered (first, second; and so on), as is their compass direction (north, east, west or south). All that is required is to combine the two bearings: thus, say, 1st Avenue NE. And life in the street was not altogether pleasant. Life could be precarious, subject to the vagaries of the business cycle and seasonal work. There was little to ameliorate the lot of those whose savings were meagre, and whose needs could not be met. Homes were hardly habitable, with not much in the way of heating, plumbing and sanitation. There was little home ownership. Houses were also crowded. Only the public house provided some solace (for the men), and after the 1920s the local cinema provided temporary respite from the drudgery (Offer 2008: 540).

The rationalisation of space can be seen also in the many office buildings which arose during the twentieth century (and not just within capitalist societies), especially after the 1930s. Particular floors were associated with particular divisions, sections or departments. Often, the status of the department correlated with the height of the floor, as befits a hierarchy. This segmentation – this correspondence between (architectural) structure and function – was deemed to be highly systematic, and therefore to be commended. To be sure, there was an architectural isomorphism among manufacturing, commercial, educational and medical structures. All were solid. 'Solid' because size mattered, as did durability. The 'weight' of solid modernity is symbolised in the architectures of factories, hospitals, schools, railway stations and post offices. They were substantial, built to last, in the same way that the earlier power and permanence of the church had been revealed in the great cathedrals of the middle ages. People knew the form.

Just as space was associated with particular functions, so also, as discussed earlier, was time. Complex endeavours are required to be coordinated. To know the time is as important as to know where you are. It has been argued that this quest for order is a revelation of a technocratic consciousness (Berger *et al.* 1974). Although the elaborate coordination of time and space is functional for the modern workplace, it can 'spread' to those leisure endeavours which have nothing to do with work. A few examples can illustrate the point. Sometimes we feel guilty if we are late for a social engagement; or, conversely, we become annoyed if someone else is late. Punctuality is important. Even if we are not required to meet a deadline, we may create one. Say you are on holiday, and you wish to drive to your destination. You might remind yourself that the last time you made the journey it took two hours and five minutes. That now becomes a 'target' which is to be bettered. Throughout the journey, you constantly check the time in order to measure your progress; and anxieties arise if you are 'running late'. There is a sense of constantly being 'against the clock', in competition with oneself. 'For good measure', you might even think to record your car's fuel consumption for the journey. It is remarkable how fascinated some of us are when 'time stands still'. This can be seen in busy city-centres when someone (usually in disguise) mounts a soap-box and stands still; completely still, as if a statue. Looks of amazement are exchanged among the onlookers.

It used to be the case that the factory hooter, or the school bell, sounded the stages of the work-day. Jobs were then full-time, and permanent. Apprentices 'served their time'. By 1961, three-quarters of those employed in England and Wales had manual or low-pay clerical jobs, and usually they were paid an hourly wage, each week, in cash. Particularly in the industrial north, manufacturing prevailed. There remained the Victorian-era residue of metals, machinery, shipbuilding and textiles. To these were added the inter-war manufacturing of cars, aircraft, household appliances, together with packaged goods such as soaps and sweets. Later came pharmaceuticals, and nationwide railway-building and mining industries. Women tended to work before marriage, and some on a part-time basis thereafter. All this has been deemed a 'proletarian way of life' with little spatial or temporal flexibility (Offer 2008: 538). Since then, time-management has been more the preserve of the individual: alarms have become more personalised and private.

The modern period which spans much of the nineteenth and twentieth centuries was typified by an 'ethic': the Protestant work ethic. Its essence was to value 'deferred gratification'. Self-discipline was seen as a virtue, to be inculcated and sustained. The sense of self becomes more pronounced. Individuals come to regard themselves as unique, in pursuit of a project to become someone (Bell 1972: 26). The suppression of the emotions in favour of the application of reason was the order of the day. By the middle of the nineteenth century, the 'bourgeois world-view' had come to prevail, both in the workplace and gradually in the school. It was 'rationalistic, matter-of-fact, pragmatic; neither magical, mystical, nor romantic; emphasizing work and function; concerned with restraint and order in morals and conduct' (ibid.: 29). The general view was that men were more able to curb their emotions than women. Men were regarded as being more rational, and able to distance themselves from the moody mentalities which had prevailed during the pre-modern period. Indeed, the emergence of the scientific method, and the expansion of the disciplines (especially economics, sociology and psychology), gradually asserted itself, setting aside the earlier attachment to dogma, doctrine and belief which had prevailed in the pre-modern era. Science increasingly deploys a questioning mind-set; it questions all forms of authority, even itself. In the post-Enlightenment period – say, after 1750 – all aspects of the physical, social and psychological realms became the subject-matter of the scientific method. Social phenomena were deemed to have the same ontological status as physical phenomena. Nature and society could be understood (that is, theorised) and, where necessary, could be altered, preferably for the common good, though not always. In sum, the laws of the social world were thought to be no less intelligible than those of the physical world, and nor were they contingent upon time or place. Thus it was that the notion of progress increasingly took root. We became more future-oriented, less accepting of the natural order, less inclined to explain things as the 'will of God', less fateful and faithful. For example, no longer do we attribute the approach of thunder and lightning as being the expression of the wrath of God, or as the presence of the devil. No longer do we rush to the sanctuary of the church, or ring its bells to warn everyone of the presence of evil. Instead, we can actually predict the coming of the storm. We can read the weather forecast. Science, therefore, provided the modern world with a coherent world-view, a set of explanations which could be tested empirically for their truth-value. This world-view is as persuasive for us today as was the theological world-view of the medieval period for its people then.

The social sciences are the intellectual expression of the culture of modernity. For the most part – and especially until the mid-1960s – both sociology and psychology had tended towards an epistemological position which is akin to that of the natural sciences, or positivism. 'Positive' in the sense that, having explained social and psychological phenomena, it is possible to intervene 'positively' in these realms. This epistemological position implies that social and psychological phenomena have a real ontological status, and that they can be apprehended empirically. Theories in psychology such as behaviourism and Piagetian genetic epistemology, and theories in sociology such as structural functionalism and some branches of Marxism, all tend to give primacy to structural 'forces' over individual agency. They are to varying degrees 'deterministic'. Not always have these structuralist positions prevailed. For example, the 1920s and 1930s saw the Chicago School of Sociology established. Symbolic interactionism explored the interrelationship between structure and agency. Even so, it was not to challenge the structuralist orthodoxy until the 1970s. During the first half of the twentieth century, scientism – the view that it is only science which offers the 'immaculate perception' of the world; other interpretations are no more than subjective belief and opinion – held sway.

Science does not have answers to questions about morality. Its findings can inform our decisions in a limited way, but no more. The questions which it asks, the funds which support its research, the uses to which its findings are put – these are value-laden concerns about which science can justify no firm conclusions. All the same, the science of solid modernity does lay claim to 'positive' effects. It can put aside enchantment and emotion in favour of rational argument and empirical verification. Whereas before there had been uncertainty, thereafter there would be certainty; whereas before there had been ambiguity, thereafter there would be clarity; and whereas before the likelihood of chaos existed, thereafter there would be rational planning (Beck and Lau 2005: 536–7).

Modernity and education

In 1816, Jeremy Bentham, the author of *Panopticon*, set out his ideas on education in his book *Chrestomathia*. It contained his 'principles of school management', most of which will have a very familiar ring to them (Bentham 1816). It is all about 'performativity' (Ball 2003). The monitorial schools applied these principles. In effect, the school was to be run on efficiency lines, as if it were a business (that is, a factory). It is sometimes argued that the schools 'imported' the managerial 'grammar' of the factory. But the affinity between the management of businesses and the management of schools may be more to do with the fact that they each faced similar problems. When Bentham wrote *Panopticon* in 1787, schools were not publicly funded. In effect, many were businesses, just like the factories. They too had to generate cash-flow, to allocate scarce resources, to be accountable to parents, and to maintain order. It is little wonder that the solutions to these problems – common to both factories and schools – were similar (Miller 1973: 18).

In the early twentieth century, business principles went on to be applied rigorously, particularly in American schools during the 1920s, a period when educational administration as a sub-discipline of education was establishing itself (Callahan 1962; Nasaw 1981; Tyack and Tobin 1994). Take, for example, the question of 'classroom management'. It was a problem of economy: it seeks to determine in what manner the working unit of the school plant may be made to return the largest dividend upon the material investment of time, energy and money. From this point of view, classroom management may be looked upon as a 'business' problem.

(Bagley 1910: 2)

This quest for scientific efficiency is writ large in the reform of America's schools. The district school superintendents, the state officials and the professors of education – many of whom subscribed to Taylor's scientific management theory – were attracted by the efficiencies of scale and hierarchy to be seen in the factories. Why could it not be applied to schools; why not, for example, group children of the same age and ability into one 'grade', there to be taught by one teacher? (Tyack and Tobin 1994: 476). It is a 'grammar' of schooling which has persisted throughout the twentieth century.

One of the most widely cited analyses of this structural accord between schooling and capitalism is that by Bowles and Gintis (1976). It is referred to as the 'correspondence principle', a 'structural correspondence' between the social relations of schooling and those of production. In sum, the school 'develops the types of personal demeanour, modes of self-presentation, self-image, and social-class identifications which are the crucial ingredients of job adequacy' (Bowles and Gintis 1976: 131). The modes of regulation which apply between employers and workers are anticipated in the hierarchical relations that apply within the school. In both locations, the rewards are said to be extrinsic (that is, the payment of wages or the awarding of grades for compliance; and the threat of unemployment, exclusion or non-promotion for unsatisfactory work or behaviour). Bowles and Gintis conclude: 'Thus, at least for this sample, the personality traits rewarded in schools seem to be rather similar to those indicative of good job performance in the capitalist economy' (ibid.: 138). For example, supervisors at work disapproved of 'creative' and 'independent' behaviour; and they approved of those same behaviours which were rewarded at school, namely: 'being perseverant, dependable, punctual, predictable, tactful, temperamental and consistent; and identifying with school, empathizing with orders, and deferring gratification' (ibid.). In both work and school, the lack of intrinsic rewards, argue Bowles and Gintis, is thereby alienating.

Neither workers nor pupils give their consent to this alienation willingly. On this, compare Bauman's perception of the worker–employee relationship with Waller's sociological account of the school. In production, labour is tied inextricably to capital. They need each other, and the relationship is a recipe for outbursts of enmity during an otherwise persistent 'trench war' (Bauman 2000: 176). Something similar exists in the school: a 'despotism in perilous equilibrium', vulnerable to disruption, but the means whereby order is sustained can be vetoed by the parents. 'It is a despotism resting upon children, at once the most tractable and the most unstable members of the community' (Waller 1932: 10).

Jackson's 1970s study of the American elementary school revealed that not much had changed since Waller's study in the early 1930s. Nowhere in society are so many individuals confined together for so long in such a small space as in a school. Students are a captive audience. They must pretend to be alone when they are not (Jackson 1990: 16). Imagine, says Jackson, what would happen if a factory the size of a typical elementary school contained three or four hundred workers (ibid.: 8). Or take Seldon's contemporary commentary on English schools. It is, he states, 'the apogee of Fordism gone mad' (Seldon 2010: 15–16), except that it is the government, not the capitalist, which controls it by decree.

Most schools today are surprisingly similar to the schools created by the industrial revolution. At that stage, it was the function of state schools to prepare the newly urbanised children for their future life in the factory, and so the parallels between the organisation of schools and the organisation of factories were strong. The school may now be ripe for radical workplace redesign; one option would be to examine the most impressive of today's workplaces and then redesign schools to serve as a preparation for life in the companies of tomorrow's knowledge economy (Hargreaves 2003: 29).

In sum, despite intermittent attempts to change it, the basic 'grammar' of schooling remains little changed (Tyack and Tobin 1994: 454). Similarly, as we have suggested, the form of other organisations outside of education has undergone periodic revisions. Organisation theory, like educational theory, appears to oscillate between rational and normative modes of regulation: rational and didactic during the late phase of an economic down-swing until near the peak of the following upswing; and normative and 'progressive' during the latter phase of the upswing and the early phase of the downswing (Hartley 2010). Notwithstanding these normative and progressive 'aberrations', throughout the solid modern period the underlying principle has been that of instrumental rationality. Behaviourism informed the psychology of education, and structural functionalism informed the sociology of education (or educational sociology). The curriculum was arranged in aims and objectives (Kliebard 1970). As for the management and administration of education, it too drew heavily upon Taylorism, Fordism and systems theory: the administrative structures in education were hierarchical, and the administrative units (school divisions in the US and local education authorities in the UK) were centralised. The adjective 'mass' had typified the education 'system' in the hundred years to 1970: mass elementary/primary education; mass high/secondary education; and a move towards mass higher education. It was the counterpart to mass production and mass consumption.

During the solid modern period, the social structure was of a piece with that of culture. This 'accord' is now coming to an end (Beck and Lau 2005: 527). Nearly 40 years ago, the 'cultural contradictions of capitalism' – a 'radical disjunction of culture and social structure' – were emerging: 'The one [social structure] emphasizes functional rationality, technocratic decision-making, and meritocratic rewards. The other [culture], apocalyptic moods and anti-rational modes of behavior [*sic*]' (Bell 1972: 38; brackets added). For Bell, rational orders were in disarray, especially in the arts: nothing is framed, or on a plinth; narratives avoid a linear beginning, middle and end; the euphony of melody and harmony in music is disrupted (ibid.: 14). The bourgeois 'personality' – that is, self-disciplined and self-motivated, rational and materialistic – had never fully prevailed: it had its detractors, but they tended to sequester themselves in bohemian enclaves, defining themselves as an *avant-garde*. During the 1960s, that began to change; they moved out into the mainstream. The taboos were fewer. The arbiters of aesthetic taste no longer held sway. Order and impulse vied for position, the former no longer dominant. The boundaries of convention were taken to the limit. As Bell put it: 'There is no longer an avant-garde, because no one in our postmodern culture is on the side of order or tradition. There exists only a desire for the new' (ibid.: 30).

Since then it is a 'sensate mentality' which is writ large: values and morals are malleable, never absolute; gratification is not to be deferred; life is to be lived for the moment; pleasure is to be sought; material and the empirical are to be privileged; everything has its price (Sorokin 1985: 34–5). But these are matters for fuller consideration in the following chapter. Meanwhile, it is in order to remind ourselves of the 'premises' of 'solid' or 'first' modern societies: they are nation-states with fixed boundaries; they reveal individualisation, an individualisation which is in theory unlimited, but which in practice is 'moulded by social institutions'; they are 'full-employment societies' (though mainly for males); they are societies wherein nature is to be exploited and mastered; they appeal to scientific rationality and control; they admit continual specialisation and differentiation, all of which is finely calibrated (Beck, Bonss, and Lau 2003: 3–4).

3 The economic crisis
Surfacing contradictions

> When a world order collapses, that's the moment when reflection should begin.
>
> (Beck and Grande 2010: 409)

In September 2007, long queues formed outside the branches of Northern Rock, a bank in the UK. Depositors were anxious about the security of their savings, and so they withdrew them, hurriedly. The UK government went on to nationalise the bank in February, 2008. Its collapse was, in retrospect, the canary in the coalmine, a harbinger of what was to follow, but few at that time knew what it portended. Among them was Nouriel Roubini, an academic at the Stern School of Business in New York. His warnings went unheeded (Mihm 2008). After all, had not Gordon Brown, Chancellor of the Exchequer in the UK government, earlier declared, 'No more boom and bust' (Wilcox 2007)? Roubini turned out to be right; Brown, wrong. In the following months, the banks were to lose the trust of their customers. Almost a year to the day of the collapse of Northern Rock in England, the American bank Lehman Brothers filed for Chapter 11 bankruptcy in September 2008; the largest bankruptcy in American history.

Capitalism had been in crisis before. During the first modern period (since about 1800), there have been a series of powerful surges which have ended in a financial crisis and a stockmarket meltdown, most notably the collapse of 1929 which heralded the Great Depression. Each surge – of which there have been five – is associated with a technological revolution, i.e. canals and the original industrial revolution; steam and railways; steel, electricity and heavy engineering; oil, the automobile and mass production; and, now, information and telecommunications (Perez and Rutherford 2009: 30). Usually – but not always – upward surges in the economic cycle tend to occur in response to a technological innovation, which attracts short-term, risk-capital investment. Perez (2009a) refers to this expansionary phase as the 'installation period' when the potential of the new technology is demonstrated. During these rapid and steep up-swings of the economic cycle, the writ of the financier runs. Governments tend to stand back, and to allow the market to regulate itself. The accumulation of wealth becomes its own justification. Wealth is flaunted. 'Irrational exuberance' – a phrase coined in the 1990s by Alan Greenspan, the then chairman of the US Federal Reserve

Bank – takes over. Stockmarket values become inflated in relation to their underlying worth. Warnings are ignored; ridiculed. Inevitably the bubble bursts. This time, it was not just some economists who saw the writing on the wall; so, too, did some sociologists (Adler and Heckscher 2006: 73). Earlier, the economic historian Avner Offer had also predicted another bubble. Each technological innovation – canals, water supply, gas, railroads, tramways, telegraphs, television, underground railways and electricity – had spawned its own 'mania' of excessive speculative investment, or what he calls 'surges of "excess entry"'. In 2003, he too predicted that the same was about to occur in relation to digital telecommunications (Offer 2003: 5).

This 'next rush', as Offer called it, was triggered initially by the micro-processor which had been developed during the early 1970s, and which was to be the instigator of what has come to be termed the information and communications technology (ICT) industry. Many forms of communication gradually became digitalised, thereby enabling their convergence. Again – as during the 1920s – financiers invested heavily in the new technologies. Governments in the US and the UK, both based on an ideology of economic neo-liberalism (or monetarism), once again provided light-touch regulation. Again, the market took its course. Global – or transnational – corporations proved difficult to regulate, notwithstanding the work of the World Trade Association (WTO) to do so. Again, credit became easy to obtain, and by more people. The 'internet mania' or the 'dot.com' bubble was the first to burst: technology shares trading on the New York NASDAQ exchange collapsed in 2000. That turned out to be the first of two bubbles to burst. Thereafter, credit itself became a commodity. Many complex and little-understood financial 'products' came to the market, and large commissions were paid to those who sold them (MacKenzie 2011). Often the collateral required for loans was ignored. Matters unravelled quickly after the failure of Lehman Brothers bank in 2008. So ended what Perez calls the 'installation' phase of the new ICT and digital technologies.

In the downturn which follows the collapse of an expansionary phase, it is necessary for the state to intervene so as to enable what Perez calls the 'deployment period'. In this endeavour, typically (but not inevitably) the excesses of the financiers will be regulated, and the needs of the producers will be attended to, if necessary with the assistance of the state. The technological innovation is, of itself, insufficient to move the cycle beyond the pre-crisis 'installation period'. In the aftermath of a financial crash, when the frenzy has subsided, the long-term goals of the producers tend to supersede those of the financiers. It is during this period that the most radical organisational and social innovations occur (Sterman 1986; Bullen *et al.* 2006; Perez 2009a: 802; Perez 2010). To elaborate – major technological breakthroughs trigger two phases: the 'surge' or 'installation' phase, driven by the financiers (and which ends in the bursting of the bubble); and the 'deployment' phase thereafter (which is enabled by the state) (Perez 2009a). It is the 'deployment' phase of information and communications technology which now beckons. We are, in Perez's terms, at the 'turning point'. It will, she states, require a new and compatible organisational form, a new collaborative and social technology which is itself supported by information technology. And these new collaborative organisational forms will required a new interactive social character (Maccoby 2006), or identity, which may be structured isomorphically within education and its related fields. In other words, there will emerge a new 'techno-economic paradigm' which will represent the best articulation of economic, technological and organisational practices (Perez 2010: 198).

Financial crises bring into sharp focus the anomalies which had hitherto gone unnoticed; or, even if they had been noticed, they were ignored. In the wake of these shocks to the capitalist system, nation-states must intervene to limit the damage and to prepare again for economic growth. Financial crashes such as those which followed 1929, 1973 and 2008 trigger a 'fiscal crisis of the state'. By 'fiscal crisis' is meant 'the tendency for government expenditure to outrace revenues' (O'Connor 2001: 2). Put plainly, at the very time when the calls upon the state's resources are the heaviest, the ability of the government to raise the necessary taxes to provide them is at its weakest. The state must do more with less; or it must enter into public-provider arrangements, or even privatise services which hitherto it had funded; or it must make cuts in services (Hood *et al.* 2009). All of these cuts and re-balancings must be made in such a manner that they will be accepted by those whose lives may be affected adversely as a result of them. In order to ensure the legitimacy of the reductions in public expenditure, the government must deploy a rhetoric which resonates with the public mood. The 'cuts' must be justifiable. They must be seen as fair. In October 2009, the UK Chancellor of the Exchequer, in his speech at the Conservative Party Conference, referred no fewer than seven times to the fact that 'We are all in this together': that is, the forthcoming budgetary burdens were for all to shoulder (Osborne 2009). However, not only must government legitimate the reductions in public expenditure, but also it must at the same time provide the conditions for 'accumulation' (to use O'Connor's term), or for 'deployment' (to use Perez's term). That is, it must provide the conditions for economic growth.

But – this time, post-2008 – will it be different? All of the previous cycles have occurred during that period of modernity which Bauman (2000) has called 'solid modernity', or which Beck and Grande (2010) refer to as 'first modernity'. Recall that the previous chapter was informed by Daniel Bell's three realms of social analysis: the *structural*; the *political*; and the *cultural* (Bell 1987: 1). Whereas these realms were broadly compatible during the period of first or solid modernity, now – as intimated at the end of the previous chapter – they are not. To use a term which is fast becoming fashionable in ICT circles, these realms are out of 'sync'. Why?

Take the *structural* realm which comprises technology and economic institutions. In his 1987 speculation, Bell had stated that by 2012 the third technological revolution would have arrived: 'the joining of computers and telecommunications (image television, voice telephone, data information computers, text facsimile) into a single yet differentiated system, that of the "wired nation" and even the "world society"' (Bell 1987: 10–11). Bell's speculations have come to pass. These technologies provoked a more profound change than either those of the industrial revolution or that of the printing-press before it; and this is but the beginning of a process whereby a shift occurs from computer-centred to networked internet-based technologies (Castells 2000a: 10). Profound because it portends a 'world society' enabled by the process of globalisation: that is, 'the process that constitutes a social system with the capacity to work as a unit on a planetary scale in real or chosen time' (Castells 2000a: 10). Of these capacities, there are three types. *Technological* capacity refers to information and communication technologies (ICTs) which permit connections to be made everywhere, at any time. *Institutional* capacity refers to the deregulation by nation-states of the regulatory regimes which control economic activity. *Organisational* capacity means that ICT-technologies enable organisational structuring to be flexible, interactive and international (Castells 2008: 81). Information-sharing enables customers, distributors and producers to work seamlessly and synchronously in project-based endeavours. This last capacity – the organisational – means that the optimum organisational structure is that of the network, which can operate either within large corporate structures (effectively de-centralising their activities), or they can serve to connect hitherto disparate small and medium-sized enterprises (Castells 2000a: 10). This does not mean that these enterprises will necessarily be networked as wholes – it is more likely that sections will be networked, and that the organisational configuration will depend upon the nature of the project at hand.

All this is highly disruptive of 'first' or 'solid' modernity. Its strong boundary demarcations – spatial, temporal, social and organisational – no longer serve as the viable means of categorisation. In first modernity, agreement about what was natural and what was of human construction was usually possible; one knew who 'belonged' and who did not; it was clear where the boundary between public and the private realms was drawn; and similarly where the responsibilities of the nation-state lay, and where they did not (Beck and Lau 2005: 534). But there now exists a range of global risks the management of which is unclear. The structural and political arrangements of first modernity are no longer functional for efficiently managing the risks of international terrorism, of pandemics, of sovereign debt crises, and of climate change. This is a 'crisis of efficiency' (Castells 2008: 83). Nor are they able to deal with a 'crisis of equity': that is to say, there is no global regulatory means whereby the effects of rampant neo-liberalism can be curbed and compensated for (ibid.). In response, it may be argued that there are indeed various loose structures – bilateral and multilateral arrangements and accords; major charities, foundations and social entrepreneurs – which can mitigate these crises. But the evidence that they do so is not persuasive (managing the sovereign debt crisis is a case in point) (Beck and Grande 2010: 410–11).

Social technologies and the new work order

There is now an emerging view about the kind of worker which the new economy needs, and about how that worker is to be educated. In his *End of*

Millennium, Castells distinguishes between two kinds of labour: 'generic' and 'self-programmable'. Generic workers are the classic 'hands' of the nineteenth-century factory floor: these 'human terminals' are, as individuals, expendable and irrelevant, to be replaced either by others, or by machines: 'While they are collectively indispensable to the production process, they are individually expendable [. . .]' (Castells 2000b: 372). But not so the self-programmable worker: here is a worker steeped in flux and flow, a worker willing and capable of adapting to the fluctuations of the market and to those of the production process (Gallie 2007). The emergence of programmable labour marks a decided shift in the demeanour and dispositions of the worker. Production during the past 100 years has been largely along Fordist lines: that is, mass production, typified by routine and the repetition of tasks. The price to be paid for this ruthless efficiency was disenchantment. Cold, hard calculation – the suppression of the affects – is the concomitant of instrumental rationality. Weber described the 'nullity' which had filled our lives: 'Specialists without spirit, sensualists without heart; this nullity imagines that it has attained a level of civilization never before achieved' (Weber 2003: 182). Weber's disenchantment, Durkheim's anomie and Marx's alienation were the intellectual expressions of this condition. Now 'the common man' has come to similar conclusions:

> The alienation and utility that characterized the perceptions of a handful of intellectuals at the beginning of the century have come to characterize the consciousness of the common man at its end. Jobs are stupefying, relationships vapid and transient, the arena of politics absurd.
>
> (Berman 1981: 17)

In his interpretation of Weber, Gellner (1987: 153) reminds us of the nature of the deal we have struck: on the one hand, we have acquired 'cognitive, technological and administrative power', but that has been at the expense of 'our previous meaningful, humanly suffused, humanly responsive, if often menacing or capricious world. That is abandoned for a more predictable, more amenable, but coldly indifferent and uncosy world.'

The changes in the labour force during the twentieth century were considerable. At the turn of the century, the UK had completed its industrial revolution, and already had 24 per cent of its (mainly male) workforce in manufacturing and textiles. Only 12 per cent of the UK workforce in 1900 remained in agriculture, but in France, Germany and the US the corresponding figure was 40 per cent. By 2000, the percentages employed in both agriculture and manufacturing had declined: in manufacturing, to 14 per cent; in agriculture, forestry and fishing, to only 2 per cent. But the percentage employed in services had risen markedly to 75 per cent (Lindsay 2003: 137). As indicated in the previous chapter, the decline of manual working has been rapid. Within a generation, by 2003, only a quarter to one-third were in manual occupations (Offer 2008: 3). The *Employment in Britain* survey, conducted in the early 1990s, found that only 6 per cent of workers were doing assembly-line work, and a further 11 per cent worked mainly with machines. From the 1950s, the British working class (particularly the male) underwent a rapid process of individualisation, especially from 1980. The decline of traditional manufacturing brought with it a decline in the collective bargaining power of the working class, and with it a reduction in their capacity collectively to disrupt production. Until then, they had retained the knowledge of production – it was not codified, or incorporated within automated technologies; it was not therefore easily replaced (Offer 2008: 540). The rapid decline of traditional jobs correlates with a rise in trade-union membership in the UK. In 1900, the membership-rate had been 11 per cent of those in employment, but it peaked in the late 1970s at 50 per cent. By 2000, it had declined to a 60-year low of just under 29 per cent (Lindsay 2003: 133). The miners' strike of 1984 in the UK was the 'proletarians' last stand': thereafter they were dispersed geographically to suburban estates, some to buy up the stocks of public housing under 'right-to-buy' legislation. There they mingled with others who were not of their ilk. The once-solid collective identities – no mean political and civic force – dissolved (Offer 2008: 544).

The services which attract the most economic activity are those of finance, and the professions of health, social services and education: 'The core of the postindustrial society is its professional and technical services' (Bell 1987: 8). The new economy is a 'relational economy' (Nahapiet 2008). What is central to the production process of the new capitalism are not commodities, but design: how to design and market new 'identities', 'affinity spaces' and 'networks' (Gee 2004: 97). An affinity space may be virtual or real (or a combination) wherein individuals interact, primarily for a common purpose, and less so on the basis of their social and cultural affinities (ibid.: 98). These activities have been referred to as *high-touch*, as opposed to *high-tech*, knowledge-based activities (Turner 2002). Many 'high-touch' services require emotional labour. This is nothing new. Nearly 50 years ago, in *White Collar: the American Middle Class*, C. Wright Mills noted the pressures of emotional labour on white-collar workers:

> They sell by the week or month their smiles and their kindly gestures, and they must practice the prompt repression of resentment and aggression.
>
> (Mills 1951: xvii)

Today, the emotions are being rationalised so that workers will be 're-enchanted' (Ritzer 2000). In *The Managed Heart: the commercialization of human feeling*, Hochschild asks 'How do institutions control how we "personally" control feeling?' (Hochschild 2003: 219). Her analysis incorporates Weber's concept of bureaucracy and Marx's consideration of whose interests are served by that bureaucracy. It is not, she argues, a question of the personality simply being 'sold' (which is the position taken by C. Wright Mills in *White Collar*), but that 'people actively manage feelings in order to make their personalities fit for public-contact work' (ibid.). The have-a-nice-day smiles and personalised greetings seem to be sincere, but often they are scripted. This is 'false fraternisation' (Ritzer 2000). In short, front-line workers must instrumentalise their affects – for profit, pay or preferment – by appearing to be genuine in their quest to elicit 'customer delight'. Thus it is that emotion and capital are now linked productively: emotional capital.

In the 'high-tech' sector, workers are required to be creative. (The same applies in the emerging 'culture industries', the latter requiring creativity of a more artistic kind.) Whereas in the high-touch economy the emotions are more to the fore, within the high-tech economy the matter of creativity looms larger. This is not to say that in the emerging 'culture' industries creativity is not essential; on the contrary. But it is to say that in the emerging new knowledge economy, creativity becomes crucial. Of course, workers have always had to have knowledge, but it tended to be fixed, and linked to known raw materials, predictable markets, well-understood treatments and stable products. The contemporary knowledge economy seeks a 'learning worker' (Jacques 1996: 143). Here is a worker who has the capacity and inclination to revise continually the content of their knowledge, as required (ibid.: 144). The 'learning worker' approximates the 'self-programmable' worker (Castells 2000b: 340). This is distinct from the 'generic' worker who simply applies knowledge and routines, as directed. All this represents a shift in the worker's mode of consciousness. Formerly, it was 'mechanical' in its orientation. It had emphasised 'instrumentality, emotionless, accumulation, skepticism, individual consciousness, standardization and objectification' (Jacques 1996: 37). This mode of consciousness will not suffice in the knowledge economy, one wherein creativity produces innovation and new products. It requires not only a 'maximally creative' worker, but one who can also generate short-term returns (Thrift 2000: 675).

We have said that the knowledge economy is a 'relational economy' (Napahiet 2008). It is also an economy which relies upon collaboration, at least to some extent. The social, like the emotional, is now a form of capital. Networks – Gee's affinity spaces – are not necessarily communities. They tend not to generate affective bonds; they are calculative associations which centre upon a project. The paradox is that while the *rational* rhetorics of neo-liberalism have undermined trust, the deployment of the knowledge economy will come to rely upon it. The 'twentieth-century firm' is being superseded by what Heckscher calls the 'emerging enterprise'. The strategy of the twentieth-century firm was mass production; that of the emerging enterprise is solutions. The organisational structure of the twentieth-century firm was bureaucracy; for the emerging enterprise it is collaborative enterprise. Finally, whereas the culture of the twentieth-century firm was paternalism, that of the emerging enterprise is contribution (Heckscher 2007: 21). Insofar as 'contribution' is concerned, it portends new cultural dispositions and linguistic repertoires, a new identity or 'character', a character at ease with interdependence; an 'interactive social character', not – as before – a 'bureaucratic character' (Maccoby 2006). This character cannot simply be called for; it must be acquired tacitly through exposure to the hidden curriculum of schooling and to the regulatory regime of the workplace. It will be a matter of learning to co-labour, to be a collective practitioner rather than an individual reflective practitioner. The central concept which informs this is 'collaborative community' (Heckscher and Adler 2007).

Post-Fordist flexible production can provoke stress and uncertainty among workers. Job-security is lessened, and this can lead to a reduced commitment and motivation on the part of workers. If the employers seek short-term contracts, then workers will provide short-term commitment. Cynicism may ensue (Scase 1999). As pay levels decline, stress levels increase, as occurred in the US during the 1990s (Cappelli 1997: 206). How, under such conditions, can the commitment of workers be assured? How is their consent to be managed? All this matters much if a knowledge and creative economy requires collaboration and trust if it is to flourish. And trust reduces transaction costs; it requires fewer contracts (Biggart and Castanias 1997). This kind of economy requires what Coleman (1988) refers to as 'social capital': unlike physical capital, it is not tangible; unlike human capital, it does not reside in the individual. Bureaucracy alone will not suffice, and rational management practices have limits (Biggart 1989: 169–70). In short, cultures of imposed compliance are unlikely to allow for the creativity of workers to be expressed. Work, like consumption, must serve the 'pleasure principle'; it must be the opportunity for variety, for excitement, for some measure of risk (Bauman 2004: 33–4).

Just as the product is marketed so as to resonate with the emotional 'needs' of the consumer, so also is the very process of production 'sold' to the worker. Work should have an emotional appeal. This is referred to as internal marketing. If managers can somehow 'delight' their workers, then the latter may go on to 'delight' their customers in the same way. For these workers, their relationship to their jobs may become emotional, not just calculative. But not all transactions which customers make have the opportunity for eliciting pleasant emotions, as anyone buying groceries in a busy supermarket can attest to. Cost-cutting efficiencies can even lead to computerised self-checkouts being installed. And managing staff on the basis of internal marketing and relationship management is limited in its possibilities for affording 'enchantment'. The products on offer to consumers far exceed the 'product' range on 'offer' to the worker. And consumers choose to shop, wherever and whenever they wish. Even the 'flexible' worker has no such discretion. Nevertheless, this has not stopped some managers looking towards injecting a dose of the spiritual in their attempts to re-enchant the worker (Thrift 1999: 148).

The realm of polity

Bell's second realm is polity. In Western modernity, this is based on liberalism – on the universal rights of individual citizens, enshrined in written constitutions. These rights of the individual should not be such that they undermine the public good. And the notion of the individual implies here an essence – a universality. But this essence is difficult to sustain because, increasingly, the self is seen to be a construction, a project to be undertaken, not a given, not fixed. This quest to accomplish selfhood is partly prompted by a constant flow of media-messages which seek to unsituate the self so that new products and services will be sought and bought. For those who can afford continually to 'buy into' these new identities, there is an implicitly shared consumerist world-view. That is to say, they share the view that by consuming they can accomplish selfhood, at least for a while. But those who, for whatever reason, cannot or will not beat a path to the shopping malls – for them, theirs is a quest for a collective effervescence which seeks solace within a shared moral community, and wherein dispositions are shared, wherein the familiar is favoured over the strange, wherein empathy is privileged over reason. This is a 'community of trust' (Seligman 2010: 8). Faced by continuous uncertainty, disruption and risk, individuals today may be seeking the certainties of pre-modern modes of community. The signs are to be seen in the re-emergence of religious fundamentalism, ethnic movements, and sub-nationalist movements (Lash and Friedman 1992: 355–6).

The result of these social movements is difference, not only among 'communities of trust' themselves, but also – and increasingly – between 'communities of trust' and those 'communities of confidence' which adhere to modern multicultural values, to individual rights and to disparate moral values (Seligman 2010: 8). Thereby emerges a problem:

> At the heart of these issues then is the problem of difference and of living and sharing public space with individuals and groups who are, in certain critical and important ways, different and whose difference makes us uncomfortable.
>
> (ibid.: 9)

It prompts a question: can we live together? (Touraine 2000). The difficulty is that by appealing to 'identity' and 'difference' we imply the exclusion of others; we imply that we are unable to communicate with them (Touraine 2009a: 47). Tolerance is required in order to live together in a society typified by both 'communities of trust' and 'communities of confidence'. It is not sufficient simply to fall back on an extreme relativist position which privatises or trivialises all differences (Touraine 2009a: 6). Tolerance requires that we live with – acquiesce in – that which we regard as different *and* as objectionable. Mere difference does not of itself require tolerance; it is only when that difference provokes our distaste or fear that it becomes objectionable. Tolerance means that we suffer in discomfort; we are not at ease with the difference. But there is another position to take. We may intend away the difference, or trivialise it, so that tolerance no longer becomes necessary. We can say that we and that which is different are really of a piece – that we all share a universal property or characteristic (Seligman 2010: 10). On this, consider Touraine's view on the contemporary education system in France. It – the education system – 'refuses to take into consideration the characteristic of its pupils and identifies completely with the universalism of the knowledge it has to transmit' (Touraine 2009a: 37). State schools in France are required not to recognise differences in the personalities and social backgrounds of their pupils. The central challenge for modern, diversifying societies is to create a new, broader sense of 'we' (Putnam 2007: 140).

The realm of culture

Within contemporary culture, we are facing uncertainties in relation to each other, to our place of employment and to ourselves. It has been argued that the 'characteristics' of the bourgeois individual – self-disciplined, sober, self-motivated, rational and materialistic – had never completely held sway. This Protestant ethic – this work ethic, no less – had not been without its detractors, but they had tended to inhabit enclaves, away from the run of the mill, on the periphery. Until about 1930, there had prevailed an industrial society whose maxims were those of cost–benefit analysis, efficiency and instrumental rationality; it was a technocratic mind-set. Thereafter, what hitherto had begun as the *avant-garde* was gradually to become convention. The 'anti-bourgeois' world-view came to supplant that of the 'bourgeois'. What remains from the nineteenth century is the continuing emergence of the unique individual, one increasingly bereft of traditional ties to family and to a local community. It is an individual who lives alone in a mass-society which is undergoing de-socialisation and de-institutionalisation (Riesman *et al.* 2001). What counts as the 'family' is no longer the agreed concept it once was; it now has many permutations. Marriages are less durable. Religion is in decline, but there are signs of re-emergent 'collective effervescences' based on tribalism, spiritualism and nationalism.

We are on short-term loan to ourselves. Identities seem fragile, forever in need of a makeover. Since the 1960s we have lived in a consumer society. The turning point in the US appears to have been the economic downturn of 1958 during which the meaning of affluence as 'comfort, luxury, and sensual gratification' came to be doubted. It was an expression of 'post-material discontent' with mass consumption; it sought instead more 'sophisticated forms of distinction and self-expression; [. . .] it presented a more dynamic view of consumption, as a psychic balancing act, which oscillates between comfort and pleasure, between gratification and prudence' (Offer 2006: 221). Capitalism has widened its product-range so as to include cultural, not just material, goods. The advertising agencies and the media – especially television and the Internet – set out their market of cultural 'products'. But our identities must have a sell-by date. They must never be laid to rest as fixed and final. No customer must be truly satisfied with their existing purchases, for therein lies the path to corporate decline. Repeat business is needed with the same company, but for a different 'personalised' product, one that will at last accomplish the 'look' and 'feel' that will provide emotional satisfaction.

Companies are at pains to forge 'relationships' with their consumers. We are continually encouraged by the media to reflect upon our identity, and thereafter to redesign it with new symbolisations of ourselves, thereby gaining a stylistic edge over others. We are encouraged to choose anew these material and cultural products. The need to reflect is relentless, and it is meant to be so. The 'symbolic possibilities' which are afforded to those who can afford to have them is now very considerable:

> The fact that we relate to the entire world in a planet-wide interaction and that our culture is marked by an ever-increasing quantity of messages and

information in flux translates into an explosion of symbolic opportunities for individual experience.

(Melucci 1996a: 125)

We are in a continuing mission of 're-selfing', or of 'becoming somebody' (Wexler 1992). We are forever on the move, 'free-floating', 'unencumbered' (Bauman and Vecchi 2004: 29).

Effective consumers must be emotionally intelligent, in touch with themselves. We have seen earlier that emotional labour is required of the flexible worker in the service industries. But there seems to be an increasing salience of the emotions in contemporary culture. Rationality no longer enjoys the status it once did; social theory has embraced the 'body'; lifestyle advisers and other purveyors of therapy promise to steer us through life's never-ending uncertainties; the media serialise and sensationalise the emotions (Williams 2001: 12). But the prospect of personal fulfilment comes at a price. It comes as no surprise that advertisers have now moved their emphasis from the technical to the emotional when selling their products. The technical details of many mechanical or electrical products are now little in evidence. Instead, we must feel the appeal; the producers must somehow resonate subliminally with those emotions which we find to be pleasurable. Products must engender desire, now. Their only 'use' is instant satisfaction; nothing less will suffice (Bauman and Vecchi 2004: 64).

These products are 'visceral', as distinct from 'prudential'. Visceral goods are consumed immediately – payment for them is at the point of delivery; they satisfy drives; their novelty and pleasurable effects are short-lived; they are compelling, thereby giving rise to addictive behaviour. They can be regarded also as 'arousal' goods (Offer 2008: 542). Food, alcohol and entertainment are examples. Prudential goods, on the other hand, require social cooperation for their provision. They involve the promise of delivery at some point in the future. Health, education and social care are examples. While it is not axiomatic that the state should provide prudential goods, nevertheless from about the 1870s to the late 1970s the provision of these services was indeed publicly funded. Thereafter, 'Prudential fatigue gave rise to a public sector stand-off, between the taxpayer as consumer and as investor' (Offer 2003: 20). That is to say, the preference for prudence waned, and that for gratification waxed. As the expectations of the public provision of prudential goods increased, the willingness to pay for them through taxation lessened. Voting patterns followed suit (Offer 2003: 24). The public concerns of the citizen are muscled to the margins of public discourse, giving way to those of the preoccupations of the individual consumer (Bauman 2000: 36). Even governments that wish to retain their commitment to prudential goods run a risk: high welfare provision may attract the 'homeless and disinherited' (thereby raising welfare expenditure), but at the same time they may provoke corporations into relocating elsewhere (Bauman 1998: 54).

One of the quick-fix modes of consumption which is literally visceral is that of food (alcohol is another). In a meta-analysis of 11 countries between 1994 and 2004, it has been found that affluent 'market-liberal welfare regimes' are most likely to have the highest incidence of obesity because overeating is a response to the stress caused by competition, inequality and uncertainty in market-liberal societies. The effect of economic insecurity was found to be almost twice as powerful as that of the impact of cheap, accessible high-energy fast-food (Offer *et al.* 2010). Offer and colleagues' analysis admittedly uses aggregated data, but they raise also the intriguing possibility (not explored) that the roots of excess and risk-taking may be historical. This has an affinity to Campbell's socio-historical analysis of consumerism. He argues that during modernity 'there is a sense in which the disenchantment of the external world required as a parallel process some "enchantment" of the psychic inner world' (Campbell 1989: 73). The bourgeois individual was prone to suppress the affects and emotions, so that their expression could only be imagined. Their 'release' could be enabled by consumption. Campbell argues further that the locus of the emotions has been historically contingent. This was different from the pre-modern period when the emotions were regarded as 'inherent in aspects of reality, from whence they exert their influence over humans'; they '"filled" him [*sic*] with those distinctively aroused states called emotions' (ibid.: 72). Even so, the act of choosing and consuming has yet to re-enchant those who can 'buy into' consumerism, which may be why there are signs of an association between, on the one hand, games of chance, astrology and the 'restoration of the natural', and, on the other hand, the 're-enchantment of the world' (Maffesoli 1996: 39). While science prevails, enchantment will be elusive. We are caught in 'the deep contradictions of Romantic feeling and Enlightenment rationalism' (Inglis 1982: 23), between private feelings and public bureaucracy. In its quest to remove uncertainty, science generates more uncertainty. Science does not endow the world with meaning; it is meaningless, unlike other world-views. Its 'inner logic' is that it erodes the world of meaning, and it cannot replace that which it has removed (Schroeder 1995: 233). We remain ill at ease with ourselves. Nothing is fixed. No harbour for the self is safe (Melucci 1996b: 2). Contemporary culture has few taboos. Images of suffering attract an aesthetic rather than an ethical reaction, and to take a moral standpoint may attract accusations of not being liberal.

The writing of this book began when UK and US banks in 2008–9 were failing. It ends during a period when large cuts in public expenditure are being pronounced in the UK (especially in England) and in other parts of Europe. This is the cost of dealing with the banking crisis of 2008. Hitherto, before the crash, the profits of the banks had been privatised, but now the costs of re-capitalising them are to be socialised from the public purse. And although many of the failing banks had global interests, it is to nation-states that they turned in their time of need; and so national sovereign-debt levels have soared to levels which do not seem manageable. As a result, there has been a resurgence of public unrest – and particularly by school and university students, and by the urban unemployed – the likes of which have not been seen since the 1960s. Does this mark an end of the apathy of the young towards what might be called social (as opposed to individual lifestyle) issues? It is young people who look beneath the surface of society's demands and contradictions. They deal with them as best they can in ways which may appear to be mysterious and troublesome to adults (Willis 2003: 391). For Melucci, the young are, in his words, 'the primary subjects of dramatic transformations that affect contemporary society, and they experience them most immediately. By listening to their sharp voice, adults can learn about themselves' (Melucci 1996a: 123). Since the 1960s the issues for the young have changed from the right to equality to the 'right to *difference*' (Melucci and Keane 1989: 177). Their concerns have shifted from making a difference, towards being different and tolerating difference. Are they about to start to make a difference again?

Summary

Throughout this chapter, it has become clear that there exists an attentuation – a lack of correspondence – between what Daniel Bell has called structure and culture, or between Enlightened rationalism and Romantic feeling. Structure – economy, markets and technology – seems to have detached itself from that of collective and individual identities (Touraine 2000: 49). To be sure, the fiscal crisis of 2008 has thrown into sharp focus the anomalies and contradictions which for the most part had lain dormant during what Perez has called the 'installation' phase of the economic cycle. As in the aftermath of 1929, so it is now. The tensions are plain to see: those between the responsibilities of the nation-state and those of the global 'community'; those between what O'Connor called 'accumulation' policies and 'legitimation' policies – or, put differently, between the deregulated pursuit of profit and its deleterious side-effect of growing inequalities among nation-states, and within them. There is also the tension between, on the one hand, a culture which is fragmented and unstable, and whose maxim celebrates a market-driven emphasis on consumption, identity and difference; and, on the other hand, a government whose wish will surely be to prune expenditure, and with it a resurgence of standardisation, surveillance and accountability. The centrifugal forces at work in the cultural realm will engage uneasily with the centripetal tendencies of government. And finally, there is unease about individualism, self-centredness. Are the emotions which bind communities now giving way to the short-term calculative associations of networks?

4 Markets, bureaucracy and education

Schooling during the industrial age was marked by firm categorisations and boundaries: between one national system and another; among school subjects; between teacher and taught; among age-groups; between the sexes; and between society and school. Much was predictable, sustainable and containable – even parochial. Since the 1960s, however, there has emerged a discontinuity between this isomorphic structural form and emerging cultural patterns. Gone are the predictable pathways which used to chart the direction of life. The industrial mind-set came to be seen as resting uneasily with an increasingly market-generated commodification of the lifeworld. A synthesis between the two was sought. The beginnings of this synthesis are revealed in the post-1980 education policies of those nation-states which adopted economic neo-liberalism, in particular the US, New Zealand and England. This chapter charts the first phase of this process of what came to be known as the 'marketisation' of education. Put simply, it was an engagement between bureaucracy and markets.

Bureaucracy

For the past century or so, we have been living in the age of the machine. Especially during the period influenced by Taylorist management theory (after 1911), workers were regarded as somewhat inert, as raw material, to be manipulated. Little was left to chance: time, space, materials and workers were all subjected to specification and to supervision. All was itemised and costed; nothing was wasted. The optimal organisational form was bureaucracy. Bureaucracy is best suited to an organisation which fulfils the following conditions: the product is stable and fixed; the raw material from which it is derived is clearly understood; the processes of production are tried and tested; and the product can be recognised easily and objectively by the market, without ambiguity. Even during leisure time, this bureaucratic and technical way of thinking had a way of suffusing consciousness, prompting list-making, coordinating, monitoring, measuring and classifying (Berger *et al.* 1974).

The school is a monument to this mind-set. If the metaphor of a manufacturing process is superimposed upon the school, then this association becomes clear. Let us say that we have a *raw material* called a child. The process of production – the *technology* – is pedagogy. The *organisational structure* for production is the classroom (itself within a school, arranged bureaucratically). The *product* is a recognised credential which represents the child's understanding of the formal curriculum which was to be transmitted. What has characterised much of the history of formal schooling has been a school system which has emphasised the homogeneity of pupils: that is, there has been a presumed homogeneity about the 'nature of the child'. Virtually everything was arranged rationally: architecture, time, curriculum, assessment. Rules regulated everything. Children were to be rational and sensible, not silly. They were to sit down in their place. For all activities there were set procedures. This was deemed to be natural: *the* school, *the* classroom, *the* pupil, *the* curriculum, *the* teacher. And the pupils literally wore a *uniform*. It is true there have been periodic deviations from this – such as child-centred education and open-plan architectures – but these have been short-lived, and were more rhetoric than reality. This standardised state of affairs – this 'soulless standardization' (Hargreaves 2003: xvii) – has prevailed since the introduction of mass elementary education in the late nineteenth century. It has mattered little whether or not the nation's economy leaned towards capitalism or to socialism. What mattered was that this was schooling which was arranged on rational lines, for efficiency (it was cheap), and for effectiveness (it anticipated the 'mass' nature of production and consumption).

During the 1960s, what came to be known as 'industrial society' had to face many difficulties, both external and domestic. Of the former there was international competition from Asia, and (in the UK) opposition from once-compliant Commonwealth countries which came to realise that the wealth was not so common after all. Of the latter: demands for a more benevolent welfare state, and for higher wages and more flexible working conditions; calls for reform by the civil rights movement (in the US) and by the women's movements; and concerns about the Cold War and the war in Vietnam. The 1973 oil-crisis brought these matters to a head. In 1983, the National Commission on Excellence in Education reported in *A Nation at Risk*:

> If an unfriendly foreign power had attempted to impose on America the mediocre educational performance that exists today, we might well have viewed it as an act of war. As it stands, we have allowed this to happen to ourselves. We have even squandered the gains in student achievement made in the wake of the Sputnik challenge. Moreover, we have dismantled essential support systems which helped make those gains possible. We have, in effect, been committing an act of unthinking, unilateral educational disarmament.
>
> (National Commission on Excellence in Education 1984: unpaginated)

This indictment was made after a long period of reform, and after increasing per-pupil expenditures. Eventually, Prime Minister Thatcher and (later) President Reagan both called for reductions in the size of the state, and insisted upon a more market-based provision for public services. One of the most widely cited examples of a market-based solution in the US was *Politics, Markets, and America's*

Schools: 'the most important prerequisite for the emergence of effective school characteristics is school autonomy, especially from external bureaucratic influence' (Chubb and Moe 1990: 23). John Maynard Keynes was now forgotten, Milton Friedman and the monetarists favoured. The financiers were let loose; markets were de-regulated. In a 'new spirit of capitalism' (Boltanski and Chiapello 2005), the neo-liberals cleverly co-opted the new cultural 'norms': that is to say, in production, 'flexible' working practices were introduced within a neo-Fordist managerial regime; in consumption, businesses set out their stalls of 'niche' goods and services which appealed to identity-seeking customers. Marketing became a business unto itself. Minds, bodies and emotions – even spirituality – became open to its gaze and reach.

Politics at the national level is today mainly about lifestyle issues. Culturally, almost anything goes. There is an inclination towards relativism (Gellner 1992). If, during the middle ages, life was lived in fear of the after-life, now it is lived in fear of the salvation of the self in this one. The concerns of today are more immediate, and they seem to elude definitive answers. Even the certainties of science seem uncertain. In a sense this should not be surprising, for it is the quest of science forever to question what claims to be convention. Some scientists succumb to 'normal science', but there are sufficient numbers of others who can disrupt it. The effect is sometimes that the public bears witness to the competing claims which the research reveals. Scientists at times give conflicting messages: drink red wine, don't drink red wine; eat eggs, don't eat eggs. Indeed, many of the stories of certainty – the 'grand narratives' of science – were said to be in disarray (Lyotard 1984). And, as one might expect in a scientific and democratic society, deference to once-hallowed 'authorities' has waned: those who cannot count themselves as able-bodied, white, middle class, male, liberal and heterosexual continue their claims for recognition, and for their voices to be heard. No longer will appeals to biology, to religion, to tradition or to the law silence these voices. And when there are no absolutes, confusion sets in. But help is not far away. Anxieties can be assuaged. The lifestyle gurus and the makeover merchants are ready with their solutions, at a price. For those who cannot afford to partake of these wares – they literally cannot 'buy into' them – there beckons another type of guru, a pre-modern guru, whose message is that the rewards for faith and compliance are not to be found in the mundane.

The global financial crisis of 2008, as we saw in Chapter 3, has presented international politics with a new urgency. Contrary to expectations, the end of history (Fukuyama 2006) has not come to pass. Modernity's path to progress now looks to be littered with obstacles. Within a very short space of time – no more than about 20 years – there has been a global awareness of common and contemporaneous concerns: international terrorism; the regulation of global finance; the likelihood of 'resource' conflicts, especially over oil and water; and the effects of climate-change. The banking crisis of 2008, and the sovereign debt crisis which followed, brought them into sharp focus, but the structures for dealing with them are not yet in place. To be sure, after decades of derogatory comments about the 'state' by neo-liberals, how ironic it was that the response to the economic crisis was decidedly national; for it was to national governments that failing banks turned in their hour of need. Suddenly 'throwing money' (that is, public funds) at a pressing problem seemed to be no bad thing in the eyes of those who hitherto would have had no truck with it (Clarke 2010: 387).

Bureaucracy and markets

During the early 1980s, different societies adopted different positions about the welfare state. In the US, New Zealand and in the UK (especially England), the view was taken that bureaucracy was a source of limitation to the smooth functioning of public services. In short, the professionals who worked in these public service agencies had 'captured' them. On the other hand, the customer, or the consumer, had simply the right to take what was on offer, not to demand what he or she actually needed or wanted. In particular, in the UK, the power of local authorities was regarded as being excessive, especially if they were controlled by the opposition Labour party. In Scotland, where the writ of Thatcherism did not run, there was a particular nationalist resistance to neo-liberal policies.

Since 1944, expectations of the welfare state had been rising, but the capacity to fund them was declining. As economic globalisation gathered pace, there was competition from the Indian sub-continent and from some Asian countries. Entrepreneurship (especially in the UK) was said to be in need of reassertion. Competition was back in vogue. In response to economic globalisation, different societies adopted different positions about their welfare states (Bronk 2000). On the one hand, flexible labour market policies in the US produced very considerable psychological, financial and social costs for the unemployed. On the other hand, in some of the less 'flexible' European economies, whose welfare provision was more generous (as in Germany, a 'corporatist welfare' regime), higher levels of unemployment were regarded as politically sustainable (Esping-Andersen 1990), though only up to a point (Carnoy 2002: 248–9). To be sure, modern economies require efficient state agencies which socialise the costs of the infrastructures upon which capitalism depends. And capitalism needs structures – religion, family, nation – which will enable the social cohesion which will serve to lessen the centrifugal tendencies of competitive and narcissistic individualism. In Europe, Bauman has succinctly summed up the problem: 'The governments who insist on keeping the standards of welfare intact are therefore haunted by the fear of a "double whammy": the homeless and disinherited flocking in, the capital (and so potential income sources) flocking out' (Bauman 1998: 54).

In the 1990s, the problem of the welfare state and its relationship to economic globalisation attracted a new solution. It was informed by the concept of 'governance', a term commonly associated with international relations:

> I understand 'governance' to mean the capacity to get things done without the legal competence to command that they be done. [. . .] Governments

exercise rule, governance uses power. From this point of view, the international system is a system of governance.

(Czempiel 1992: 250)

Within some nation-states during the 1990s, the concept of governance was introduced, not with the intention of replacing government, but of refining it. While government relies upon formal authority, governance does not, for it must gain the consent of a majority of those whom its activities affect; government, on the other hand, can, if necessary and up to a point, continue to function even when this consent is not forthcoming. Governance, therefore, steers at a distance. It lessens the emphasis on the nomenclature of bureaucracy; it deploys a discourse of 'ownership', 'involvement', 'empowerment', 'devolution' and – especially – 'choice'. Thus, whereas within the international system there is no government (only governance), within national systems there is government, but with an orientation and practice towards governance. And whereas governance refers to the networked *inter*-relationships between public and private providers, the new public management confines itself to the reform of management at the *intra*-organisational level (Rhodes 1996).

Governance has an elective affinity to what became known in the 1990s as the 'new public management'. It assumes that bureaucracy of the Weberian ideal type is deemed to be unsuitable for the delivery of services which Osborne and Gaebler call 'rowing', as distinct from deciding policy, which they term 'steering' (Osborne and Gaebler 1993: 35). The new public management was akin to 'entrepreneurial governance' which

> demands institutions that are responsive to their customers, offering choices of non-standardised services; that lead by persuasion and incentives rather than commands; that give their employees a sense of meaning and control, even ownership.

(ibid.: 15)

It drew a ready endorsement from President Clinton, whose Vice-President, Al Gore, was given oversight of the National Performance Review which commenced in 1993, and whose aim was to enable this entrepreneurial government. In the UK, by the end of the Conservative government in 1997, this new public management was reported to have taken root, nationally and internationally. The 1996–7 OECD survey of 28 countries reported common 'reform strands'. These were: devolving managerial authority; a focus on results; a service-quality orientation; effective leadership; and, crucially, a *strengthening of the steering functions at the centre* in order to implement strategic reforms and to promote policy-coherence in the face of complex policy problems and a more devolved public sector environment (OECD 1997: 86–7). These strands comprise the 'audit society' (Power 1997) and the 'evaluative state' (Neave 1988: 11). Within the evaluative state, strategy is set by government, which sets goals and targets. It specifies products rather than processes, and it monitors the achievement of these products (Neave 1988: 11). The evaluative state is similar conceptually to the new public management:

> First NPM can be understood as primarily an expression of sigma-type values. Its claims have lain mainly in the direction of cutting costs and doing more for less as a result of better-quality management and different structural design.
>
> (Hood 1991: 15)

'Sigma-type values' mean that they endorse the maxim: 'keep it lean and purposeful' (ibid.: 11). It stands for 'payment by results', what Neave calls a posteriori evaluation. '*A posteriori* evaluation works then through control of *product* not through control of process' (Neave 1988: 11).

As far as education was concerned, the new public management seemed to go in two directions: on the one hand, towards more school-based decision-making, especially of financial management and staffing; and, on the other hand, towards greater central control and inspection of both the curriculum and of the school (Hartley 2008: 368). Gradually, in England, more of the pedagogical process of primary schooling came to be prescribed. This, therefore, was no free market; it was a 'quasi-market', not a normal market. Not normal, because it is the state, not the user, who pays; and the provider's funding is related to the number of users who choose it. The quasi-market is, therefore, said to be a 'fundamentally egalitarian device, enabling public services to be delivered in such a way as to avoid most of the inequalities that arise in normal markets from differences in people's purchasing power' (Le Grand 2007: 40). To repeat: at one and the same time, the state directs policy, but does not appear to do so; it steers. It defines strategy from the centre, but it devolves the 'ownership' and the choice of the tactics whereby this strategy will be accomplished. It is more concerned with the 'product'; it is less concerned with the 'process' whereby the product is accomplished. Of importance, too, is the causal linkage which is made between funding and monitored performance. Funding follows performance; no longer is it an up-front investment which is entrusted to the professionals who will use their good judgement to spend it wisely and efficaciously.

So began a process which revealed a new synthesis between bureaucracy and markets. This was no bureaucracy–market binary, but rather a necessary conjunction of the two. The new public management and the quasi-market were of a piece. At first glance, the continuation of bureaucracy seems to fly in the face of the notion of a market. After all, is not the market supposed to be free, to be not encumbered by bureaucratic procedures? But the reason for the continuation of bureaucracy as a mode of regulation was that it was seen as necessary for the market to operate smoothly. That is to say, the parent required knowledge – *objective* knowledge, not hearsay – which could be trusted, and which would enable a comparison to be made among schools. That being the case, it would be necessary – insofar as schools were concerned – to standardise the curriculum. Since the Second World War, and before 1988, the curriculum in England had resided quietly in its 'secret garden', a garden sequestered from the state's intervention, save for the requirement to provide religious education. Only the examinations of pupils at the ages of 16 and 18 had not been not set by the schools; they had been set by examining boards. It was argued also that a national curriculum would ensure a fair entitlement 'for all', and it would have the benefit of furthering a One Nation conservatism. In sum, the national curriculum could be seen as progressive, but also – because it allowed for national testing – it appealed to economic neo-liberals who were determined to structure the education system according to market principles.

This standardisation of both curriculum and assessment was not introduced at the outset of the journey to the market. In England it occurred only with the Education Reform Act (1988). Before then, the government's policy had been directed towards redefining the parent as a consumer of schools for their children. That is to say, parents after 1980 (in England; in Scotland, after 1981) could express a preference for (not choose) a school which was not their local one. On this, there were certain caveats made, such as the architectural limitations on the capacity of the school to take in more pupils than it had been designed for. The difficulty – as argued by the government – was that parents, the would-be consumers, had little objective evidence with which to compare schools rationally. In England, the national curriculum and national testing allowed for these comparisons to be made; and publicly so, in the form of league tables. (In Scotland, the curriculum was not legislated; there were merely curricular guidelines, although they were seen as requirements; and there were no primary-school league tables.) In England, therefore, school league tables were produced which provided a ready-reckoner for parents to consult when making their so-called rational choices, out of self-interest. In addition, parents could consult the individual school inspection reports published by the then Office for Standards in Education (OfSTED), since renamed as the Office for Standards in Education, Children's Services and Skills. Even so, many decisions which parents made were on the grounds of proximity to the friendship groups to which their children belonged, or for other reasons which were not necessarily connected to the so-called objective data that the league tables publicised. For example, whether or not parents resided in urban areas (which have a greater selection of schools from which to choose), or whether or not they could afford the transportation costs to a distant school. The policy assumed, too, that all parents had the same capacity and inclination to seek and to interpret the data, which was not the case (Gewirtz *et al.* 1995). There was also the difficult issue of how to define and to monitor school effectiveness. As a general observation, schools which had middle-class catchment areas performed better than schools which were in working-class catchment areas. But to rely simply upon the raw achievement data as an indication of the effectiveness of the school was thought to be a misrepresentation. There needed to be a so-called 'value-added component' to the league table publications, not just reliance upon absolute attainment. That, it was argued, would be the fairer method with which to compare schools. Even so, there is a very strong correlation between value-added scores and absolute attainment scores: 'Value-added scores are no *more* independent of raw-score levels of attainment than outcomes are independent of intakes' (Gorard 2006: 241; emphasis in the original). Indeed value-added analyses themselves require near-perfect measured information at the two points in time. And even in England, where central government undertakes an annual school census (which includes attainment data for all pupils), at least 30 per cent of cases contain errors (Gorard 2010: 54). Besides all this, there remain very difficult issues about closing 'failing' schools, about when to do so, and about what must be done with the pupils and teachers who will be displaced.

Academies and free schools

Between 1979 and 2010, the broad intention had been to extend the quasi-market in education. The process was begun by the Conservative government (which ended in 1997), and thereafter by the Labour governments, which arguably furthered competition and central control (Whitty 2008: 166). Labour also extended the possibilities for schools to achieve greater autonomy. Previously, the Conservative government had enacted the right to establish grant-maintained schools in 1988, and thereafter City Technology Colleges (CTCs) allowed for private-sector sponsors to partly fund them. To these were added the 'city academies', the first of which was opened in 2002. Like American charter schools (of which more below), they are independent and publicly funded schools which are partnerships or joint-ventures between central government and sponsors, be they individuals, faith-based organisations or businesses. Ten per cent of their intake may be selected on the basis of their aptitude and ability, and they offer a curricular specialism.

They resurrect the nineteenth-century paternalism and philanthropy which marked education in England before 1874 (Gleeson 2010: 200). In England, the Coalition government which succeeded the Labour government in May 2010 is even more committed to academies than its predecessor. It has now allowed primary schools to achieve academy status, and it has streamlined the application processes. It wishes academy-status to be the norm for state schools, which in turn means that they will be funded directly from central government (Department for Education 2010a: 52). It defined academies as

> publicly funded independent local schools that provide a first class free education. They are all ability schools established by sponsors from business, faith or voluntary groups working with partners from the local community. Academies provide a teaching and learning environment that is in line with the best in the maintained sector and offer a broad and balanced curriculum to pupils of all abilities, focusing especially on one or more subject areas (specialisms). As well as providing the best opportunities for the most able pupils and those needing additional support, academies have a key part to play in the regeneration of disadvantaged communities.
>
> (Department for Education 2010b: unpaginated)

On the face of it, there seems to be little to separate the Thatcher and Blair governments' education policies. They contain similar discourses: of standardisation (accountability, audit, competition, standards, targets, efficiency, effectiveness and excellence); and of differentiation (individual, choice, diversity). Blair's New Labour, however, sought to revive their social justice agenda, preferring a pragmatic Third Way approach, one which sought to reconcile the 'old left' and the 'new right'. The 'old left' believed in the pervasive involvement by the state in social and economic life. It set great store by 'collectivism', with a welfare system which protected citizens fully from birth to death. As for the 'new right', it was all for 'minimal government', for an 'autonomous civil society', for 'market fundamentalism', for 'moral authoritarianism, plus strong economic individualism', for the 'acceptance of inequality'; and for a 'welfare state as safety net' (Giddens 1998: 7–8). In short, the Third Way sought to reconcile neo-liberal (that is, accountability, competition and choice) with progressive social democratic (that is, 'equity') principles (Whitty 2008). The neo-liberals wished to position parents as informed, rationally-choosing consumers who would prompt schools to maximise their performance, and thereby attract pupils. The progressive 'equity' position, however, seeks to break the association between schooling and housing, thereby ending 'selection by mortgage'. Sometimes ignored is a libertarian position: choice is, in itself, a good thing, of intrinsic value (though not if it leads to neglect or to abuse) (Goodwin 2009: 272).

Have these 'quasi-market' policies in England reduced social segregation? Place of residence should not determine which school is attended. This is not something which the relatively prosperous have to put up with, and so nor should others have to. Indeed, when – within the state sector – there *is* attenuation between residence and schooling then the middle class moves quickly to recover its position. They resort to 'exit'. In a city, this can take the form of moving to a property within the catchment area of a high-performing school. This in itself pushes up house prices in that catchment area, which in turn generates a catchment area whose middle-class parents have amassed both financial and (usually) cultural capital. The *School Admissions Code* in England provided for 'random allocation' if a school is oversubscribed. *Section 2.33* of the code stated:

> Random allocation of school places can be good practice particularly for urban areas and secondary schools. However, it may not be suitable in rural areas. It may be used as the sole means of allocating places or alongside other oversubscription criteria, but only after criteria giving priority to children in care and the admission of children with a statement of special educational needs. Random allocation can widen access to schools for those unable to afford to buy houses near to favoured schools and create greater social equity.
>
> (Department for Education 2007c: 34)

Random allocation had been practised in the US (the District of Columbia, Milwaukee and Chicago), in New Zealand, in The Netherlands and in Sweden (Stone 2008: 268).

Take a landmark policy in one English local authority. In 2007, in the City Council of Brighton and Hove in the south of England, some schools were oversubscribed. Parents had to participate in a lottery ('random allocation') which would determine which school their children went to. It was intended to put an end to 'selection by mortgage', and to inject impartiality into the process. Furthermore, parents who previously had 'bought into' the catchment area of a high-performing school could also run the risk of their house-prices falling, given that their exclusive right of access to the school was no longer secure (Paton 2007). The initial consequence was that local independent schools reported increases in applications of up to 44 per cent (Curtis 2008). The middle class was not prepared to run the risk of being randomly rejected. However, a more recent study of the effects of that lottery has reported 'no significant change in student sorting: if anything, the point estimates suggest a rise in socio-economic segregation' (Allen *et al.* 2010: 16). A revised admissions code, which was implemented in England in September 2011, required local authorities to end the use of area-wide lotteries.

The case of Sweden provides a germane example – germane because not only was Sweden a bastion of welfarist principles before 1992, but also because its experience of for-profit free schools has been closely followed, especially by the Conservative party in England. In Sweden, these free schools co-exist with municipal schools. Both types of school operate within a national regulatory framework, and they must hire only trained teachers. Even so, the independent schools are less regulated in a range of aspects to do with staff competence; with health and social care; with facilities for physical education, science and home economics; and with school meals and library facilities (Arreman and Holm 2011: 232). Both independent and free schools are state-funded, and the free schools cannot charge top-up fees. They must work within the value of the state-funded vouchers, which are disbursed by the municipalities. Their profit accrues from any 'savings' in salaries, and in the cost of both materials and premises. In the post-16 sector, a report by the state-funded Swedish Public Service television service estimated that in 2007 the 300 independent school companies achieved a turnover of more than 1,000 million euros (Arreman and Holm 2011: 233). In the municipal schools, any such savings remain within the municipality. In sum, the free schools are for profit; the municipal schools are for the public (Fredriksson 2009: 303).

A report, *School Choice and its Effects in Sweden,* by Skolverket, the Swedish National Agency for Education, surveyed parents, the majority of whom reported greater school segregation, as did senior administrators in cities and suburbs. The report notes that in the two cases which were specifically studied, 'the results also show fairly unambiguously that segregation has in fact increased' (Skolverket [The Swedish National Agency for Education] 2006: 32). Moreover, the higher the educational achievement level of the parents (especially city-dwellers), the higher the likelihood that they would make a choice of school. They were 'considerably more favourable' in their attitude towards both independent schools and to competition among municipal schools (ibid.: 31). The report concludes by expressing the concern that if, as is the case, there is increasing uncertainty about the effects of school-choice, and particularly so if they undermine 'positive values such as enhanced democracy, educational development and justice', then the legitimacy of the reforms may be withdrawn.

To return to the UK, on the point of social segregation, Gorard and colleagues' national study of the period between January 1989 and 1995 concluded that segregation by poverty in all secondary schools in England had declined annually. Moreover, when they operationalised other measures of socio-economic status (such as statements of special educational need, first-language use and ethnicity) they found the same trend – that is, reduced segregation (Gorard *et al.* 2003: 184). After 1996, however, school segregation by poverty in England did rise until 2001–2, and it remained at that level until 2005–6 (Gorard 2009b: 648–9). The centrifugal tendencies marked by the weakening of the national curriculum, the extension of vocational tracks, and selection by faith, by 'aptitude' and by the ability to pay – all this may explain the rising socio-economic segregation among schools since 1997 (Gorard 2010: 60).

Has an education policy which has been informed by 'quasi-market' principles reduced the social stratification of academic achievement? A major report, *How Fair is Britain? Equality, human rights and good relations in 2010*, published by the Equality and Human Rights Commission, revealed the persistence of the effects of relative poverty, as measured by the eligibility for free school meals (FSM). These effects occurred as early as the age of five years, and widened by the age of 16 (Equality and Human Rights Commission 2010: 326). For example, at the age of five years, 55 per cent of pupils who were not eligible for free school meals 'achieved a good level of development in 2008–9, compared to 35% for pupils known to be eligible for FSM' (ibid.: 305). These effects became greater throughout the school years, so that FSM students were 'only half as likely to have good GCSE results as those who are not'. The report continues:

> The combination of being eligible for FSM and being part of another group with a lower probability of obtaining good qualifications (for example boys, those with an identified SEN [special educational need] and certain ethnic minority groups) leads to extremely low results.
>
> (ibid.: 325; square brackets added)

As for the academies programme, an analysis of the progress of those schools which converted to academy status between 2002 and 2006 raises doubts about the ringing endorsements which have been made of them. Gorard, in a follow-up to his earlier study (Gorard 2005), concludes that academy schools perform not much differently from their non-academy counterparts *in similar circumstances*, albeit as measured narrowly by performance at Key Stage 4. That said, it begs the question whether or not all of the time, effort and energy which was expended on academies has been worth it (Gorard 2009a: 113).

This kind of evidence has not deterred the Coalition government in the UK from nailing its colours ever more firmly to the mast of the academy. And, inspired by Swedish policy, the government in June 2010 invited proposals for 'free schools', referred to above. In Sweden about ten per cent of lower secondary school pupils attend free schools. The majority are operated on a for-profit basis, thereby producing some social stratification. As stated, they have proved to be more attractive to affluent and educated parents. As for their effects on pupil attainment, a recent meta-analysis concluded that pupils in Sweden 'do not appear to be harmed by the competition from private schools, but the new schools have not yet transformed educational attainment in Sweden' (Allen 2010: 4). The government in England invited proposals from 'charities, universities, businesses, educational groups, teachers and groups of parents'. The English free schools are to be 'inclusive': that is, they will provide for all abilities and backgrounds. They will 'improve choice and drive up standards for all young people, regardless of their background'. As with academies, they will be 'free' to set the pay and conditions for their staff; to have greater control of their budget; to not have to follow the national curriculum (but it must be a 'balanced and broadly based curriculum' and both academies and free schools are required to teach English, mathematics and science, and to make provision for the teaching of religious education); to vary the length of school terms and days; and to be free from the control of their local authority. Their funding will be on a 'comparable basis' to that of academies and other state-funded schools; and – so far, unlike in Sweden – they will not be for-profit. By February 2011, the government had received 323 proposals. In September 2011, 24 free schools had opened.

Charter schools: engines of progress?

In England, the Coalition government gave charter schools in the US a ringing endorsement: as 'engines of progress' no less (Department for Education 2010a: 51). The emerging evidence suggests that this is something of an over-simplification. In the US, there are about 5,000 charter schools. They are publicly-funded, beyond the control of local school districts. Their charter allows them greater autonomy over curriculum, pedagogy and operations. Those students who attend them choose to attend them, instead of being assigned to them (Zimmer *et al.* 2009: xi). The first charter schools were formed in the city of Milwaukee in 1991.

Have charter schools reduced social segregation and increased standards? The results are at best inconclusive. The research on charter schools is beset by a lack of conceptual agreement. Moreover, it is not easy to generalise at the national level, given that education is mainly a state and local matter. In the US, the research evidence in favour of school choice as determining academic outcomes is 'rather thin indeed' (Lubienski 2008: 40). In a sense, the research appears not to matter to policy-makers, for it is argued that 'school choice in the USA is growing rapidly regardless of what research "says"' (Lubienski 2008: 42). It is a matter of policy-based evidence; not evidence-based policy.

The early studies drew no consistent conclusions – some negative, others positive. Of the former, Bettinger's study of charter schools in Michigan raised doubts about their benefits: they did not improve academic attainment as quickly as had those traditional public schools whose 'pre-charter' test scores were similar (Bettinger 2005). On the matter of 'cream-skimming', the RAND study of charter schools in eight states found no evidence that they systematically attracted above-average students: 'In all seven sites, students transferring to charter schools tended to choose schools with demographic characteristics not dramatically different from those of the TPPs [that is, traditional public schools] they left' (Zimmer *et al.* 2009: 87; brackets added). There were no 'dramatic shifts in the sorting of students by race in any of the sites included in the study' (ibid.: 90–1). But there were some positive outcomes for charter schools. In relation to attainment there were two states – Florida and Illinois (Chicago) – which had data. In those states: 'Attending a charter high school is associated with statistically significant and substantial increases in the probability of graduating and of enrolling in college' (ibid.). There was no evidence that charter schools 'negatively affected' the achievement of students in nearby traditional public schools (ibid.); but nor were there any 'positive competitive effects' (Texas excepted) on traditional public schools near to a charter school (ibid.: 90–1).

The more recent and much more extensive findings of the Center for Research on Education Outcomes (CREDO) study at Stanford University are less supportive of charter schools. Its sample was far larger than that of the RAND study, and it comprised a longitudinal student-level study of the effects of 70 per cent of charter schools in the US. Each charter school student was matched with a 'virtual twin' based on demographic data, English-language proficiency, subsidised lunch eligibility and participation in special education (Center for Research on Education Outcomes 2009: 1). The purpose of the study was

> to test whether students who attend charter schools fare better than if they had instead attended traditional public schools in their community. The outcome of interest is academic learning gains in reading and math [sic], measured in standard deviation units.
>
> (ibid.)

Some 17 per cent of charter schools (a 'decent fraction', according to the authors) outperformed a matched TPS, but 37 per cent of charter schools 'deliver learning results that are significantly worse than their students would have realized had they remained in traditional public schools' (ibid.: 43). (The results refer to 'math gains'.) The authors conclude that these latter results are 'both alarming and regrettable' (ibid.: 46). The remaining charter schools (46 per cent) performed no differently than their local TPS (ibid.: 43).

There were significant state-by-state differences. The authors conclude: 'Our national pooled analysis reveals, on the whole, a slightly negative picture of average charter school performance nationwide. On average, charter school students can expect to see their academic growth be somewhat lower than their traditional public school peers, though the absolute differences are small' (ibid.: 45). There is also a chronological consideration: first-year charter students have significantly smaller achievement gains than their TPS counterparts, but in the second and third years this trend is reversed (ibid.: 45). It appears that the hyped and hoped-for gains which would accrue from charter schools look to be unconfirmed by recent meta-analyses of the research, most notable that by Loveless and Field (2009). At best, the matter remains unresolved: after 15 years the academic outcomes of charter schools are so far 'mixed' (ibid.: 111–12). None of the studies detects either large positive or negative effects, and they may produce – contrary to the public interest – the unintended consequence of increased racial segregation (ibid.).

The responses to the major studies have produced some surprises. An early and prominent advocate of marketisation in American education, Diane Ravitch, has recently recalled how easily she had been convinced of its claims: 'I too had jumped aboard a bandwagon, one festooned with banners celebrating the power of accountability, incentives, and markets. I too was captivated by these ideas' (Ravitch 2010: 3). Her conclusion now is that business leaders mistakenly regard schooling as consumer-driven, like shopping. Schooling, like policing, or fire-fighting, may in theory be privatised, 'but it is not wise' (ibid.: 221). In this she might well have concurred with the point made in 1862 by the Duke of Marlborough when the House of Lords was debating 'payment by results'. He stated:

> One grave objection to the new system was, that instead of the education of the country being conducted as heretofore religiously and conscientiously, it would introduce into it a mercantile spirit – that there would be a danger of its engendering and fostering a feeling in the minds of schoolmasters which would induce them to look upon their pupils as having a certain money value, and to neglect those whose instruction was not likely to be remunerative. The schoolmaster's pecuniary interests rather than the moral training of the child would be rather attended to. It would also prevent managers from giving to the schools that constant notice and attention which they had hitherto bestowed upon them, and would expose teachers to the temptation – one which he hoped and firmly believed would never be yielded to, but which would nevertheless exist – to falsify returns in order to secure money payments.
>
> (Hansard 1862, cc 1012–13)

There remain also the considerations that charter schools – because they rely so much upon financial sponsorship – are vulnerable to the whims and fads of those who fund them. And some of this research seems to be touched by 'advocacy researchers' who may circumvent traditional peer-reviewing. That is to say, a new and powerful research infrastructure – comprising influential think-tanks which are well funded by pro-charter, pro-choice foundations – has emerged (Lubienski and Garn 2010: 42).

Naming, shaming and gaming

A 'reign of terror' is said to best describe what the English education system was subjected to during the 1980s (Scott *et al.* 1999). It was 'ruthlessly policed' (Alexander 2001: 352), and very rapidly so – within a ten-year period. The Conservative government denied this; if anything, it argued, the opposite was the case because financial management had been devolved mainly to the school, away from the local authority. Indeed, the policy of local management of schools (LMS) had served to give the impression that the government had set aside the mundane matters of administration, preferring instead to steer at a distance, to confine itself to strategy. How, therefore, could these policies attract descriptions such as 'reign of terror' and ruthless policing (Hartley 2008: 367)?

When the stakes are high, the players must deploy all of the moves which will mitigate their loss and maximise their gain. Hood makes the point that in 1998 Prime Minister Blair adopted in a modified form the mode of economic management by 'targets' which the Soviet Union had abandoned about a decade before. In England, this 'target and terror regime' was to be applied to the management of the public services. For education, some six 'top-level targets' comprised 90 'conditions' which thereafter would apply to all of the state schools in England. In response, managers would adopt 'gaming' tactics in order to cope. One such behaviour was the *threshold effect*

> whereby a uniform output target applying to all units in a system gives no incentive to excellence and may indeed encourage top performers to reduce the quality or quantity of their performance to just what the target requires.
>
> (Hood 2006: 516)

For example, if schools were set a uniform attainment target, then the school might put a disproportionately high effort into bringing up to the required attainment level those pupils who were just below the level, to the possible detriment of those at the highest and lowest ends of the attainment distribution (Hood 2006: 518).

There is also the matter of marketing and impression-management. How does an ordinary school (and, more crucially, a school deemed to be failing or in special measures) present itself to its 'consumer-base'? And this is particularly so when nearly all English secondary schools attract 'specialist school' status. ('Specialist Schools' are publicly funded state schools in England which are financed to provide a specific curricular specialism.) If 'specialist' status is thereby normalised, how then can a school position itself as positively extraordinary, and therefore as attractive (Maguire *et al.* 2011)? Or, if needs be, how can a school re-present itself positively if it has received an unfavourable external inspection report? The school web-site and the school brochure must become the means whereby the *flâneur* can be lured into 'buying into' the educational imagination which the school seems to symbolise. Through a process of fabrication, the 'ordinary' school must filter the gaze of its viewers so that its attractions are highlighted and its shortcomings are shrouded in opaqueness and opacity.

Other 'moves' occurred. In the US, the No Child Left Behind (NCLB) legislation required that all students from grades three to eight achieve proficiency in reading and in mathematics. State-wide tests measure this, and the scores for each school must be categorised on the basis of the pupils' race, their proficiency in English language, whether they be disabled, and whether they come from low-income families. It is a legal requirement that every child must reach 100 per cent proficiency by 2014. This is a tall order, and inevitably each state defines proficiency as it sees fit, and chooses its own appropriate tests; and administrators will wish to ensure that their students can reveal their proficiency. So there is much variation, and there may be a temptation to construct tests with a level of difficulty that will allow for a good pass rate.

The consequences for a school not coming up to the mark – that is, by not making Adequate Yearly Progress (AYP) – are considerable: it must allow students the choice to go elsewhere. The school might even be handed over to direct state control, or be privatised; its teachers may be dismissed. So this is indeed high-stakes testing. In addition to state-based tests, the federal government administers biennially to an unannounced sample of students its National Assessment of Educational Progress (NAEP) tests. The federal government's influence on education is set to strengthen under President Obama's *Race to the Top* programme (US Department of Education 2009). Among other proposals, it seeks to link individual teachers to students' attainment data. The data-gathering procedures to do so are said to be in place. The National Education Association (NEA), the main teachers' union, was predictably wary. The measures portend the end of tenure. In a speech to the NEA in 2009, Arne Duncan, Secretary, US Department of Education, emphasised his purpose:

> I came here today to challenge you to think differently about the role of unions in public education because, when thousands of schools are chronically failing and millions of children are dropping out each year, we all must think differently.' Choosing his metaphor well, he proceeded to elaborate: 'I believe that teacher unions are at a crossroads. These policies [which preserve tenure] were created over the past century to protect the rights of teachers, but they have produced an industrial factory model of education that treats all teachers like *interchangeable widgets*.
>
> (Duncan 2009; brackets and italics added)

To be sure there will be some who will take the targets seriously, and will desist from 'gaming', and may take no comfort from the 'failures' of others. But even those who may think that they are performing well may find – literally to their cost – that they are not, after all, on the side of the angels. In 2008, the government in England suddenly required that the five GCSE subjects which had comprised its 'floor target' should thereafter include English and mathematics (hitherto, so-called 'soft' subjects would have counted for just as much as English and mathematics). Some 638 schools in England suddenly found themselves below the 'minimum standard': that is, more than 30 per cent of their 15-year-old pupils fell short of this 'floor target' of five GCSEs at grades A*–C; and if they should fail to meet that target by 2011, then either closure or conversion to academy-status beckoned. A year later, on 14 January 2009, the government was pleased to announce that the number of 'National Challenge' schools had fallen to 440 (Department for Children Schools and Families 2009a). The policy may work. But at what cost? The failure to comply and to perform has consequences, and – ironically – certain 'special *measures*' or sanctions will ensue, and will be for all to see. Perryman's study of 'Northgate', a school in 'special measures' in England, reports that the school underwent eight inspections within 18 months – which although technically 'continual' seemed to be 'continuous' and 'constant inspection'. She reports that teachers referred to the process as a 'treadmill', 'jumping over hurdles', 'jumping through hoops', 'a crazy cycle of working like mad followed by a period of near collapse' (Perryman 2006: 154).

The endorsement of marketisation, standardisation and testing looms large in the Report of the New Commission on the Skills of the American Workforce, entitled *Tough Choices or Tough Times* (National Center on Education and the Economy 2008). This title has something of the tenor of *A Nation at Risk* which was published in the Reagan era. It constructs a crisis, and it insists on a solution which seems to exacerbate the very problem which it purports to solve (Hargreaves and Shirley 2009: 25). It bears noting that *Tough Choices* warned of 'tough times' if its recommendations were to go unheeded. Its publication in 2006 anticipated the 'tough times' of the 2008 economic crisis, a crisis not brought about by the presumed failings of the over-regulated school system, but by the failure to regulate the world of finance. In England, in September 2007, in the very same month that the customers of Northern Rock bank were queuing anxiously to withdraw their savings, McKinsey and Company published *How the World's Best-Performing School Systems Come Out on Top* (McKinsey and Company 2007). It reached the unexceptional conclusions that the best school systems 'get the right people to become teachers', 'develop them into effective instructors', and 'ensure that the system is able to deliver the best possible instruction for every child'. It endorsed the benefits of comparative analysis, and drew upon the high-performing systems of education in Finland, Singapore and The Netherlands – none of which endorse 'standardized and market-driven solutions' (McKinsey and Company 2007: 40).

Consider the OECD analysis *A Family Affair: intergenerational social mobility across OECD countries*. It reports the strength of the association between individual (son, *not* daughter) and parental (only the father) earnings across OECD countries, or 'intergenerational earnings elasticity'. It finds the association to 'be particularly pronounced' (and persistent) in the UK, Italy, the US and France. In the Nordic countries, Australia and Canada, 'persistence is comparatively low with less than 20% of the wage advantage being passed on from fathers to their sons' (OECD 2010a: 184–5).

To return to charter schools: fewer than five per cent are unionised, and their teachers' conditions of service seem less secure than those of their TPS counterparts. Nor are the charter schools themselves in as predictable a financial situation as the traditional schools. This is because the charter schools rely on philanthropy: the 'causes' which benefactors give priority to may change. Ravitch concludes that charter schools have been supported financially by 'hedge-fund managers, the Walton Family Foundation, the Eli and Edythe Broad Foundation and other major benefactors' (Ravitch 2007: unpaginated). As stated, the traditional public schools must now become adept at marketing themselves. This costs money, and it needs expertise to be effective. For example, the Harlem Success Academy network, a chain of four charter schools has a reportedly annual marketing budget of $325,000, a spend of roughly $900 *per applicant*. The typical marketing expenditure for each nearby traditional public school is a mere $500 *per school* (Medina 2010). Take similar marketing strategies and costs in Sweden at the post-16 level. These include radio and television advertising, the distribution of leaflets and brochures, and advertisements on public transport and on buildings. Free gifts – driving licences, computers, holidays, a shorter school-day and 'free Wednesdays' – are some of the enticements which beset the would-be student (Arreman and Holm 2011: 231).

Markets, mandarins and makeovers

Since the early 1980s education policy has been informed largely by economics. This has marked a profound disciplinary shift in education policy from what had obtained previously. No longer was it the case that the psychologists of education held sway (as in the 1920s, 1930s and 1940s); and the same could be said about sociologists of education whose heyday had been in the 1960s and 1970s. It is true that a bureaucratic mind-set has prevailed throughout, but it has been appropriated for different political agendas. For the 1960s Fabian-inspired social democrats, bureaucracy may have endorsed a dry standardisation, but it was in the interests of equity 'for all'. Not so for the economic neo-liberals: for them standardisation and bureaucracy were the necessary conditions for a quasi-market to operate. All the same, the New Labour governments in England sought to strike an accord between the needs of an emergent post-Fordist managerial regime and a political position which espoused equity.

For the neo-liberals, the extension of choice to rational consumers would, of itself, cause schools (be they profit-based or not) to get their businesses in order. It seemed to be a win–win situation: private providers would make money; students would be taught more effectively when schools had to compete for the funding which they, the students, attracted; and all of this would result in efficiency-gains (and arguably lower taxes). The Third Way position has sought to 'incorporate' the market through strategic private-finance initiatives, and through a curbing of the entrenched powers of the 'producers' – the professionals – who would now be publicly audited and (if need be) sanctioned. The Third Way approach has been to retain 'choice' to parents as autonomy-seeking citizens and users of publicly-funded services. Having said this, the amount of choice remains rather limited. Recall Le Grand's questions about 'choice': is there choice of provider (where); of professional (who); of service (what – that is, in education, of curriculum, pedagogy and assessment); of when (that is, the time when the services can be accessed); and finally, of 'access channel' (how)? (Le Grand 2007: 39).

For the most part, what has been on offer has been a 'choice' (actually a declared preference for) of structures, of schools (charter schools, academies, and free schools). There has been little choice of curriculum, pedagogy and assessment (though, in England, secondary schools may offer a specialism, and free schools need not abide by the national curriculum), and virtually none about when that curriculum shall be 'delivered'. In England, it has been mainly the middle classes who have had the wherewithal and the inclination to exercise choice. In all these endeavours, the assumption is that education shall be an individual, not a collective, 'good'. Quasi-markets in education appeal to opportunism, and they may result in greater social segregation. There still does not appear to be much evidence that charter schools, free schools or academies produce higher academic achievement than traditional schools which have similar intakes. Even so, whatever the assumptions which have underpinned 'choice' – be they libertarian, neo-liberal or social democratic – it is a term which attracts little negative appeal. And when viewed within the context of the consumer boom which led to the crash of 2008, it resonated well with those self-indulgent, credit-fuelled consumers who sought an endless succession of personal makeovers. Thereafter the loans and the leveraging have all but dried up. But an economy requires both producers and consumers; if not, it will stagnate. How will education now foster the 'means of consumption' *and* the 'means of production'?

5 Towards personalisation

Markets connote choice. They purport to privilege the consumer, not the producer. The marketisation of education has been a limited market; even rigged, in the sense that governments have put in place high-stakes tests (which are used to ensure 'standards'), especially of attainment in language, mathematics and science. Thereby the curriculum is necessarily narrowed, a set menu, not *à la carte*; and the pedagogy is fine-tuned to the test. The test results – be they at the school or the national level – are what 'count' for policy-makers. What counts is what is measurable, and is therefore comparable. These results are collected and collated, and the 'stock' of a school or country can be charted for all to see, just as the Dow Jones Industrial Average monitors the sentiment which investors place in quoted companies. It breeds competition.

When viewed from a neo-liberal position, the broad purpose of education shall be to support the economy, in this case an economy whose mode of production is capitalist (Cuban 2004: 123). Just as economies compete, so too will their schools (both pupils and teachers) and universities. For neo-liberals, individual failure is the consequence of individual attributes, especially a lack of entrepreneurial spirit. Individual failure may not be attributed to system factors (Harvey 2007: 65). If schools fail to perform, then the consequences are deemed to be falling national productivity, slow economic growth, a lack of competitiveness in global markets and rising unemployment. Viewed thus, an education system becomes a kind of global positioning device where its position (and therefore its fortunes) may be 'tracked' on the OECD's Programme for International Student Assessment (PISA) charts (Hartley 2003a). The inference to be drawn from the league tables, therefore, is that high-scoring nations will *ipso facto* be better able to compete economically. Policy-makers relentlessly refer to these league tables in the hope that their teachers and pupils will be motivated to accomplish ever-greater things. The high-fliers such as South Korea, Shanghai-China, Singapore and Finland are cited approvingly; those which languish in the depths are chivvied to 'catch up'. (As stated in the previous chapter, according to the McKinsey Report, the other high-fliers are Belgium, Canada, Hong Kong, Japan, The Netherlands, New Zealand and Australia (McKinsey and Company 2007).)

The purpose of these 'testing times' (Stobart 2008) has been to motivate supposedly recalcitrant and self-serving 'producers' (that is, teachers) to perform more effectively. Recall the concept of 'performativity': Performativity is a technology, a culture and a mode of regulation that employs judgements, comparisons and displays as a means of incentive, control, attrition and change – based on rewards and sanctions (both material and symbolic) (Ball 2006: 144). Performativity, which derives from (Lyotard 1984), is redolent of the panoptical control originally envisaged in Bentham's *Panopticon*, as discussed in Chapter 2. It is intended to structure self-discipline; it is, therefore, a producer of anxieties, not to say fear. No task can be put to rest; no-one can be put at ease; the bar can always be raised, or the goal-posts moved; excellence, by definition, will always be a step too far. To repeat, how ironic it is, therefore, that none of South Korea, Singapore and Finland above have thought to adopt 'standardised and market-driven solutions' (Hargreaves and Shirley 2009: 25). Sahlberg (2011) puts the question: 'Are those education systems where test-based accountability has been one of the main drivers of educational change showing progress in international comparisons?' Using the OECD PISA data-set, he assumes that the following countries typify such systems: the US, England, New Zealand and some parts of Canada and Australia. Drawing upon three PISA data-sets generated between 2000 and 2006, he discerns a pattern: the trend in mathematics achievement in all 'strong-accountability-policy' nations is down; and the same is true for science and reading literacy. Not so in Finland, which has stressed trust in, and collaboration among, its teachers (ibid.: 11). Nor does 'time on task' correlate positively with high pupil attainment: in high-performing systems, such as Finland, South Korea and Japan, less reliance is put on formal teaching time than in far lower-performing countries such as Italy, Portugal and Greece. This allows the teachers in Finland more time for curriculum development, school improvement and professional development.

The neo-liberal view that the broad purpose of education shall be economic invites two further questions. First, has the consumer-driven marketisation of education produced future workers who will have the knowledge, demeanour and disposition to function effectively in the so-called 'new economy'? Put differently, has the alliance between bureaucracy and markets produced the most appropriate type of worker for what Gee *et al.* (1996) call the 'new work order'? Have standardisation and marketisation allowed for what Lingard (2007) has called 'productive pedagogies' – pedagogies which are productive not for an age of mass production and mass-customisation, but for the globalised knowledge economy and society? Second, an economy comprises both a means of production and a means of consumption. While the first question addressed whether or not the neo-liberal reforms contributed to *production*, this second question asks whether the neo-liberal reforms – for all of their talk about privileging the 'consumer' – do indeed prepare the child for *consumption* within the new economy. That said, the neo-liberals have positioned the *parent* as the consumer, but it is less clearly the case that they have positioned the *pupil* as a would-be consumer. To be sure there is a strong literature on the commercialisation of childhood (Pugh 2009). The average child in the US sees some 40,000 commercials a year (Linn 2005). Moreover, the relationship between education and consumerism in the US has been a long time in the making, and was explicitly part of what used to be called home economics (Spring 2003). Complementary to these analyses is a further question: is there a 'consumer' complement to Lingard's concept of the 'productive pedagogy': that is, is there a *pedagogy* for consumption? In other words, does the *hidden* curriculum prepare the pupil for personalisation?

Education as a global positioning device

In the emerging economic order of globalised 'fast capitalism', education takes upon itself the purpose of a positioning device. How well education systems 'transform' themselves will determine their position (Hartley 2003a). This is a technical-functionalist approach which argues that the provision of skills, demeanour, disposition and value-orientation for a modern economy and society is too important and complicated to be left to those agencies which had hitherto provided it, namely the family and the church. Human capital theory is a development of this approach. It informs particularly the work of supra-national agencies such as the World Bank and the OECD, organisations wherein economists are prominent:

> In a nutshell, globalisation enters the education sector on an ideological horse, and its effects on education and on the production of knowledge are largely a product of that financially-driven, free-market ideology, not of a clear conception for improving education.
>
> (Carnoy 1999: 59)

Even so, how marketisation as policy is expressed as structure and process varies (Barber 2000: 3). Globalisation is a constructed and contested concept: there are globalisations (Kellner 2000: 310). Notwithstanding these variations, the influence of supranational organisations on national systems is developing apace. The data-categories and discursive frameworks of these agencies have become increasingly standardised, normalised and diffused within and across nation-states (McNeely and Cha 1994; Grek *et al.* 2009).

On balance, human capital theory would predict that nation-states with similar economies would have similar education systems: the latter could be 'read off' from the former. But this is not as clear-cut as the theory implies. Take, for example, the education systems of England and Scotland. They reveal considerable differences, notwithstanding the similarity of their economies and their geographical contiguity. Unlike England, Scotland has not beaten a path to the market with quite the same fervour as England has. Scotland has no national curriculum, no league tables of primary schools, no academies, no 'failing schools' and no heavy-handed surveillance of schools. As with nation-states, so with individuals: human capital theory would predict that the rates of return for individuals on a given educational credential would be similar. But this fails to take into account the fact that the social characteristics of the individual may 'intervene', to the advantage of some, and to the disadvantage of others. It is often assumed, too, that nineteenth-century public mass elementary school systems were a response to the economic demands of industrialisation. Not so in Scotland, where literacy levels were related to religion; and nor in Prussia where the needs of the military prevailed. Indeed, Rubinson and Browne conclude that 'Technical-functional and human-capital theories actually produce little convincing evidence that education increased national economic growth or that education has expanded in rhythm with industrialization' (Rubinson and Browne 1994: 585). Have the marketisation and standardisation of education since the 1980s 'produced the producers' of the new economy?

Pedagogy for production

Recall what the social relations within production now require. The employment relationship is shifting from Fordist to post-Fordist patterns. That said, many private- and public-sector organisations are structurally of a piece with the highly bureaucratised economy of mass production, but nevertheless they look towards the 'new economy'. Fewer workers now manipulate materials; instead, they 'manipulate' symbols and people. They are less given to being controlled explicitly; their consent must be managed, not demanded. Here arises what has been called the 'core dilemma of the new capitalism'. How shall 'empowered "partners"', in the absence of visible, overt top-down power', be prepared for work? It may occur, perhaps, by being exposed to a pedagogy informed by cognitive science (Gee *et al.* 1996: 60). Alternatively, take Clegg's preferred pedagogy for the new economy. No longer acceptable is 'exploitative learning' which demands that tasks be explicit, that require a short completion-time, and be routine – in sum, a Taylorised pedagogy. Instead 'exploratory learning' is required. It 'is associated with complex search, basic research, innovation, variation, risk-taking and more relaxed controls' (Clegg 1999: 261–2).

Notwithstanding these requests for a pedagogical shift, the evidence appears to be that the pedagogical relationship remains largely didactic – a 'transmission' pedagogy, one which anticipates the managerial regime of Fordism rather than that of the new work order (Hartley 2003b). Examples of its entrenchment can be drawn from England, and from parts of the US and Australia. Take England. If anything, the prevalence of 'whole-class' teaching has become more entrenched during the past 20 years. To some extent this may be attributed to the introduction in 1996 of the National Literacy Project. This was taken further by the incoming Labour government in 1997 which introduced the 'national strategies' for literacy (1998) and for numeracy (1999). In literacy, it meant that more emphasis be placed upon phonics and grammar, and on interactive whole-class teaching. From the government's standpoint, the strategies appeared to have had the desired effects. First, the government prompted a rethink among primary school teachers that their once-hallowed child-centred pedagogy was as effective as more teacher-directed work. A replication study of 50 primary schools in England was conducted between 2003 and 2005. It comprised 188 in-depth interviews with teachers, together with the observation of 51 lessons. Among teachers who had been trained before 1990, a discernible shift was noted. They have come to argue for a more structured and planned approach to their teaching, and for sharing these with their pupils (Webb and Vulliamy 2007: 577). Or take Hardman and colleagues' finding that the national literacy strategy has seen more whole-class teaching which is 'dominated by teacher-led recitation'. For much of the time, teachers' questions were of the 'closed question' type, thereby affording little opportunity for the pupils to become more actively engaged, or to elaborate and explore (Hardman *et al.* 2003: 212). That said, the second desired effect was that the introduction of the national strategies *did* mark an upward trend in the national curriculum tests at Key Stage 2, at least until the end of 2001, but thereafter the scores levelled off (Galton 2007).

If these pedagogical interventions are added to the raft of accountability measures introduced by the 1997 Labour government in England, then according to the government's position an improvement in educational achievement should accrue. But it remains hotly debated. Michael Barber (former head of the Prime Minister's Delivery Unit under the Blair government) and Peter Tymms (Director of Curriculum, Evaluation and Management, at the University of Durham) each gave evidence in December 2007 to a House of Commons Select Committee. Tymms took issue with Barber's view that standards had improved between 1995 and 2000 because of the national testing of pupils and the inspection of schools. Nor was Tymms persuaded by the motivational effect of league tables:

> Q22: *Professor Tymms:* A league table position is largely determined by the intake of pupils to that school. It might vary depending on how you analyse it, but if you had measures of pupils on intake, that would certainly explain more than 50% of the variants [sic] in the results, and maybe up to 70%. The amount that is due to the quality of teaching is typically quoted as being about 10 to 15% of the variants [sic] in secondary schools, after intake is taken into account, *which means that we are down to about 5 to 7% of the variation in the league tables being due to the quality of the school* – maybe less, once everything is taken into account. In primary schools it is slightly more, but it is still dominated by the intake.
>
> (House of Commons Children, Schools and
> Families Committee 2008, Ev 9; emphasis added)

Test-scores are easily conveyed indicators of the achievement (or not) of targets, but they do not convey the details of the hidden curriculum which is associated with them. Beneath the surface impressions of the numbers are other messages. One is about teacher education: if university schools of education are themselves required to 'teach to the test', then it may come as no surprise that the students whom they teach (and who themselves go on to teach in schools) may also be disinclined to engage in critical dialogue and creative activities (Department of

Media Culture and Sport 1999: 153). If teacher educators and teachers are treated bureaucratically, then it is little wonder that they might treat their students and pupils in the same way. It was a theme echoed ten years later by the authors of the *Cambridge Primary Review*: 'Children will not learn to think for themselves if their teachers are expected merely to do as they are told' (Alexander *et al.* 2010: 496).

A similar range of concerns has been expressed about No Child Left Behind in the US. The testing regime instigated by NCLB in the US leads not to what Lingard would call 'productive pedagogies' but to what McNeil and Valenzuela (2001) call 'defensive pedagogies'. Their research in Texas draws some stark conclusions. The curriculum is aligned to the Texas Assessment of Academic Skills (TAAS) drills, especially in the poorest schools. The tests are multiple-choice and computer-marked. The 'drills' reduce the curriculum to discrete, isolated bits of information. The need constantly to prepare for the tests means that incursions upon the time formally assigned to subjects such as history and art are common. The authors conclude that the TAAS testing regime is rigid and prescriptive, is wedded to 'discredited learning theories', and pays no heed to the culture of children (ibid.: 19). A similar meta-analysis concludes that the quality of student learning has not improved under NCLB. The curriculum has been narrowed, the pedagogy has been akin to teaching to the test. The morale of teachers is decreasing, and the drop-out rates of students are increasing (Hursh 2007: 512). The onerous testing regime in America's schools generates high levels of anxiety, and the temptation to cheat is thereby the greater (Amrein-Beardsley *et al.* 2010: 27).

These doubts about the pedagogy which associates with market-driven high-stakes testing regimes suggest that – at best – this pedagogy is not suitable for the new work order. It is of a piece with a Fordist managerial regime. It is not, to repeat, a 'productive pedagogy' (Lingard 2003: 8). To elaborate: a productive pedagogy has four dimensions. The first dimension is 'intellectual quality': that is, does the lesson emphasise conceptual depth and not just content, as expressed in critical and negotiated understandings? The second dimension is 'connectedness': that is, does the lesson make meaningful connections to the pupils' own background knowledge; and does the lesson identify and engage with intellectual and real-world problems? The third dimension focuses on whether or not the classroom environment is supportive: that is, is there mutual respect among teacher and pupils; are the criteria against which pupils are to be judged made explicit, and are the pupils engaged fully in their academic endeavours? The fourth dimension of a productive pedagogy is 'recognition of difference': that is, is the classroom inclusive, and does it instil a group identity whereby no single cultural code prevails?

Even in Queensland, Australia – and well before the onset of national high-stakes testing in Australia – research commissioned by Education Queensland investigated the extent to which productive pedagogy was in evidence. The Queensland School Reform Longitudinal Study (QSRLS) undertook detailed observations and ratings of some 975 classroom lessons offered in 24 state schools between 1998 and 2000. It observed the following: commendably supportive and caring teachers whose concerns were therapeutic for the children. But while supportive, these pedagogies were not productive; they were 'pedagogies of indifference', lacking intellectually demanding work (Lingard 2007: 257).

The progressive possibilities of schooling in Queensland – however limited their realisation, as reported in the QSRLS – now look to be even more limited. For it is the case that Australia has recently tightened its grip on its constituent states. It has begun to tread the path of high-stakes testing. There is now a National Assessment Program – Literacy and Numeracy (NAPLAN), and national standardised tests in literacy and in numeracy are administered to all students in the third, fifth, seventh and ninth year of their schooling. The Australian Curriculum, Assessment and Reporting Authority (ACARA) has the responsibility for this. From January 2010, how an individual school has performed in relation to other schools of similar socio-economic composition can be viewed on-line on the *My School* web-site: http://www.myschool.edu.au and there are data for almost 10,000 schools. Lingard, who was instrumental both in the QSRLS study and the subsequent *New Basics* trial of productive pedagogies, remains unimpressed by Australia's adoption of neo-liberal education policies from England and the US: a twenty-first century education and society 'does not require schooling reduced to better test taking on a narrow subset of school curricula (Lingard 2010: 135).

A similar call to Lingard's has been made by the think-tank DEMOS (Birdwell *et al.* 2011: 18–19). They discern five 'premiums' which enhance the employability of people: the *character premium*, which comprises soft skills such as the ability to communicate effectively and to be team-workers; the *literacy and numeracy premium*; the *work premium* acquired by 'early experiences of work'; the *technical premium* acquired by education and training to A-level standard, or its equivalent; and the *graduate premium*. Consider the character premium. It consists of the 'character capabilities' which are akin to Lingard's productive pedagogy outcomes. These 'character capabilities' comprise application and self-motivation, self-regulation, resilience, self-direction, self-understanding, the ability to acknowledge one's strengths and weaknesses, the ability to acknowledge one's responsibilities to other people, the possession and deployment of social skills, empathy, and the ability to 'understand and enjoy difference, pay attention and listen to others' (ibid.: 49).

Pedagogy for consumption

The study of education during the current neo-liberal phase has been mainly concerned with the relationship between education and capitalism. We have said that there is an assumption that a nation's productivity can somehow be read off from the ranking which it has achieved in international league tables. But this economistic view has focused upon the presumed causal relationship between schooling and production, and not upon the relationship between schooling and consumption. The evidence of schools adopting 'productive pedagogies' for a new work order so far looks to be very limited. But is it the case also that schools are adopting – to use an infelicitous term – 'consumptive pedagogies'? While it is true that the marketisation of education gives the impression of an association between schooling and consumption, this association has so far been limited. It is limited because for the most part the 'consumer'-parent has been given the opportunity to state a preference for particular schools (assuming there is more than one school available to choose from). On this, there are two considerations to note. The first is that the consumer is assumed to be the parent, not the child; and the second is that the choices available are largely those of structures – that is, of schools as organisations. Put differently, the 'choice' is of the 'where', not the 'who' (which teacher), not the 'what' (the curriculum), and not the 'how' (the pedagogy and mode of assessment). On the 'what' – the curriculum – there is some element of choice in that most secondary schools in England have a stated curricular specialism, but the national curriculum remains for most schools. Even free schools, though not required to teach the national curriculum, must nevertheless offer a 'broad and balanced curriculum'.

That said, there has been a clear commercial incursion into schools, especially in the US (Molnar 2005) and particularly so in charter schools (Molnar 1996). Here marketing has been in evidence in a fairly explicit way. The activities include the commercial sponsorship of programmes, electronic marketing, the designation and appropriation of space, the corporate sponsoring of teaching materials, fund-raising and incentive programmes. But this explicit commercialisation of public schools may soon be complemented by a new 'consumptive pedagogy' whereby the consumerisation of the child may be a *tacit* process – a part of the hidden curriculum no less. Whereas the marketisation of education has thus far been largely confined to the choice and consumption (by the *parent*) of structures (that is, schools), the supplementary phase of marketing commercial products to the *pupil* (as referred to by Molnar) is but a first step towards the normalisation of a 'consumerist ethic' among pupils and students. The basis of this position turns upon the emergence of a new relationship between production and consumption, a matter addressed below.

Production and consumption: towards prosumption?

Social theory has until recently been relatively concerned more with capitalist production than with consumption (Pietrykowski 2007). Marx – though by no means ignoring consumption – focused mainly upon the alienation of workers in factory-based production during the industrial revolution. At the point of sale, producers realise 'exchange value'. Consumers, on the other hand, realise the intrinsic 'use value' of their purchases after the transaction has been completed. Only in the sense that workers needed to consume the necessities of life in order to be able to work could their purchases be said to be indirectly productive. In the traditional sense, therefore, a person acts as a producer and as a consumer *in a separate way*. Weber, in *The Protestant Ethic and the Spirit of Capitalism*, was also concerned with production: that is, why was it the case that Protestants were dutiful and diligent? And – of relevance to consumption – why did they value frugality, preferring to accumulate wealth rather than to spend it? In relation to Weber's analysis, we considered in Chapter 3 Campbell's historical analysis of the social origins of consumption during the Romantic period. His question was: how could the Protestant 'work ethic' (derived from Puritanism), and the ethic or spirit of consumerism (associated with Romanticism) co-exist (Campbell 1989: 8)? Surely they were contradictory? Campbell argued that the source of the emotions varies historically: in the pre-modern period, the emotions had been 'inherent in aspects of reality, from whence they exert their influence over humans' (ibid.: 72). But during the dis-enchanted modern period, the Protestant work ethic suppressed the emotions. They could only be imagined, not expressed – except through consumption.

Weber was referring mainly to factory-based production and to bureaucracy, both of which typify industrial society, be it capitalist or socialist. More recently, there has been reference to 'post-industrial society' (Bell 1976) and – relevant here – to 'consumer society', as analysed by Baudrillard (1998) and by Bauman (2007). For Bell, the defining aspect of post-industrial society was that it codifies theoretical knowledge, and it makes explicit the connection between science and technology. The industries of the twentieth century – for example, telecommunications, optics, transistors, computers and biotechnologies – were all derived from developments in theoretical physics and biology. Contrast this to the nineteenth century when nearly all of the new industries were the brainchildren of what Bell calls 'talented tinkerers' (Bell 1976: xiv–xv). Other dimensions of 'post-industrial society' include the following: the shift from manufacturing to services; the rise of the professional and technical classes; the importance of formal education as an occupational requirement; the importance of human capital, not just financial capital (land and money); and the prevalence of communications over transportation (ibid.: xvi)

The path from producers to consumers has been a long one. In the UK, the 1980s saw the celebration of 'choice', when only individuals mattered. The 'intuitive solidarities of the proletarian economy' of the 1950s and 1960s could not be sustained as the traditional manufacturing base failed (Offer 2008: 545). The 'society of producers and soldiers' had been preoccupied with the fitness of the *body* for life in the factory and the military; the spirit was contained and – if need be – broken. Not so now: it is the management of the *spirit* which matters. It must be made fit for self-centred consumption (Bauman 2007: 54). Contemporary society is a consumer society, and individuals are now morally obliged to act more as consumers than as producers (Bauman 1988: 807). The consumerist lifestyle is a 'condition of membership' in consumer society (Bauman 2007: 53). Those who cannot consume are deemed to be failing in their duty; and, lest their desires can only be realised by stealing that which they cannot afford to consume, their compliance is elicited by surveillance and coercion. The 'contented' middle classes meanwhile sequester themselves in gated residences, their properties and possessions protected by alarms and cameras (Galbraith 1993). Their children become distrustful; they themselves are anxious. Their doors and minds are closed to the Other. Once-public spaces are now privatised, and they offer little opportunity to linger or to sleep. The poor and their plight are now often regarded as an aesthetic – as a spectacle to behold briefly, then to be forgotten. In short, the poor are thereby deemed to be abnormal, for they lack the 'norm of consumer competence or aptitude' (Bauman 2007: 33). The consumer 'ethic' has little time for those who do not subscribe to it and, in the neo-liberal mind, the poor are deemed to have chosen their poverty.

For Bauman, postmodernism – the culture of postmodernity – is not a culture; indeed the notion of the culture of postmodernism is an oxymoron (Bauman 1988: 798). Others take a similar line. America, argues Baudrillard, 'lives in perpetual simulation, in a perpetual present of signs' (Baudrillard 1993: 76). There is an emergent 'digital narcissism', a society of self-broadcasting bloggers who 'flatten' truth and create 'an on-demand, personalized version that reflects our own individual myopia' (Keen 2007: 17). All this said, there is an argument to put that it would be incorrect to say that in consumer society the producer is kept at bay. That is to say, what we are witnessing is a movement wherein the consumer and the producer are simultaneously involved in both production and in consumption (Ritzer 2010). The neologism 'prosumer' has been coined to describe this (Toffler 1980; Toffler and Toffler 2006; Ritzer 2010). It will be introduced here, and explored more fully in Chapter 6.

A prosumer is someone who contributes to the exchange-value of a product without being paid to do so. In traditional production, it is the worker is who paid for his or her labour, and the difference between the costs of that labour (and other costs incurred by the owner) and the price paid by the consumer remains with the owner, as profit. So in this relationship there is a clear demarcation between the producer and the consumer. The concept of the prosumer brings these together; it conflates them. Of course, this is by no means new: for a long time, customers have served themselves in fast-food restaurants, at filling-stations and at ATM machines. And more recently, customers may engage in self-check-in at airports, and in self-check-out at supermarkets. The media make use of reality-TV participants, and of 'listeners' on talk-show radio programmes. Customers often submit reviews of products sold by on-line retailers. Not having to pay waiters, garage attendants, bank tellers, cashiers, shop workers, actors and ticket agents adds exchange-value for the producer. What could be better than a low-paid worker than a 'consumer as prosumer' who works for nothing? To be sure, the worker does produce a good deal of surplus value, but the consumer who 'works' for nothing 'produces nothing but surplus value' (Ritzer and Jurgenson 2010: 26). Whereas before, consumers derived only use-value from a purchase, now prosumers may generate both exchange value for producers and use-value for themselves. And in these endeavours the prosumers appear to be willing contributors. The question arises whether or not the prosumer is but an add-on, or temporary worker, in what largely remains the preserve of producers (Humphreys and Grayson 2008); or whether the arrival of the prosumer marks something of a fundamental shift in the very nature of capitalism (Ritzer and Jurgenson 2010: 26). The latter position alludes to the opportunities created by Web 2.0 for user-centred design and collaboration. The Linux open-source operating system is an example which is often referred to. But there are other examples – such as *eBay*, *Facebook* and *YouTube* – whereby the corporation will provide and maintain the infrastructure of a web-site, but thereafter allow the content to be devised by 'users', or prosumers.

Summary

The neo-liberal ideology which has informed education systems in England and the US assumes that schools can be made to be efficient, effective and excellent. Efficient, because through competition, schools will drive down costs; effective, because – if not – schools will, so to say, go out of business; and excellent, because funding shall be contingent upon performance. In short, schools will be productive for the economy. In these endeavours, there is an emphasis placed on competitive individualism: individual pupils will be tested; their schools will be ranked in league tables. In all of this, there has emerged a somewhat unexpected mix of bureaucracy and markets. Unexpected, because the notion of a market implies the freedom to choose; and, in education, this implies the freedom to choose the curriculum, pedagogy and modes of assessment. But in order for the parent to be informed about the schools 'on offer', they need to be able to make comparisons among those schools. However, these comparisons can only be objective if like is compared with like: that is, a like curriculum and a like test requires a national curriculum and national tests.

We have seen that the evidence from research on charter schools in the US and from academies in England is that if the socio-economic character of the school-intakes are similar then these schools perform no better than their traditional counterparts. The weight of this evidence is now persuading some, like Diane Ravitch, who once advocated them, to pause for thought. Moreover, the highest-performing education systems have not followed the path taken by England and the US. Neither the US nor the UK is placed within the top ten of the 2009 PISA rankings for science, mathematics or reading literacy (OECD 2010b). Paradoxically, for all of their rhetoric about the presumed causal relationship between education and economic growth, both England and the US (as well as Australia) seem set to prepare for what has been termed an 'industrial society' marked by Fordist managerial regimes and factory-based production. They lack 'productive pedagogies' for a knowledge economy. They also appear to prepare pupils for an economy of mass consumption. There is little synchronisation between the standardised offerings of schools and the increasingly customised and personalised products which the market presents outside of them. Curricular choice is limited. Pedagogically, there remains a strong demarcation between teacher and pupil, notwithstanding the rhetorical preference for 'learning'. There is little individualisation of provision. In the economy, however, there is an increasingly blurred and porous relationship between producers and consumers; there is, in some sectors of the economy, a co-production. All of this is not to say that there should be a necessary and overriding structural accord among education, production and consumption. But it is to say that the neo-liberal agenda has purported to effect such a correspondence, and that it has failed to do so; if anything, it set aside in the early 1980s that very child-centred and learner-centred pedagogy which might have been more of a piece with an emerging new work order. There are now some indications, however, that the effects of consumer society, rather than of industrial society, are beginning to surface in the policy lexicon of education. The preferred term is 'personalisation', the subject of the next chapter.

6 Consumption, personalisation and education policy

We may think of personalisation at two levels: first, it is a mode of regulation or governance, the successor to the 'new public management' in the provision of public services; and second, personalisation is a basis for 'learning', as in the phrase 'personalised learning'. In broad terms, the emergence of personalisation accords with consumerism, and especially with what has been termed 'customisation' or 'personalisation'. Personalisation is an extension and elaboration of that marketing discourse which the previous school-choice legislation had initiated. It does not supersede or supplant the 'choice' associated with charter schools, with academies and with free schools; rather, it complements and deepens the extent to which marketisation has suffused education policy. The quasi-market of schools was by and large a structural endeavour, but the now-touted personalisation of learning is an interpersonal and cultural quest. It takes a step further towards the integration of structures and agents; it is about re-culturing; it resonates with consumer culture. As a legitimatory rhetoric, it strikes a chord: 'Cultural theory suggests that [policy] rhetoric has to mesh with culture and interact with it' (Hood 2000: 178; brackets added). It enables a new rhetorical twist: whereas the standardisation discourse makes much of the rational, the personalisation discourse speaks to the emotional – to voice, to well-being, to the personal: 'In its present consumer phase, the capitalist system deploys the pleasure principle for its own perpetuation' (Bauman 1988: 808).

An emergent phase of consumerism is in train. During the 1950s and 1960s, the decline of both traditional manufacturing industries and trade unions had corresponded to a change in the basis for political action. Consumption practices appear now to be more individualised, and less homogeneously aligned to broader social categories, particularly to social class. Put differently, production-based politics gradually seems to have lost ground – but by no means completely – to consumption as the basis on which 'issues' emerge (Trentmann 2007: 148). In late modernity, the *agora* may not be the hitherto-designated political spaces, but elsewhere – and especially in the virtual spaces of the internet wherein consumers 'reside' and communicate. It is as if citizens can 'cast their ballot', so to say, on a global scale. It prompts a question: 'Are consumer society and *direct* politics thus beginning to come together and to bypass parties, parliaments and governments?' (Beck and Beck-Gernsheim 2002: 44, italics in the original).

There are two complementary social trends emerging: first, reflexivity and with it the project of the self; and second, 'sub-politicization', a process whereby new non-traditional political spaces are emerging as a response to the perceived ineffectiveness of the traditional ones (Sassatelli 2006: 223). All this is no less than the 'reinvention of politics' (Beck 1997). This trend is sometimes seen as a sign of a shift from the citizen to the consumer. But this is an overstatement, for a number of reasons. First, notwithstanding the government's propensity for positioning the public as a constellation of 'choosers', most users of public services do not agree that they are indeed 'consumers' or 'customers'. In the UK, there is scant evidence that users in the health service, in social care and in the police service define themselves as consumers; and nor do managers of these services regard users as consumers. For example, in the UK, only 1.4 per cent of a sample of managers in the health services deemed their users to be 'consumers'; and similarly, in the police service and in social care the corresponding percentages were 2.9 and 5.0 respectively. More importantly, the users themselves, when interviewed, were reluctant to define themselves as 'consumers': only 3.19 per cent of health service users, 1.6 per cent of police service users, and none of the social care users did so (Clarke *et al.* 2007: 126–8). The New Labour Third Way in the UK had thought to merge the social democratic notion of the citizen and the neo-liberal notion of the consumer, with the latter dominant and the former in a continuing transition towards the latter (Hall 2005). This raises the question whether or not it remains appropriate to speak of *public* services when it is the case that the provision of them increasingly straddles the public, private and not-for-profit sectors, and when the maxims of managerialism and the ethos of entrepreneurship continue to be applied to them (Newman and Clarke 2009: 110).

The emergence of the prosumer (a notion introduced in Chapter 5) portends a question: how will the prosumer be 'produced'? The question is of a piece with Trentmann's more general statement: 'Consumers did not arise effortlessly as an automated response to the spread of markets *but had to be made*' (Trentmann 2006: 6; emphasis added). The concept of customisation implies that the customer be involved in designing or configuring the product. Given this integration, the chances increase that the consumer will be 'delighted', and, this being so, will act as an (unpaid) advocate of the brand (Kumar and Stecke 2007: 560). Of late, customisation has been transformed from 'mass customisation' towards 'mass personalisation': that is, towards the 'market of one' (Kumar 2007: 560). The 'mass' in 'mass personalisation' means that the needs of individual customers can be met, but with 'near mass production efficiency' (Tseng and Jiao 2005: 685). On the face of it, this sounds like an impossibility. But if the technologies are 'soft' or electronic, then mass personalisation is possible. Electronic retailers are examples. If not, as in manufacturing at present, then mass personalisation is less likely (Kumar 2007: 540). But 3-D printing, or additive manufacturing, may change this. Using digital technology, it enables customised products – a bespoke pair of shoes for example – to be produced more quickly and cheaply than mass-produced products. Many products can be easily customised at home and then sent for 'printing', as easily as sending a document file to be printed. This would allow personalisation to be incorporated into 'hard' manufacturing technologies, and with greater efficiency and effectiveness than current mass production processes (The Economist 2009; 2011).

Consider further the roots of personalisation in marketing theory. Capitalism appears to be set upon commodifying 'everything' (Strasser 2003: 3). It 'flows': there is a shift from the occasional acquisition of products to the continuing quest for service and value (Hawken *et al.* 2011). Contemporary capitalism, as argued earlier, is increasingly a 'relationship economy'. Consumers demand that goods and services accord with their needs and tastes, and so to focus only on the supply-side in the public services no longer suffices. In the prosumer vein, a co-creation – a 'direct involvement in the production process by what we still call the consumer' – is now required (Miller 2003: 117). In effect, this process comprises the combination of co-configuration and co-customisation (Victor and Boynton 1998).

Victor and Boynton present a five-fold typology of industrial work: *craft, mass production, process enhancement, mass customisation,* and *co-configuration.* Each type of work associates with a particular form and content of knowledge. Thus it is that *craft* work generates tacit knowledge, arrived at intuitively, out of experience. It is not codified, but if it is then 'best practice' can be made formal, as in 'manuals' and 'handbooks' which define procedures, and which can be used as the basis for monitoring. Such is the case in *mass production.* But it is not always so that the set procedures are effective in all circumstances. Refinements to practice, suggested by the workers themselves, may be made. This gleaning of a collective-worker wisdom can be formalised in team-based arrangements: a *process enhancement.* This in itself enables a more insightful analysis of the needs of clients: that is, not so much a provider-customer division, but a working towards a relationship between the two; a *mass customisation.* Co-production also has the purpose of retaining customers, thereby tailoring products in order to meet their changing needs (Victor and Boynton 1998: 14). Thus it is that personalisation is not so much a one-off deal, but a lasting relationship. Thus it is, too, that *individual* personalisation requires for its accomplishment new *collectives* and new collaborations; the latter perhaps enabled by ICT.

The quest for ever-greater customisation prompts ever-greater collaboration and inter-dependence, not just between the producer and the customer, but also among the producers themselves who strive collectively to meet a customer's requirements over a prolonged period; a *co-configuration.* It is not the product itself which is crucial; rather, it is the identity, the experience and the relationship which are associated with it. So, by retaining the relationship with the consumer, the provider can offer new imaginings and new identities (Gee 2004: 97), even new 'sensations' and 'transformations' (Gilmore and Pine 1999: 177). In sum, 'with co-configuration we can imagine creating products that are not only made to order for you but continuously remake themselves as your needs change' (Victor and Boynton 1998: 196). But this is a relationship born of calculation rather than sincerity. It resonates with what has been termed 'synthetic personalisation', which denotes the tendency for corporations (and now governments) to present the impression that the individual really matters even when those individuals are being processed *en masse* (Fairclough 1993: 199–221). It is not dissimilar to 'false fraternisation' (Ritzer 2000).

Co-production, personalisation and governance

Since the 1980s, the consumer-centred 'market' has emerged as an 'order' or mode of governance in education, complementing the existing producer-centred and allegedly self-serving 'bureaucratic' mode. To this was added a new 'network' mode of governance and regulation. The three modes of governance regimes are to be found in Thompson's typology of 'orders': the *hierarchical order*, the *market order* and the *network order* (Thompson 2003: 48). To elaborate: the *hierarchical order* has pre-specified and designed outcomes; its organisational structure is bureaucratic; its products and processes are monitored and measured. The *market order* is driven by spontaneity, and by private competition; it is self-regulating, with an 'unseen guiding hand'. The *network order* is open both to designed outcomes and to those generated spontaneously; and similarly it is open both to formal coordination and governance, and to informal non-governance. What it requires for its accomplishment are cooperation, consensus-seeking, trust, loyalty and reciprocity.

After 2004, a refinement of the 'market' order was introduced. It was not to replace the other two orders, but to supplement them, and it has come to be known as personalisation. In 2004, the UK Cabinet Office published a discussion document entitled *Personal Responsibility and Changing Behaviour: the state of knowledge and its implications for public policy*. It declares:

> policy-makers have sought out more sophisticated means of building more effective relationships between citizens and government which can influence public behaviour, particularly with a view to increasing personal responsibility in areas like health and welfare, and encouraging greater partnership between users of services and service providers ('co-production').
>
> (Halpern *et al.* 2004: 3)

In a similar vein, in 2006, Sir David Varney published *Service Transformation: a better service for citizens and businesses, a better deal for the taxpayer* (Varney 2006). Throughout, the term 'citizen' prevails over the term 'consumer', but the report advocated the 'personalisation of services': that is, 'tailoring the service to the needs of the individual on the basis of previous information and the behaviour of the individual' (ibid.: 8). (The previous version of the 'consumer' was someone who had expressed a preference for, or chose from, what was on offer.) The report's notion of personalisation accorded with that adumbrated by Leadbeater, a leading consultant and policy adviser. He had defined the dimensions of personalisation as follows. The *ethos* of personalisation is declared to be 'democratic, personalised, user-centric'; its *users* are defined as 'co-producers, creating solutions with professionals'; its *mode of delivery* includes a 'mixed market of providers'. 'Solutions [will be] assembled from a variety of sources around user needs'; the *role of the professional* will become that of 'adviser, broker, advocate, solutions assembler' (Leadbeater 2004a: 62–5; brackets added). In the same year as Varney's report, the government produced a structure for the reform of the public services (Prime Minister's Strategy Unit 2006: 6). It shows the complementarity of bureaucracy, markets and inter-agency working. In the government's model, 'top down performance and management' is expressed as in 'targets, regulation, inspection and intervention', which corresponds to Thompson's *hierarchical* order of governance. The government's 'market incentives to increase efficiency and quality of services' and its 'users shaping the services from below' both correspond to Thompson's *market* order of governance. And third, the government's 'capability and capacity' approximates to Thompson's *network* order. The government's model thereby implies a consensus: that is to say, bureaucracy, markets and networks are in mutual adjustment, each segment being functional for the others, all in a self-improving equilibrium.

Thompson's 'market' order privileges the consumer as an individual who chooses (after being informed) from what is on offer. In this, the stress is on *individual* choice, and on a *separation* between consumer and provider. But the government thereafter introduced *personalisation,* which it calls '*users shaping the services from below*' (Prime Minister's Strategy Unit 2006: 6). This, in turn, logically requires some form of networked multi-agency working so that personalised needs can be met. In other words, personalisation – notwithstanding the implication of *individual* choosing – requires for its implementation not a separation between customer and provider, but two kinds of *co-production* or *collaboration*. The first is between consumer and provider so as to identify the need; and the second, if necessary, is a co-production among the providers themselves in some kind of networked configuration of inter-professional working.

The modes of regulation, therefore, are complementary. Contemporary public policy reveals that the market suffuses all of them, either directly (as in 'market incentives to increase efficiency and quality of service' and in 'users shaping the services from below'), or indirectly (as in 'top-down performance management'). The new public management had combined 'market incentives to increase efficiency and quality of service' with 'top-down performance management'. That is to say, the 'new public management' had required 'self-managing', 'flexible' professionals and workers to decide upon the tactics whereby government-defined strategies could be put into practice locally. Public-sector professionals were assigned 'ownership' of the means whereby centrally set targets would be achieved. Their performance was top-down managed, and their budgets turned upon their 'delivery' of the targets. Institutional comparisons were thereafter made available so that the discerning 'customer' would have comparable and robust evidence with which to make an informed choice of provider. These bureaucratic endeavours, therefore, were in the 'pay' of the market. Now the market seems set upon making further inroads, allowing 'customers' to choose not just organisations (this or that school or hospital), but to become a co-producer of solutions with professionals – these solutions are to be configured from a variety of sources drawn from a mixed market of providers (Leadbeater 2004b: 59–68). The customer thereby becomes not so much a chooser of what is 'on offer', but a co-producer of 'solutions' of what is wanted; a 'prosumer'.

But the prosumer must make a decision about what is needed and wanted. This is central to the matters of personalisation and co-production. Clearly, the sentiment behind personalisation is not coercion; on the contrary. But not all matters can be left to the individual to decide upon; the public interest must be taken into account. For instance, once the dangers of passive smoking became widely known, the right to smoke in public places was withdrawn by legislation: this is hard paternalism. But matters to do, say, with diet are less clear-cut. Yes, nutritional information can be required to be displayed on the food-package, but still the waistlines expand, and the attendant medical costs increase. If 'education' fails to elicit the behaviours deemed to be most beneficial to the consumer, then what? On the other hand, if there is little desire on the part of the public for hard paternalism, again – then what? Since 2004, a new 'libertarian paternalism' has been mooted – an emergent 'avuncular state': 'worldly-wise, offering a nudge in the right direction, perhaps pulling strings on your behalf without your even noticing' (The Economist 2006). 'Libertarian paternalism' is the preferred term for this 'nudging' (Thaler and Sunstein 2009); 'soft paternalism' is the term preferred by their main critic, Glaeser (2005).

In the UK Coalition government, since 2010, the theme of libertarian paternalism has been developed in *Better Choices: better deals – consumers powering growth* wherein the 'soft' approach is indicated:

> In developing this strategy, we have drawn upon insights from both traditional economics and behavioural science, which recognises that not all consumers respond in an economically rational way to financial or other incentives – for example because we have limited time, desire or cognitive resources to make a fully informed decision.
>
> (Cabinet Office Behavioural Insights Team 2011: 11)

But co-production and personalisation present a problem for government: what if the consumers (in schools, pupils) want something which government deems to be neither in their own nor in the government's interests? Should they not be 'nudged' towards a choice which is deemed by government to be appropriate for the individual? This question has not escaped the attention of governments in both the UK and the US. In December 2010, for example, the UK government's discussion paper *Applying Behavioural Insight to Health* stated:

> There has been the assumption that central government can only change people's behaviour through rules and regulations. Our government will be a much smarter one, shunning the bureaucratic levers of the past and finding

intelligent ways *to encourage, support and enable people to make better choices for themselves.*

(Cabinet Office Behavioural Insights Team 2010: 4; italics added)

A subsequent discussion document, *MINDSPACE: influencing behaviour through public policy*, outlines further the new synthesis between liberal and paternalistic approaches. To take an example: on the matter of tobacco and alcohol, it would say that the purchase of these should continue to attract high taxation and other regulations (the hard paternalistic approach), but that also 'sophisticated behavioural programmes' to reduce their consumption (the 'nudge' or 'avuncular' approach) should be developed and implemented (Dolan *et al.* 2010: 77). Take another, more specific, example from *MINDSPACE*: how to get motorists to reduce their speed when approaching a dangerous bend in the road. The nudge approach involves a simple 'environmental design' modification. That is to say, a series of white stripes are painted in the centre of the road. Some distance from the bend, the stripes are spaced evenly, but as the bend approaches the stripes are placed closer together, so as to give the illusion and sensation of speed, thereby 'nudging' the motorists to pay heed to their natural instinct to slow down. Their illusion of being in control remains intact. Here, therefore, is a very cost-effective method of influencing driving behaviour (Dolan *et al.* 2010: 16).

Personalisation has been explored most fully within the area of social care in England. A review of the National Health Service recommended a pilot scheme whereby up to 5,000 people with long-term conditions could have 'personal budgets'. Its implications are considerable: if, in a period of post-crisis financial constraints, the personal budgets are insufficient to meet stated needs, then what happens? Would for-profit providers come to dilute the public-service ethos, and would they be more likely to opt for cheaper, standardised solutions rather than bespoke solutions? (Beresford 2008; Needham 2009).

Personalisation in education: an emerging revised code?

We have said that personalisation in education may be thought of at two levels. The first is as a mode of regulation whereby consumers of public services no longer choose from what is on offer, but seek what they want, co-productively, with providers. This deepens the marketisation process in education, and it draws upon marketing theory for its intellectual underpinning. The connection with the emergent avuncular state is that it follows logically that in the co-productive process the would-be consumer must somehow be 'tutored', but in a very subtle manner so that the choice is in the interests of both the consumer and the government, with consumers under the illusion that the choice is theirs, and no-one else's. The work of the Behavioural Insights Team, which drew upon so-called 'nudge' approaches in behavioural psychology, is less explicitly focused upon schooling, but it has an elective affinity to personalisation in education. The following section gives a short account of the emergence of personalised learning in OECD countries, especially in England.

One of the earliest references to the personalisation of education was that by David Miliband (the then Schools Minister in England) at the North of England Education Conference in Belfast on 8 January 2004. The title of his speech was 'Personalised learning: building a new relationship with schools' (Miliband 2004). As a graduate student, Miliband had been influenced by the ideas in *The Second Industrial Divide* (Piore and Sabel 1984), wherein it was argued that the end of mass production and consumption was nigh, to be followed by flexible specialisation and customised product-marketing. In 2005, Horne, a member of the Department for Education and Skills Strategy Unit, asked: 'Where has personalised learning come from?' In answering, he cited changes in marketing theory (Horne 2005).

During the period of mass customisation, customer-satisfaction surveys were used to generate ideas for products which would have mass appeal. Thereafter, the task of marketing managers was to inform consumers about their 'offers'; and the task of the consumer was to choose one. Applied to school-choice, the consumer-parent was an information processor, a rational and discerning analyst of these 'offers', which came in the form of published performance data, usually league tables. But the parent had to know where to find this information, and had to have the financial means to live in the 'right' catchment area; or, if not, to have the resources to transport their children to it. The parent was not only deemed to be a rational analyst of the information, but also to be in possession of a sophisticated cultural repertoire that would enable negotiations with the relevant professionals (Hartley 2008: 371). Personalisation emerges clearly in *Excellence and Enjoyment: a strategy for primary schools* (Department for Education and Skills 2003). This continued in the White Paper *Higher Standards, Better Schools for All: more choice for parents and pupils* (Department for Education and Skills 2005).

Miliband outlined 'five components of personalised learning'. First, it requires 'assessment for learning and the use of data and dialogue to diagnose every student's learning needs'. Second – and somewhat vaguely – it is the importance of developing 'teaching and learning strategies that build on individual needs'. Third, it means 'every student enjoying curriculum choice, a breadth of study and personal relevance, with clear pathways through the system'. Fourth, there are 'radical' organisational consequences: that is 'the starting point for class organisation is always student progress, with opportunities for in-depth, intensive teaching and learning, combined with flexible deployment of support staff'. And finally, it means the support and involvement of the community and other local institutions, including the social services (Miliband 2006: 24–6). But its clearest explication occurs in *2020 Vision: report of the Teaching and Learning in 2020 review group*, chaired by Christine Gilbert, Her Majesty's Chief Inspector of Education, Children's Services and Skills. Therein the implementation of personalisation was deemed to be 'a matter of moral purpose and social justice': that is to say, not only would personalisation serve to alleviate the educational plight of the most disadvantaged groups, it also 'reflects wider changes in society, which are likely to continue at an increasing rate' (Department for Education and Skills 2007a: 7).

The policy of personalisation in education raises the question of who shall be the consumer: the parent and/or the pupil? We have said that during the 1980s and 1990s, the marketisation of education had focused clearly on the informed, rationally choosing *parent*; under personalisation, what counts as the consumer is arguably more the *pupil* who, following the logic of personalisation, should be the co-producer of his or her own pedagogy and curriculum (Hartley 2008: 372). Leadbeater (2006), however, stated that 'Personalised learning does not apply market thinking to education' (ibid.: 111). But, elsewhere, he declared that 'young people are far more *avid and aware consumers* than they used to be. This culture is bound to have an effect on how they view education' (ibid.: 110; emphasis added).

To be sure, the initial conceptualisations of personalised learning were deemed to be decidedly elastic (Pollard and James 2004). A number of attempts to provide a typology of personalisation have emerged. The first is Paludan's (2006) typology, which comprised four 'scenarios', each associated with a particular kind of socio-economic condition. *Total personalisation* associates with a strong economy and a high degree of cultural integration. In these circumstances, there would be not only personalisation of each pupil's 'route' through the education system, but also of the 'content'. *Personalised timing* associates with high economic growth, but also with immigration controls, and a desire to reassert national identity. The consequence would be a national curriculum, but with a personalisation of the timing by which it would be acquired. *Automated teaching,* the third scenario, accorded with low economic growth, and with high levels of outsourcing to other countries. Here would be required highly motivated pupils and a high-skill workforce, best enabled by information technology. This technical solution, Paludan argues, would be efficient, would resonate with youth culture, and it could provide for the personalisation of both content and timing. The *status quo* is the fourth scenario. This would associate with a low-growth economy, with an uncertainty about national identity, with reluctance to experiment, and with an economy which has few resources.

The second conceptualisation was undertaken by Leadbeater. Overall, he states that personalisation is most appropriate for those services which are face-to-face: that is, education, non-emergency health care, social services and housing (Leadbeater 2004a). These are services which necessarily entail a continuing relationship between the user and the producer, thereby allowing for the former to significantly 'shape' the service provided by the latter (ibid.: 66). He also drew the distinction between 'shallow' and 'deep' personalisation. 'Shallow' personalisation allows for 'modest modification of mass-produced, standardised services to partially adapt them to user needs'. 'Deep' personalisation, on the other hand, offers to users a 'far greater role – and also far greater responsibilities – for designing solutions from the ground up' (Leadbeater 2004a: 21). Leadbeater's later typology of personalised learning is threefold. The first type is *bespoke service*, a service tailored to the imputed needs of individual clients by knowledgeable professionals who are sensitive to the client's needs (Leadbeater 2006: 102). The second type is *mass customisation*, which permits a degree of choice on the part of the user from 'standardised components and modules' (ibid.: 104). The third is *mass personalisation*, where a co-production is undertaken by a community of users who 'co-create value'. In this respect, Leadbeater cites the open-source Linux operating system, and the SIMS on-line gaming community (ibid.: 106–7).

The third conceptualisation was that by Hargreaves who produced a series of publications on 'personalising learning' (Hargreaves 2004; 2005a, b, c, d; 2006). In keeping with the sentiments of the marketing theorists, he likened personalisation to customisation in the business world. As an example, he refers to the difference between Henry Ford's one-colour car and the later user-driven approach which was developed in the post-war Japanese car industry (Hargreaves 2004: 2). For Hargreaves, schools are informed too much by a 'nineteenth-century imaginary', not a twenty-first century imaginary (ibid.: 2–3). Drawing upon Hargreaves' publications, in 2008 the Department for Children Schools and Families in England (2010a) established a *Space for Personalised Learning*. It was a multi-disciplinary team comprising experts from design strategy, education, architecture, research and technology. Ten pilot schools worked with the project. Following Hargreaves' conceptualisation, the project generated a three-fold typology of personalisation. Its definition of 'high personalisation' accords strongly with Hargreaves notion of customisation. The elements of 'high personalisation' are as follows:

- Learners are 'prosumers', co-constructing and co-designing their own programme of learning, identifying with facilitators what they want to learn, and also co-determining the method of delivery.
- Learners progress to appropriate content when they are ready to do so, for different levels of the curriculum. They are not constrained by their age, but can attend content designed for younger or older age groups as needed.
- Learners have a high degree of individual flexibility, joining groups as required to experience curriculum content.
- Learners are involved in scheduling and attending their own diaries. Some session lengths are fixed, others are flexible and depend on the work taking place.
- Learners attend the school in the core hours relevant to the options they are studying and access to staff they require.
- A high degree of space in the school is owned by learners, with staff providing services to those spaces.

(Department for Children Schools and Families 2010a: 43)

'High personalisation' is of a piece with Paludan's total 'personalisation'. Two other types are generated: 'medium personalisation' and 'low personalisation'. Medium personalisation would reveal 'some flexibility in providing packets of customised experiences, but not for every student. Low personalisation would be expressed as 'relatively centralised systems and structures providing a broadly similar experience for every student' (ibid.).

A recent attempt to conceptualise personalised learning (albeit in relation to adult education) was made by a European group called LEADLAB, funded by the European Commission through the Grundtvig Lifelong Learning Programme. It comprised members from Italy, Finland, France, Germany, Greece, Spain and Switzerland. In this it usefully drew the distinction between 'individualization' and 'personalization'. Whereas individualisation has the same objective for all learners, personalisation has different ones; whereas the teachers define the curriculum under individualisation, personalisation permits the learner actively to participate in the construction of their own curriculum; whereas individualisation 'valorises' only the cognitive, personalisation also valorises the emotional and the social (Grundtvig Project 2011: 7).

In England, further education and training was also deemed to benefit from it, as indicated in the government's *Personalising Further Education: developing a vision:*

> Personalisation puts the user at the heart of education and training services. We believe that this will deliver the skills for more learners and at all levels that are needed to sustain an advanced, competitive economy and promote a fairer society.
>
> (Department for Education and Skills 2006: 10)

Australia also caught the mood (Keamy *et al.* 2007). In New South Wales, the *Report of the Consultation on Future Directions for Public Education and Training: 'one size doesn't fit all'*, was published (New South Wales: Department of Education and Training 2005). Of note is the subtitle: 'one size doesn't fit all', implying the preference for a customised or tailored approach. Two years later the Council for the Australian Federation published *Federalist Paper 2 – The Future of Schooling in Australia: a report by the states and territories* (Revised Edition). It states:

> With high-quality course material, excellent teaching and flexible organisation, it is possible to support each student to progress along a personalised pathway that reflects their specific goals, strengths and motivations, and harnesses other opportunities for learning. This process of personalisation is increasingly recognised as being an essential part of increasing retention and attainment rates.
>
> (Council for the Australian Federation 2007: 21)

In Canada (where schooling is a provincial responsibility) one of the clearest calls for personalised learning has been made in British Columbia (British Columbia Ministry of Education 2011). Its 'Curriculum in the Personalized World' seeks to 'renew' (not merely to 'revise') its existing overly prescriptive curriculum. This is not, however, an advocacy of strong personalisation whereby personal choices prevail. There remain the requirements for 'rigour', for 'higher-order conceptualisation', for 'flexibility', for an emphasis on the 'disciplines', on the 'foundation skills', and on '21st century competencies', these latter being 'collaboration, creativity and critical thinking'. Pedagogy will be informed by constructivism and will 'support co-construction and inquiry-based approaches to teaching and learning' (ibid.: 17). By co-construction is meant 'teachers becoming co-learners with their students, using inter-disciplinary approaches and working in teams of teachers to support students' (ibid.: 20).

Personalisation figures in recent policy objectives in the European Union. Prompted by the 2008 economic crisis, it has put forward its *Europe 2020 Strategy*. The Council of Europe reached conclusions on 12 May 2009 on a strategic framework for European cooperation in education and training ('ET 2020'). In relation to *Strategic Objective 3: promoting equity, social cohesion and active citizenship*, it states:

> Education and training systems should aim to ensure that all learners – including those from disadvantaged backgrounds, those with special needs and migrants – complete their education, including, where appropriate, through second-chance education *and the provision of more personalised learning.*
>
> (Council of the European Union 2009: C119/4; italics added)

The advocacy of personalisation continued in 2011. A discussion paper (Prevention policies to combat early school leaving aimed at children with socioeconomically disadvantaged backgrounds, including Roma) from the General Secretariat of the Council of the European Union stated that while basic skills, key competences and a broader curriculum were important, nevertheless teachers needed also staff development in how to teach in more heterogeneous and multicultural classes; and 'especially [in] developing more personalised teaching methods' (General Secretariat of the Council of the European Union 2011: 6). On this very matter, in a commentary on the Council of Europe's draft, the Minister of State for Schools in England appeared somewhat hesitant:

> However, some elements of the proposed policy framework do not fit with the Government's policies in England; for example, some of the emphasis on 'modularisation of courses', 'strengthening personalised learning', and 'study allowances'.
>
> (House of Commons European Scrutiny
> Committee 2011: 3.15; emphasis added)

The Council of Europe paper refers to 'more personalised teaching methods', but the English minister's concern refers to 'personalised *learning*', which might imply a concern about the personalisation of the curriculum. Indeed, the Coalition government in England in its White Paper, *The Importance of Teaching – The Schools White Paper 2010*, gives personalised learning no mention. Its comments upon the curriculum are taken with reducing central prescription, but not by much:

The National Curriculum should set out clearly the core knowledge and understanding that all children should be expected to acquire in the course of their schooling. It must embody their cultural and scientific inheritance, the best that our past and present generations have to pass on to the next. But it must not try to cover every conceivable area of human learning or endeavour, must not become a vehicle for imposing passing political fads on our children and must not squeeze out all other learning.

(Department for Education 2010: 42)

The Scottish government's position, however, retained the notion of personalisation, regarding it as a central (though undefined) principle:

Curriculum for Excellence enables schools and their partners to build a flexible system that offers personalisation and choice to meet the needs of all young people, wherever their learning is taking place. It also provides clear and supported pathways for young people to make successful transitions and to continue learning beyond compulsory schooling.

(Scottish Government 2011: 20)

Scotland's *Curriculum for Excellence* contains very little detail about curricular content, and is decidedly different from the more detailed requirements in England under the Coalition government (Priestley and Humes 2010). If anything, in England, there *is* a preference for 'freedom' – less for pupils, but more for teachers (whose bureaucratic burden will be lessened) and for parents (who may wish to form free schools). In sum, personalisation for pupils in England is – at policy level – given no prominence, notwithstanding the White Paper of 2011 to 'customise' services, including education. Instead, the Coalition government intends to 'dramatically extend the Academies programmes' such that they become the 'norm', and to enable those – be they teachers, charities, parents – to open free schools (Department for Education 2010: 52). For the Coalition government in England, 'customisation' in education now appears to revert to the choice of structures (that is, of schools), away from the personalisation of curriculum and pedagogy which had been taken further by New Labour up to 2010.

Summary

There are two dimensions to personalisation. The first is that it is a *mode of soft 'regulation'*; and the second is that it is a *type of learning – personalised learning*. The concern of this chapter has been largely with the first dimension. The changing forms of production and of consumption provide a new economic context for education. The sociological analysis of education has for the most part dwelt upon the relationship between schooling and production. But beyond the workplace, the lifeworld is becoming commodified. Identities are more open to the lure of those goods and services which will accomplish yet another makeover. And the digital convergence of the media is enabling would-be consumers to become exposed to these identity-possibilities (if they can be afforded). In its quest to transform what hitherto were 'prudential' goods (such as education and health) into what Offer calls 'visceral' goods, governments have come to rely more and more upon emotional appeals and the pleasure-principle when 'selling' policies to the public. Personalisation is such a rhetoric of regulation. It resonates with consumerism and it affirms personhood. It accords with the emerging conflation of production and consumption: that is, it is of a piece with the 'prosumer'. And it sits well with the broad policy sweep which says that no child is to be left behind (US); that every child matters (England); and that one size doesn't fit all (Australia). The very elasticity of personalisation as a concept enables it to incorporate consumption, production and equal opportunities. In sum, personalisation (or customisation) purports to produce the prosumer: that is, the collaborative worker and the collaborative consumer. And it seeks to produce a governable 'choosing' 'active' subject. At root, its intellectual heritage rests with marketing theory.

Personalisation is also a type of learning. A number of questions now arise. The first concerns how personalised learning needs shall be managed during the co-production process in education. If the customer – here, the pupil – is said to be a co-producer, then how shall this be effected? And if the co-produced needs are such that they require inter-professional collaboration, then what shall be the theoretical basis which informs this collaboration? Put differently, personalisation may require collaboration among professionals whose cultures may be different. How will this be accomplished? A second question concerns the pedagogical, curricular and assessment changes which logically might follow from an endorsement of personalised learning. Notwithstanding all of the policy declarations, the concept of personalisation – especially of personalised learning – remains elusive of a firm definition.[1]

Endnote

1 On Monday, 17 November 2008, there was an exchange on the meaning of personalisation in the House of Commons Children, Schools and Families Committee. David Hargreaves agreed that it meant 'customisation':

> Yes, customisation: We shall try to meet the needs of customers more fully – for more customers – than we have ever done before [. . .]. We took as our working definition a simple lift-over from the business world. We said that customisation, or personalisation, in education is intended to meet more of the educational needs of more students, more fully, than we achieve today. The line we took was exactly like an industry, which says that, to meet those needs, it may have to redesign its product or service. We have taken that line in schools: if that is what we are trying to do, we may have to redesign what we offer as schooling.
>
> [House of Commons Children, Schools and Families Committee, 2009. *National Curriculum: Fourth Report of Session 2008–9, Volume II Oral and written evidence.* London: The Stationery Office, Q492]

Later during the meeting, the chairman, Barry Sheerman, could no longer contain his confusion:

> *Chairman*: I am totally confused about this. This is probably the most difficult inquiry that the Committee has undertaken since I have been the Chairman. A fog seems to come up as soon as you chaps, or generic chaps – sorry, characters – come to the Committee: first, it is not useful to have personalised learning any more, although the Department has been pushing this stuff out for years.
>
> [ibid.: Q505]

7 Personalised learning

This chapter explores the curricular and pedagogical consequences of adopting the practice of personalising education in the school. (The matter of personalisation as a mode of government regulation, or governance, will not be at issue here.) Examples will be drawn from the US, Sweden and the UK. The personalisation of education represents a shift in the code, or grammar, of education (Hartley 2007a). That is to say, the form of the curriculum, the pedagogy and the mode of assessment are all undergoing change; at least at the level of advocacy, less of fact. We have seen through the work of Hargreaves, Leadbeater and Paludan that personalisation may be classified into different types. At root it is about consumer choice. Miliband, when a schools minister in England, regarded both the parent and the child as having 'choice', and to express it with a 'voice': 'The challenge is to ally choice with voice: voice for the pupil, voice for the parent' (Miliband 2006: 26). The seminal work on exit and voice is that by Hirschman (1970). Voice is 'any attempt at all to change, rather than to escape from, an objectionable state of affairs' (Hirschman 1970: 30). It can be undertaken either individually or collectively, by direct appeal either to a line manager or to a higher authority, or by protests and actions. Choice and voice, taken together, were deemed to be a new phase in the 'modernisation' of the provision of public services (House of Commons Public Administration Select Committee 2005; Her Majesty's Government 2011). In the first phase of the marketisation of education, school choice (as expressing a preference) for parents had been introduced; in the second phase – personalisation – the pupil also was assigned consumer status.

This is an example of Bauman's view that the New Labour 'modernization' project was not so much a 'one-off operation', but rather a continuing process 'further eroding the value of duration together with the prudence of long-term thinking, and reinforcing the ambience of uncertainty, temporariness and until-further-notice-ness on which consumer commodity markets are known to thrive' (Bauman 2007: 48). Bauman's analysis – his reference to the erosion of the public services as a prudential good – accords with Offer's analysis that the visceral prevails over the prudential (Offer 2003). The official discourse of personalisation has a declared affinity to the consumer.

We have stated in the previous chapter that, notwithstanding many policy documents, there remains a lack of clarity about the concept of personalisation, especially of personalised learning. Even so, it does relate to an emerging con-flation between production and consumption. The term prosumer has suffused the discussion of personalisation. There is, however, much in the discourse of personalisation which is redolent and reminiscent of what was known in the 1960s and 1970s as open education, or as child-centred education. But Miliband clearly distanced his version of personalised learning from child-centred education: 'it is not about separating pupils to learn on their own; it is not the abandonment of a national curriculum; and it is not a license to let pupils coast at their own preferred pace of learning' (Miliband 2006: 24). Despite the similarity in the discourse of personalisation in the 2000s and of 1960s' child-centred education, the reasons for the emergence of both of these 'philosophies' of education are quite different. Child-centred education emerged in the wake of the New Romantics in education (Dale 1979). For its implementation it was informed by developmental psychology; for its intellectual appeal, it drew upon Rousseau. There was nothing ado with consumerism (Hartley 2009). On the other hand, personalisation has its intellectual roots in marketing theory, not in educational psychology. Furthermore, the emergence of personalisation, as we have argued, rests on a culture in which the self is continually up for renewal. It turns on the need to re-imagine oneself, and to buy the goods and services which will contribute to the makeover of the self; it is a culture of continual re-selfing, a process akin to what has been termed 'individualisation' (Beck 1992). In order to accomplish this, a degree of reflexivity is required. It requires the capacity to be emotionally in tune with oneself, and to be creative about the possibilities for self-renewal. In this, personalisation sits well with other emergent and popular strands in educational thought. For example, there is a renewed concern about the education of the emotions: the concept of 'emotional intelligence' has readily taken root in the education lexicon. Similarly, there are appeals to creativity, and to 'well-being'. All of these are arguably centred upon the self, not upon the collective.

The justification for personalisation does not rest exclusively upon consumerism or upon the related notion of the prosumer. In addition, personalisation has been advocated as a way of bringing about greater social justice, a view taken by the European Union. So it can be said to be a moral endeavour. David Hopkins, when Chief Adviser to Ministers on School Standards at the Department for Education and Skills, but writing in a personal capacity, stated 'Personalised learning means high quality teaching that is responsive to the different ways students achieve their best. There is a clear moral and educational case for pursuing this approach' (Hopkins 2006: 1). The case for this is as follows. Unless the needs of each child can readily and accurately be appraised then the child will not be given an appropriate education. Contained within the idea of personalised learning is the concept of 'tailoring' lessons to the learning style of the child; a 'bespoke' service. This assumes that one can speak of different learning styles (as some advocates of personalised learning do, though Miliband did not), but the whole matter is complex and is not given to agreed definitions and applications, at least insofar as post-16 education is concerned (Coffield *et al.* 2004). But even if the notions of personal epistemologies and learning styles are doubtful, the notion of different personalities is on a surer footing.

Curriculum

Recall Miliband's views on curriculum and personalisation: '*curriculum choice engages and respects students.* So, personalised learning means every student enjoying curriculum choice, a breadth of study and personal relevance, with clear pathways through the system' (Miliband 2006: 24–6). In his influential series on personalising learning, Hargreaves set great store by student voice: that is, particularly it requires a private conversation between the teacher and pupil, this itself requiring a school community wherein trust has been established as a cultural norm, rather than as a range of organisational structures. Schools may regard the expression of pupil voice as possibly cathartic, as a way of defusing conflicts; or it may be managed, and channelled towards safe subjects. In Sebba and colleagues' (2007: 67) study of personalisation, 'voice' in schools was largely regarded as meaning the presence of school councils. In a related manner, the report *2020 Vision: report of the Teaching and Learning in 2020 review group* (Department for Education and Skills 2007a) refers to the advantages of allowing children to be 'given opportunities to take ownership of their learning' (ibid.: 26). (We may note that the notion of 'ownership' is a suitably consumerist notion.) In its endorsement of Hargreaves, the report states that this will be furthered when 'teachers and pupils are developing a more sophisticated language with which to talk explicitly about learning and how it can be explored and improved' (ibid.: 20). Notwithstanding the declared centrality of 'voice' in his evidence to a House of Commons Select Committee in 2009, Hargreaves appeared to diminish the importance of voice in the personalisation of learning (House of Commons Children, Schools and Families Committee 2009: 473).

Pupils do not have the right of 'exit' from school unless their parents have the financial and cultural wherewithal to withdraw them. Nor do they have the right of veto. Recall that Hirschman's concept of 'voice' is defined as 'any attempt at all to change, rather than to escape from, an *objectionable* state of affairs' (Hirschman 1970: 30; emphasis added). Lacking the right to 'exit, pupils, therefore, must resort to voice in order to counter 'objectionable' states of affairs (but they may also deploy the use of silence which itself is a political tactic). But if voice is to be restricted to the pupil–teacher level, then it requires pupils to have a linguistic competence and a level of cultural accomplishment which will enable them to have a 'learning conversation' with teachers, so as to negotiate, to co-produce, the curricular content that they require and need. But for some pupils, the expression of their personalised curricular needs may literally be unspeakable. At the outset, Leadbeater was aware of this, and warned about it. Not only is the cultural repertoire of the middle class better suited to personalisation, they have also the material resources – more space, computers and books. Unless these resources are available equally across the social spectrum then the personalisation of education could have negative consequences for equity (Leadbeater 2004a: 74–5).

A Swedish ethnographic study explores this. It analysed the consequences of personalised learning (known as *individualisering* in Sweden): that is, the consequences of the transformation from 'transmission to (co-)construction' (Beach and Dovemark 2009: 691). In the process of co-construction – and the expression of the choices which require it – some choices attract more reward and approval than others, and the 'most highly valorised choices reproduce a business-middle-class commitment to consumption which is beginning to enter everything' (ibid.: 701). Middle-class pupils are creative in making the choices which will attract a high rate of return – in this sense, they are active and successful consumers who can combine creativity and performativity. They are adept in how they deploy their 'demands' on the teacher's time and resources. In sales terms, they know how to pitch themselves so as to get a result. They are engaged in 'return thinking', an emergent category arising from twelve years of ethnographic research in Sweden's upper-secondary schools (Beach and Dovemark 2011: 316). And they are aware of having this orientation. Statements from two pupils, Kaj and Klara, reveal that they did indeed have the freedom to 'make choices and work at your own pace with your friends', or 'even talk about what you want to do and why and have some influence that way too'. But, at root, they were fully aware that they had to meet 'performance demands'. They knew the value of making the 'right choices', of 'showing interest', of 'performing well', of having a 'good attitude', of showing 'initiative' (Beach and Dovemark 2009: 692). At a time when resources in education are dwindling, the capacity to personalise oneself in a manner that resonates with the expectation of the teacher is itself a scarce resource.

In a study of 'personalising the curriculum' of 14–19-year-olds in four English schools, the authors reported that personalisation did not necessarily mean 'freer choices for students': they were, instead, 'guided onto a pathway for success, achieved through dialogue between parents, students and teachers: "Choice is a weak form of personalised learning"' (Cresswell and Morrissey 2006, unpaginated). This is some way from the concept of *high personalisation* which was referred to earlier: 'Learners are "prosumers", co-constructing and co-designing their own programme of learning, identifying with facilitators what they want to learn, and also co-determining the method of delivery' (Department for Children Schools and Families 2010a: 43). Similarly, Paludan's *total personalisation* was one whereby there would be not only personalisation of each pupil's 'route' through the education system, but also of the 'content'. The policy in England appears to approximate Leadbeater's *bespoke service*, one tailored to the imputed needs of individual clients by knowledgeable professionals who are sensitive to the client's needs.

This bespoke version of personalisation applies elsewhere: for example, in New York City, and in Sweden. Take New York City where the School of One (So1) is 'a pioneer in the emerging field of customized learning' (New York City Department of Education 2010a). The mission of So1 is to 'provide students with personalized, effective, and dynamic classroom instruction and, by leveraging technology to streamline planning instruction, allow teachers to have more time to focus on the quality of their instruction' (New York City Department of Education 2010b: 2). The leveraging of technology means that the school's 'lesson bank' contains some 5,000 lessons which have been prepared by more than 50 'academic partners' (School of One 2011). An early report of the programme in the *New York Times* ran the headline 'Laptop? Check. Student playlist? Check. Classroom of the future? Check' (Medina 2009). The child receives each day a 'playlist' which contains not only the content but also the form or 'modality' whereby it will be learnt. The content is the result of applying an algorithm to the data derived from diagnostic tests each day. Thereby, academic needs are defined and a schedule of work is tailored to meet them. The 'modality' whereby the material shall be learnt varies, again according to the perceived preferred learning style of the child. This may incorporate teacher-led instruction, one-to-one tutoring, independent learning, or work with virtual tutors (from the 'lesson banks'). The programme has received major grants from some of the foundations which have an interest in technical solutions to educational problems. They include the Michael and Susan Dell Foundation, the Bill and Melinda Gates Foundation, the NewSchools Venture Fund, the Wallace Foundation, the Carnegie Corporation, JP Morgan Global Philanthropy, Cisco and the Broad Foundation.

In 2010, the expanded School of One was evaluated by a research group of the New York City Department of Education (New York City Department of Education 2010b). The research took place during early 2010. Initially, it investigated an after-school programme with 600 sixth-grade pupils from three schools (in Brooklyn's IS339, Manhattan's MS131 and the Bronx's IS339, respectively). Thereafter it investigated a short-term, in-school implementation of the programme with sixth-grade pupils in one of the three schools. It was not a randomised controlled study. Its conclusions were broadly favourable: the gains in mathematics achievement among the after-school participants in the School of One programme 'significantly exceeded' those who did not participate in the programme. Similarly, pupils who proceeded to participate in the subsequent in-school implementation achieved a similar pattern of results (New York City Department of Education 2010b: 11). The authors were appropriately cautious about their findings, and called for a longitudinal study.

A more coordinated and commercial attempt to personalise learning comes in the form of the *Kunskapsskolan* (translated as 'knowledge schools') in Sweden. They are for-profit free schools, and they are the sixth-largest independent provider of upper secondary education in Sweden, with some 33 secondary and upper-secondary schools, teaching about 10,000 students. Their executive vice-president, Odd Eiken, had been state secretary of education in Sweden. Personalisation, he states, is about 'a combination of goal setting, weekly coaching, personalised scheduling and timing and a unique curriculum maintained on the web-based Learning Portal'. There are a variety of methods: lectures, workshops, seminars and laboratories – as appropriate. 'Voice' is expressed at the beginning of each term when parents, students and staff 'decide on each student's individual educational plan and long-term goal'. Thereafter, students meet their 'coach' every week to discuss progress and purpose. In this way, students gradually 'develop personal responsibility for, and ownership of, what they learn' (Eiken 2011: 2). The school's web-site declares that learning must be 'personalized', 'customized' and 'tailor-made'.

Unlike the School of One, which so far has focused upon mathematics, the *Kunskapsskolan* incorporates the whole curriculum, which is structured in steps, and pupils are offered cross-subject 'thematic' courses. It seeks to meet national or state standards, and comprises a core curriculum. The *Kunskapsskolan,* again like the School of One in New York City, relies very heavily upon ICT to 'deliver' the personalised content. And again, as in New York, there is a spatial and temporal restructuring of schooling which is enabled by the web-based portals. Whereas, in the School of One, the 'playlist' is computer-generated, in the *Kunskapsskolan* (which opened its first American school in New York in 2011) the plans for work are the outcome of the one-to-one meeting each week which lasts for about 15 minutes. This is similar to what, in England, Leadbeater calls 'the review day' for each year group when each pupil has a 15-minute conversation with their personal tutor, who remains with that pupil throughout their time at the school; and thereafter, they meet the pupil's parent, so as to agree targets for behaviour, attendance and homework (Leadbeater 2005: 16).

The Swedish free schools have been much-touted in England by the secretary of state for education, Michael Gove. Except in one important respect: free schools in Sweden are for-profit; in England, not yet. (Gove has been suitably evasive on the question of for-profit schools in a parliamentary exchange (House of Commons 2011: 7 February, column 18).) While the Coalition government in England is attracted to the notion of free schools at the structural level, there is now much less certainty about personalised learning at the classroom level (House of Commons European Scrutiny Committee 2011: 3.15). What is clear is that free schools and the personalisation of curriculum offer little coherence about the principles for a curriculum. Gove, for example, is an unashamed elitist when it comes to the curriculum. Subjects are subjects: given, and well demarcated from each other. He is no advocate of a personalised curriculum. He would have no truck with those whose epistemological position rests on social constructivism: that is to say, those who argue that knowledge is contingent upon the times at hand. In any case, the extent to which knowledge can be 'personalised' is surely variable: in, say, history and in English literature there is arguably far less objective truth than in the natural sciences (Campbell *et al.* 2007: 151). It is the economic neo-liberals who now prefer personalisation, for it rests easily with markets, choice, technology and instrumentalism. Scotland's *Curriculum for Excellence* comes close to this position (Scottish Government 2009). In England, Gove's position attempts to reconcile two different factions in the Conservative party: the One Nation Tories; and the economic neo-liberals. In curriculum, he seems at one with the former; in structural terms – especially in relation to for-profit free schools – he is of the latter.

Pedagogy

The term 'personalised learning' implies a pedagogical position. Reference has just been made to some of the modalities whereby personalised learning is said to occur. This matter is now considered more fully. A recent major collection by the OECD on the nature of learning (Dumont *et al.* 2010) concludes with an educational agenda for the twenty-first century. It stresses that learning should be 'profoundly personalised': that is, the learning environment should be sensitive to the background of the pupil, and should take account of prior knowledge and motivation. It should offer 'tailored and detailed feedback'. It should also be inclusive of individual and group differences, and it should be social and collaborative (ibid.: 210). This association between personalisation and collaboration appears to be paradoxical: personalisation is sometimes regarded as individualisation (informed by developmental psychology), and is thereby devoid of collaboration and a social dimension (informed by social constructivism and by sociocultural theory). But there is no paradox. Istance and Dumont (2010: 329), referring to extensive research on collaborative learning (Slavin 2010), argue that well-designed collaborative activities can be motivating and 'stretching' for individuals, provided that formative feedback is given (Black and Wiliam 2006). Personalised learning does not mean 'either the solitary individual learning in isolation or choosing a curriculum for himself or herself from a smorgasbord menu on offer' (Istance and Dumont 2010: 329).

Personalised learning is redolent not only of a consumerist perspective; it has also productive possibilities in a 'new' knowledge economy. At a consumerist level, personalised learning purports to meet the needs of the individual, and to assign to the individual greater discretion about the form, content and transmission of knowledge. But its productive possibilities turn on its emphasis on collaboration. In the 'new capitalism', so this argument runs, less importance is placed upon what individuals know on their own, and more is placed upon how collectively they can collaborate so as to add value to the business at hand (Gee *et al.* 1996: 58). And this empowerment of the worker itself implies that the mode of regulation will need to allow for this collaboration; power will have to be 'exerted' less hierarchically than hitherto (ibid.: 60). The pedagogical implications are profound, and will logically require behaviourism and constructivist theories to be set aside in favour of sociocultural theory. For different reasons, both the new capitalism and sociocultural theory argue that knowledge and learning are social, and not confined to individuals (ibid.: 67). In classrooms whose pedagogy is informed by sociocultural theory, there is a likelihood that they may

> produce students pre-equipped to work harmoniously in distributed systems by internalizing core values, values that issue from the social practices and organizational structures of the system itself and not from any visible controlling centre.
>
> (ibid.: 60)

The important point is that social constructivism does not accomplish the kind of interaction which Gee *et al.* envisage. To be sure, social constructivists speak of the social, but usually in the sense that 'social' equates with the facilitator designing the environment within which the learner learns. This is not strictly *interaction*; intersubjectivity is not in process here. Sociocultural theory, on the other hand, accomplishes learning by means of scaffolding which involves the teacher as expert and the pupil as novice. Thereby knowledge is accomplished in a community of practice (Crook 2008).

Personalised pedagogy is an elusive concept. We have seen in this and the previous chapter that a series of attempts in England to define it have wandered from the inchoate to the incoherent (Hastings 2004). A steady stream of documents has sought to get to grips with it, including the White Paper *Higher Standards, Better Schools for All*. It includes a chapter entitled 'Personalised Learning'. But its attempt to clarify personalised learning is confusing, for it refers both to 'individual needs' and to 'tailored whole-class teaching' (Department for Education and Skills 2005: para. 4.6: 51). In the year before its publication Miliband had defined personalisation as 'THE big idea'. But that did not mean that it was a radical departure from convention:

> [P]ersonalisation is not new. Our best schools provide a tailored education which combines: extra small group or one-to-one tuition for those that need it – not as a substitute for excellent whole class teaching, but as an integrated part of the child's learning; opportunities for all children to get extra support and tuition in subjects and activities they are interested in, as well as access to a range of opportunities beyond the school day, including weekend and holiday courses and online learning; exciting whole-class teaching, which gets the best from every child; setting or grouping children of similar ability and attainment; a rich, flexible and accessible curriculum and, for older pupils, one that allows them to mix academic and vocational learning; *[and]* innovative use of ICT, both in the classroom and linking the classroom and home.
>
> (ibid.: para. 4.2)

> Most important of all, *it continues*, is tailored whole-class teaching [. . .] with all the resources available – from extra support staff to improved ICT – being used to ensure that every pupil gets the education they need.
>
> (ibid.: para. 4.6; *see also* para. 4.10)

Notwithstanding the mixed messages about personalised pedagogy, a year later the government made a large financial commitment to fund the resources for personalised learning, a sum amounting to £990 million by 2007; and it called upon an 'expert team to look further ahead at teaching and learning in 2020' (Department for Education and Skills 2006: 12). The review group interpreted its remit as being 'to establish a clear vision of what personalised teaching and learning might look like in our schools in 2020' (Department for Education and Skills 2007a: 3). Its deliberations were reported in *2020 Vision:*

Report of the Teaching and Learning in 2020 review group. The report states 'that personalising learning and teaching must play a central role in transforming England's education service' (ibid.: 5). It goes on to define 'personalising learning' as:

> . . . *learner-centred and knowledge-centred* . . . Close attention is paid to learners' knowledge, skills, understanding and attitudes. Learning is connected to what they already know (including from outside the classroom).
>
> Teaching enthuses pupils and engages their interest in learning: it identifies, explores and corrects misconceptions.
>
> Learners are active and curious: they create their own hypotheses, ask their own questions, coach one another, set goals for themselves, monitor their progress and experiment with ideas for taking risks, knowing that mistakes and 'being stuck' are part of learning. Work is sufficiently varied and challenging to maintain their engagement but not so difficult as to discourage them. This engagement allows learners of all abilities to succeed, and it avoids the disaffection and attention-seeking that give rise to problems with behaviour.
>
> (ibid.: 6)

Throughout the 'vision' there is no mention of a theory which informs personalised learning. But, in the same year, the government did produce a paper which was explicitly about pedagogy and personalisation (Department for Education and Skills 2007b). It mentions a 'theoretical yet practical view'. It refers to – but does not discuss – the 'theories of learning and teaching' (ibid.: 6–7), of which there are said to be three 'families': behaviourist; cognitive; and social and constructivist. In essence, the *2020 Vision* report envisages a mix: the 'judicious use of whole-class teaching, as well as one-to-one, paired and group work'. It recommends also 'using more open-ended tasks with pupils, either individually or in groups, based on specific projects or areas of inquiry' (ibid.: 13). In not aligning itself fully to a constructivist pedagogy, the government may have been mindful of the mismatch between existing pedagogical practice and co-constructed pedagogical principles. In a study of 50 primary schools in England between 2003 and 2005 Webb and Vulliamy remind us that the 1988 Education Reform Act did *not* prescribe the pedagogical style of the teacher, only the curriculum to be transmitted. Nevertheless the national strategies for literacy and numeracy which followed did move some teachers (those trained before 1990) away from what had hitherto been a commitment to thematic topics and group-work, albeit with pupils moving at their own pace (Webb and Vulliamy 2007: 577).

One of the few systematic studies of personalisation is that by Sebba *et al.* (2007). It comprised a survey of a ten per cent sample of primary and a 20 per cent sample of secondary schools in England: in total, 2,838 schools. A response-rate of 12.8 per cent was obtained, but with the caveat that the findings refer only to those schools which themselves, in the authors' opinion, were 'likely to be more interested or active in approaches to personalised learning' (ibid.: 3).

In addition, 13 case studies (consisting of: document analysis; interviews with managers, teachers, teaching assistants; interviews with pupils and with parents/governors; and lesson/activity observation) were undertaken in five primary, five secondary, one middle deemed secondary and in two special schools. This methodology, therefore, did not seek the effects of personalisation; it was more about the perceptions of it. On this latter, 'there was widespread uncertainty' about what was meant by 'personalised learning' (ibid.: 18). In general, there was a tendency to equate personalisation with individualisation (ibid.: 66). In particular, personalisation was said to include academic tracking, individual target-setting, individual feedback, self and peer assessment, the acknowledgement of prior and outside school learning, and assessment by ICT.

Pedagogically, the emergent practice at policy level accords partly with Paludan's 'personalised timing' scenario: that is, a national curriculum, but one which admits to a flexibility in the spatial and temporal forms whereby it is acquired (Paludan 2006: 97). The pedagogical process which allows the pupil more discretion about these spatial and temporal arrangements is enhanced by 'learning platforms'. This introduces one of the recurrent themes of personalised learning: technology-supported learning. As stated earlier, it looms large in both New York's School of One and the Swedish *Kunskapsskolan*.

The association between the 'personal' and computer technology has emerged strongly since the 1970s: from the personal computer (PC), to the personal digital assistant (PDA), to the smart-phone. Now the World Wide Web – or Web 2.0 – literally opens up a new world where interactions and collaborations beckon. Echoing the 'prosumer', the so-called 'net generation' have no wish to be 'passive consumers'; instead, they are said to wish to 'satisfy their desire for choice, convenience, customization, and control by designing, producing and distributing products themselves' (Tapscott and Williams 2008: 46). Put differently, they wish to be active consumers and co-producers. In order to enable this, technology-supported learning platforms are in the offing: they are declared to be safe, ubiquitous, omnipresent; they allow for productive interactions among peers, and between students and mentors; they can better meet the interests and abilities of the individual (thereby re-engaging those once-disaffected); they allow for the sharing of resources; and they offer useful management and assessment tools (BECTA 2008: 2–3). In the US, similar sentiments have emerged in *Transforming American Education: Learning Powered by Technology* (US Department of Education 2010). It defines personalised learning thus:

> Personalization refers to instruction that is paced to learning needs, tailored to learning preferences, and tailored to the specific interests of different learners. In an environment that is fully personalized, the learning objectives and content as well as the method and pace may all vary (so personalization encompasses differentiation and individualization).
>
> (ibid.: 12; parentheses in the original)

> Personalized learning on a large scale is possible only by 'leveraging' the power of technology.
>
> (ibid.: 10)

So much for the policies. Circumstances may limit their realisation. Take an American example: the Cooltown@Roosevelt project in the Vancouver School District in Washington State received technological assistance provided by Hewlett-Packard and by Comcast. In short, the 'school' was to be an internet-based 'collaboratory'. In a single elementary school, this took the form of a laptop for each student in three classrooms, and one laptop for every two students in three other classrooms. High-speed internet to the students' homes was also provided. The catchment area was 'heterogeneous', comprising 'a high concentration of impoverished, transient, and ethnically diverse students, including English Language Learners (ELL) of Russian, Ukranian [*sic*], and Hispanic heritage' (Mabry and Snow 2006: 290). *ClassServer* software enabled teachers to deliver lessons online, and to provide assessment feedback, some of it automated, and some of it monitoring the student's performance in relation to state-wide standardised targets. Was it personalised? Not quite: in the authors' view it was the very persistence of the mandated state-wide achievement targets which was 'fundamentally in conflict with the program goal of transforming learning through personalization' (ibid.: 311). At Cooltown, 'Teachers create lessons or assignments that feature some student choice within defined parameters (e.g., choice of research topic)'. If the curriculum were to have been personalised, then assignments would need to have been individualised, perhaps even 'co-developed' by the teacher and student, and based upon the student's 'interests, goals, and current achievement levels'. As for the personalisation of time, 'Students complete lessons or assignments within somewhat individualized time-frames'. Had it been personalised, then students would have agreed individualised deadlines. But in assessment, however, there was no personalisation: work was assessed according to external criteria, including compliance with state-wide standards (ibid.: 308).

There are mixed messages about how those in English schools regard the capacity of ICT to enable personalisation. As with the policy-makers, among those in schools there is very little agreement about what personalisation actually means. A BECTA on-line survey reported little agreement among pupils (n = 3180), teachers (n = 425) and 'managers' (headteachers) about personalisation and 'e-maturity' (Underwood and Banyard 2008). Take the managers' 'institutional' view of personalisation (or 'p-Learning', as the study refers to it). Unlike policy-makers, headteachers inclined towards equating personalisation to individualisation (that is, pupil choice, voice and ownership of learning). The teachers were generally 'positive' about personalisation and the capacity of ICT to deliver it, but there were subject-specialism differences: unlike ICT and sports teachers, those of mathematics had little truck with the policy of personalisation; and design and technology teachers were the least likely to approve of ICT, unlike sports and (unsurprisingly) ICT teachers. As for the pupils' perceptions of personalisation (as defined in an online questionnaire), it varied over time, peaking in the fourth year of schooling when national attainment measures were less to the fore. Thereafter, the degree of perceived personalisation wanes. Across the three groups – pupils, teachers and managers – there is no accord among them about how personalisation is perceived, or about the role of ICT in accomplishing it. And there is some agreement with Mabry and Snow about the limiting influence of state-mandated assessment on personalisation. The BECTA study concluded that the best way to maximise test scores was to resort to a traditional didactic approach, and to *not* personalise learning (ibid.: 245).

There appears to be no necessary association between the use of Web 2.0 technologies and personalised learning. Luckin *et al.* investigated, by means of a survey and focus group, the use of Web 2.0 technologies among 11–16-year-old students in 27 secondary schools in the UK. Four categories-of-use emerged: *researchers,* who merely read the information, for the most part uncritically; *collaborators,* who confined themselves mainly to sharing files, to communicating and to gaming; and *producers* and *publishers,* who mainly exchanged experiences on social networking sites. Insofar as schooling was concerned, very few were inclined to construct knowledge collaboratively and to make it public. Instead, most confined themselves to using Web 2.0 tools for presentations and for communicating. In sum: 'There was little evidence of groundbreaking activities and only a few embryonic signs of criticality, self-management or metacognitive reflection' (Luckin *et al.* 2009: 87). It accords with Crook's eloquently put concern about being lured into 'collaborations' which consist of little more than sending emails and files to shared work-spaces: 'It seems that technology takes the intersubjective pleasure of conversational exploration and replaces it with an intermittent but relentless low bandwidth exchange that is more 'coordination' than 'collaboration' (Crook 2008: 33). Crook's point is that the presumed relationship between sociocultural theory and Web 2.0 is becoming attenuated: 'the direction of sociocultural thinking has migrated to the communal and the situated at the expense of "social" as an "interpersonal dynamic"' (ibid.: 34). Selwyn, too, observes that much has been made of the supposed – not actual – association between personalised and socially situated forms of on-line learning (Selwyn 2010: 14).

The technical fix is not just about the digitalisation of 'space': that is, it is not just about virtual spaces which allow for personalised pedagogy. The architectural manifestations of personalisation are revealed in new forms, themselves sometimes transformations of old ones. Thus it is that former offices and factories are being transformed into new pedagogical spaces which – although they might retain the term 'school' – bear little architectural resemblance to the standardised cellular form of the traditional school. Deleuze's age of clearly demarcated 'enclosures' is beginning to dissipate. The solidity and heaviness of its architecture is giving way to more ephemeral and more flimsy forms. This is in contrast with the solid-modern age when status was manifested by substantial and imposing forms which made an impression on the eyes of their beholders (Bauman 2000: 174).

The physical arrangements of the Web 2.0-enhanced school reveal little of Bauman's solid modernity. The Swedish *Kunskapsskolan* is about light, visibility and openness – all enabled by the extensive use of glass materials. The close connection of form and function is attenuated: spaces are multi-functional (for example, the cafe is a learning space); 'rooms', where they exist, are irregular in shape, and may be reconfigured for collaborative or independent working, as befits the task at hand; there are no corridors; there are no places to hide; the colour 'scheme' is not monochrome; nothing seems to be uniform. All of these arrangements are signs of the times.

In England, the Department for Children, Schools and Families (DCSF) in 2008 funded the *Space for Personalised Learning* project (Department for Children Schools and Families 2010a), referred to in Chapter 6. Its purpose clearly reveals the coalescence of production and consumption in a personalised pedagogy for a new knowledge economy:

> The project proceeds from the conviction that certain shifts in society, including the very fundamental move from an industrial to a knowledge-based economy, have pressing pedagogical and spatial implications that must be understood and met. *It adopts the term personalised learning to characterize the new ways of thinking and acting clustered round these little-understood implications.* It asks: How do we go about creating a physical environment that delivers education on the universal scale demanded – and yet allows schools to implement systems and structures that provide a *more customized experience* for young people?
>
> (ibid.: 7; emphasis added)

The project itself drew from a range of disciplines: design strategy, education, architecture, research and technology. Ten pilot schools comprised the 'research subjects'. The intention was to expose 'design truths robust enough to be applicable across the whole education sector' (ibid.: 7). The solution for one school, Chantry High School, gives a flavour (ibid.: 136). The school is a specialist humanities college of about 800 pupils in Ipswich, with a relatively high proportion of pupils being eligible for free school meals. The purpose of the project was small-scale, namely to 'test ideas of personalised learning' (that is, to 'prototype' the pedagogy before its school-wide application). Its project area comprised six 'zones': a peripheral *touchdown* area for short discussions; an *adult* area for preparation and informal work, but also one which allows for 'passive supervision of corridors and toilets'; a *chalk-and-talk* area for presentations, which could be screened off; an *informal break-out* area, with access to a digital screen; a *self-managed, independent-learning breakout* area for groups of one to four; and a *teamwork* area, 'technology-enabled', comprising group-work tables.

In its conclusion, the project made a number of caveats. First, the projects were all literally contained within existing schools. Had this not been the case – had they had *carte blanche* to construct spaces anew – then more personalised spatial solutions might have been possible. Second, unlike the School of One in New York (to which the authors refer), their own brief excluded a consideration of digital technologies, and so the possibilities for a hybrid spatial-cum-digital solution (as in School of One) were not considered. Second, they did not align themselves with a notion of personalisation which accorded either with Paludan's 'total' personalisation, or with 'high' personalisation. Instead, personalisation was deemed to be about providing 'more customised experiences at scale'. In addition, very few of the environments in the pilot projects were intended to focus wholly upon pupils working alone, as individuals, devoid of collaboration (ibid.: 145).

Summary

The period between 1970 and the financial crisis of 2008 coincided with the development of a highly productive technological advance centred upon computerisation. At first, computerisation was confined to mainframes, but after the emergence of the IBM PC the way towards digitalisation was cleared. What had hitherto been separate technologies converged: radio, television, music, film, services and finance all became digitalised to differing degrees. With digitalisation came the possibility of convergence. The prefix *inter* comes to suffuse much activity which had hitherto been *intra*. Much can now be synchronised. But the synchronisations and convergences which digitalisation enables have, in education, yet to be expressed as new organisational forms and pedagogical practices. For the most part, the structures of education are 'siloed' and bureaucratic; pedagogy tends towards the didactic so as to ensure conformity to national standards. This standardisation is about efficiency and measurement. But standardisation is not just about efficiency *per se*: it is retained because it is said to enable a 'marketplace' in education wherein would-be consumers (usually parents) can acquire the publicly available data (usually online) that will enable them to make informed choices on behalf of their children. Paradoxically, the 'free' market prompts standardisation. Choice is thereby limited.

Education remains one of the most lucrative and untapped markets for digitalisation. Those who would seek to exploit it have drawn an association between personalised web-enhanced technologies (such as smart-phones) and a consumerist culture which celebrates individual identity. These individual identities are expressed through products – some virtual, others real. The expansion of wifi and 3G networks enables these identities to be projected socially in a continual process of up-dating and synchronisation – a 'hypersociality', no less (Livingstone 2009: 25). Personalisations are produced, expressed and exchanged. They become inter-personalisations, forever provisional, portable and public.

Thus far, the 'market' has been insinuated into education at two levels, to varying degrees. First, there is some consumer choice of structures, such as schools and universities, which may themselves publicise some 'specialism'. Second, there is the beginning of some degree of permissible 'consumer' action within the pedagogical process. This is personalisation, be it of curriculum, of 'learning style', of assessment, and of temporal and spatial preferences. The expression of these preferences assumes that the 'enterprising-self' pupil has the cultural and financial wherewithal to express them in a manner deemed to be appropriate by professionals.

8 The paradox of personalisation

In the aftermath of the 2008 fiscal crisis, there were calls for the cooperative, for the Big Society and for the place of mutuals. All of these for the most part are matters to do with ownership, not with the regulation and organisation of the work process itself. In this latter respect, economic globalisation is said to require a new social (not just a fiscal or technical) relations of production, what Gee *et al.* (1996) call a 'new work order'. This 'order' prefers less-rigid rules and roles. These are said to enable organisations to deal with unstable markets and changing technologies. Expertise is said to be distributed throughout an organisation, and this collective wisdom can best be used if an ethos of trust prevails (Zuboff 1989). We may refer to these arrangements as emergent 'social technologies', or as the 'micro-processes of global economies' such as team-based work and cooperative learning (Farrell 2004). The question is how will workers and students learn to co-labour, to collaborate? What is said to be required is that there be an accord between, on the one hand, the new digitalised *technological* developments which allow for collaborative production and, on the other, the *social relations within* production which can use these technologies.

What does all of this have to do with personalisation? Was not personalisation a consumer discourse rather than a producer discourse? Was not personalisation something of a piece with individualisation, and not with social arrangements? To speak, therefore, of personalisation and collaboration as somehow complementary seems to be paradoxical at best and contradictory at worst. It has been argued in Chapter 6 that there are indications of a conflation of production and consumption, of producer and consumer, such that the combined endeavour of both can accomplish a co-production of a product or service. The term 'prosumer' was proffered as an attempt to conceptualise this entity. But let us say that the consumer's need is unable to be met by the existing configuration of providers. Let us say also that the professionals or providers are located within different departments within the organisation, or perhaps even across different organisations. In these cases, there are organisational boundary demarcations which will need to be rendered porous so as to allow the providers to collaborate – to become collective practitioners, so to say – in order to meet the consumer's needs. There will need to be intra-organisational collaborations, and/or inter-organisational collaborations. What had begun as a personalised consumer need thereafter may require collaboration among the providers.

Chapter 7 referred to personalisation as it related to curriculum and pedagogy – to what usually passes as personalised learning. The concern here is not with the pedagogical aspects of personalisation. Instead, we have also said that personalisation may be considered at another level, namely as a mode of regulation within the public services. It is mainly at this latter level that personalisation intersects with collaboration, and which is the concern of this chapter. That is to say, personalisation may have organisational consequences if it is the case that the existing organisational structures and processes cannot 'deliver' personalised services. If this is the case, then some re-formation of structures may be necessary so as to accomplish new 'solution spaces' within which personalisation can be realised. Usually, this will entail trust-based collaborations among professionals and providers, both within and among organisations. Specifically – and first – the chapter reconsiders briefly the general relationship among hierarchy, markets and collaborations as complementary modes of regulation within education policy. Second, it points up the emergence of 'tailoring' or 'personalisation' or 'individualisation' of provision in education, notably within England and within the US. Third, it addresses two questions: first, what is the theory which informs the practice of collaboration which may accomplish personalisation; and second, what are some of the questions and concerns *about* collaboration for personalisation? In the discussion of the first question, sociocultural activity theory will be considered (Engeström 2001), as will distributed leadership in education (Ritchie and Crick 2008); and, with reference to the second question, reference will be made to the work of Heckscher and Adler on collaborative community (2007).

Personalisation, collaboration and hierarchy

The quest for collaboration is not just consumer-driven; it is not only a response to the *consumer*'s personalised needs. We have referred to the concept of the prosumer in Chapter 5. Personalisation – a marketing strategy – implies co-production: a conflation of consumption and production. In part, therefore, personalisation is productive. It is both a consumer discourse and a producer discourse. And within that producer discourse will be references to the need for collaboration, at two levels: first, between the consumer and the provider; and second, if required, among providers. Collaboration is also, of itself, *productive* for an economy of knowledge-based and high-end services wherein creativity is at a premium. These require a high level of mutual trust and collaboration among producers. This arrangement has been termed 'collaborative community' (Heckscher and Adler 2007). It comprises three dimensions: values, organisation and character. First, take *values*. Whereas traditional bureaucracies stipulate loyalty, reliability and a devotion to duty (that is, to the duties which are defined by superiors), collaborative community seeks shared values. This is known as 'value-rationality'. It means that organisational members commit themselves to the realisation of common and universalistic goals. Examples would be that doctors commit to healing, and teachers to educating. In these endeavours, in a collaborative community, accountability is not just to superiors, but also to peers. The solutions to problems will be gleaned from the contributions of all who have the relevant expertise, irrespective of their formal organisational status. Heckscher and Adler make the important point that whereas in the Fordist, bureaucratic period value-rationality did not have much productive purpose outside of the professions, in a competitive knowledge economy the very value-rationality which was once associated with those professions now assumes the status of a 'practical economic imperative' (Heckscher and Adler 2007: 23). Second, consider the *organisational* dimension of collaborative community. This portends more of a collegial arrangement, though retaining something of the bureaucratic form. But with a caveat: the traditional form of community within a profession is overly insular. Collaboration should occur not only within professions, but also among them. This is 'collaborative professionalism' (Adler *et al.* 2008: 369). And so to the third dimension of collaborative community: *identity* or *character*. This is an identity at ease with interdependence, which contributes to different projects within different settings, and which thereby reveals an 'interactive social character' (as distinct from a 'bureaucratic character') (Maccoby 2006).

The foregoing points at collaborations which are based upon trust. But there are other 'collaborations' which are not. In the aftermath of the 2008 fiscal crisis, new synergies between hitherto separate organisational entities and roles were sought in order to achieve efficiency savings. The newly minted synergised entity would cost less than the sum of its parts. Appeals to collaboration and to distribution have the ring of the democratic about them, and they can seem to soften what otherwise might be called 'tough choices' and 'hard decisions'. But these are forced collaborations, imposed by management. Not much sense of trust and community is at the root of these 'collaborative' restructurings.

There is a further take on 'collaboration' which is not simply a justificatory rhetoric for mergers and downsizing. There has been during the past 15 years or so a shift in the modes of management. That is to say, there has been the gradual inclusion of a softer management rhetoric which appeals to the normative. It has by no means removed the rational discourse of formalisation, standardisation, hierarchy, monitoring, audit, impersonality and deference. This neo-Taylorist repertoire has revealed itself particularly in the education systems of those nations which have been wedded politically to economic neo-liberalism. But there are now signs of a more emollient tone in the managerial rhetoric. It is not the case that the heavy-duty audit culture has been set aside, but it is being complemented by the soft sell of the social: appeals to trust, to collaboration, to distribution, and to the soul and the spiritual.

The question for Adler and Heckscher is why now this re-emergence of a collaborative 'commitment' kind of managerial rhetoric is occurring. Their general point is that largely unregulated capitalism tends to accord with rational 'control' rhetorics. To elaborate: from about 1890 to the mid-1920s, a rational 'control' rhetoric was firmly in place, in the form of scientific management and

Fordism. Here was a period when – especially in the early 'roaring Twenties' – the primacy of the market prevailed. There was little regulation. At the same time little heed was paid to the conditions of workers, who gradually became more recalcitrant and less motivated. Rational control had reached its limits, and after the 1929 stock-market crash there emerged what has come to be known as the human relations approach which purported to elicit the commitment of workers by recognising their social as well as their financial needs. But it did not supersede the rational approach; it only complemented it.

A similar pattern prevailed in the US and in the UK after about 1980. Once again, there was a technological breakthrough – the micro-processor; and once again there was a political shift towards economic liberalism. Furthermore, in the economic upswing after about 1973, the return to highly rational management rhetoric occurred, variously attracting adjectives such as 'macho' managers and 'hero' leaders. This was explicit and formal control, back to the basics of bureaucracy. Again the accumulation of wealth justified itself; and again the effervescence of the property and stock-markets boiled over in a state of 'irrational exuberance'. As in the 1920s, the capacity of these rational management discourses to retain the commitment of workers waned. Predictably, the managerial rhetoric softened from about 1997. The shifts were clear to see: from vertical to horizontal power relations; from structure to process; from strong boundaries to permeable; and from 'command and control to connect and collaborate' (Nahapiet 2008: 95). But even all this was not enough. What the management gurus had failed to recognise was the centrality of trust as a requirement not only for a 'new' economy, but also as a basis for social order (Putnam 2001). Heckscher and Adler foresaw the conditions which would allow for the 2008 economic collapse. That is, they gave the warning that prolonged periods of unfettered capitalism generate not only dynamism and innovation, but also the undermining of trust, inequality, cynicism and alienation:

> The tension between economic transformation and traditional values is growing more fevered. It thus seems likely, on this analysis, that we will soon move towards institutional reconstruction, whether out of crisis (like the Depression) or through some more orderly process.
>
> (Heckscher and Adler 2007: 73)

To summarise thus far: the concern in the chapter has not been with personalised learning as pedagogy; it has been concerned with the collaboration among professionals and organisations which is a necessary consequence of personalisation. It has been with the productive aspects of collaboration as a response to personalisation, especially so in putative knowledge economies. Personalisation and collaboration are interrelated in the matters of consumer choice and its productive realisation.

To continue: in a more general way, at the level of the *governance of the public services*, personalisation and collaboration again form a symbiotic relationship. Personalisation/collaboration form part of the regulatory framework of the public services, including education. We have already referred in Chapter 6 to Thompson's framework of modes of regulation: the *hierarchical order*, the *market order* and the *network order* (Thompson 2003: 48). We have just considered Heckscher and Adler's *collaborative community*, which has some affinity to Thompson's *network*. The other parts of Heckscher and Adler's framework are *hierarchy* and *market*, which are inter-related (Heckscher and Adler 2007: 16: Table 1.1). If there is *hierarchy*, then coordination is on the basis of a formal hierarchy. If there is a *market*, then coordination is on the basis of price. So, for example, in education the market mode of regulation has enabled parents to express preferences and choices from what was on offer. They were choosers of schools. But from about 2005, however, a new supplementary phase in the market mode of governance began. This is 'personalisation'. Thereafter, consumers are not merely choosers of this or that school, but are seekers of solutions which are 'tailored' to their expressed needs, and – to repeat – if these needs cannot be met by existing providers and configurations then the latter will require to be reconfigured into a new solution-space. Which brings us back to collaboration. The regulatory framework, therefore, comprises hierarchy, market and collaborative community. Each has its advantages: *hierarchy* ensures formal control; *market* promotes flexibility; *collaborative community* generates trust, knowledge-generation and sharing (Adler *et al.* 2008: 360). None exists in isolation: in education, for example, hierarchy (in the form of inspection, national testing, league tables) has complemented market (enabled by school-choice legislation), which in turn may require collaborations to meet personalised needs. All comprise in their entirety an overarching mode of regulation.

So much for the economic and regulatory 'drivers' of collaboration. What of the technical? On this, it must be stressed that the technical does not sit outside of the economic and the political. In order to illustrate this, reconsider the recent analysis of the 2008 fiscal crisis by Perez (2010). The period after about 1975 was what she has called the 'installation period' when the new micro-processor technologies challenged and began to replace existing ones. She stresses that during this period, easy access to finance was necessary so that entrepreneurs would invest in and develop the new and more productive technologies. But thereafter, the power of financiers should be curbed, and that of producers should be enhanced. After all, she argues, much of the easy credit which was available during 2003–8 did not get invested in technologies; instead, it went into property speculation and obscure financial products. In the wake of a fiscal crisis such as 1929 or 2008, there is a need for the state to intervene, to regulate, and to restructure institutions, including education. Speaking of 2008, she states: 'This is not merely a financial crisis; this is the end of a period' (Perez 2009b: 6). She goes on: 'The mass production model of kindergarten to PhD with various irrevocable exit doors along the way is completely obsolete and inadequate for the making the best of the Knowledge Society for all' (ibid.: 7). Flexibility seems to be her preferred solution: that is, flexibility and varieties of 'self-managed education and training' which is to be provided by a range of institutions – public and private – which use a blend of methods. Education, she argues, must become a diverse and global business; it must be 'lucrative', its professionals highly regarded; and it must incorporate the very digital technologies which had been 'installed' before 2008 (ibid.: 7). To be sure, Perez's position is an economistic one, and advocates much greater use of ICT. Although her analysis includes the importance of a compatible social and institutional restructuring so as to enable the 'deployment' phase of new technologies, it does not engage with the arguments of those who have concerns for social justice of this 'diverse, dense and gigantic industry'. There is emerging, therefore, a confluence of consumer-driven personalisation and collaborative organisational structures of production. Digital technologies purport to facilitate both.

Personalisation, the collaborative state and the collective practitioner

Since the turn of the century the lexicon of the public services in the UK has revealed a growing propensity for a range of 'collaborative' prefixes: 'inter-', 'multi-' and 'co-' are examples. That is to say, public-sector agencies are being strongly encouraged to form 'multi-' or 'inter-agency' configurations. The practice of 'workforce reform' weakens what formerly were highly demarcated professional spaces. It seeks also to re-culture workers as collective practitioners. This 're-working', this work redesign, as we have said, has occurred for a number of reasons: it is a logical consequence of a deeper marketisation process which sets great store by personalisation and the culture of consumption; it speaks to the new work order of affinity and solution-spaces; and it can draw upon an increasingly prominent range of intellectual supports from organisational learning theory and marketing theory.

Take the seminal document *Every Child Matters* (ECM) (Department for Education and Skills 2004a). Its defining principles were that services should be integrated, easily accessible, personalised, effective and of high quality. It would integrate the following: schools; general practitioners; culture, sports and play organisations; and the voluntary and community sector. The four operational components for the so-called children's trusts were defined as:

- professionals enabled and encouraged to work together in more integrated front-line services, built around the needs of children and young people;
- common processes which are designed to create and underpin joint working;
- a planning and commissioning framework which brings together agencies' planning, supported as appropriate by the pooling of resources, and ensures key priorities are identified and addressed;
- strong inter-agency governance arrangements, in which shared ownership is coupled with clear accountability.

(Department for Education and Skills 2004a: 11)

There are clear similarities between ECM and the work of Leadbeater. His work on personalisation accords with much of what in Chapter 6 we referred to as the 'prosumer'. It begins with *intimate consultation* – a conversation between the professionals and the client which seeks to surface their 'needs, preferences and ambitions'. These are not to be one-off affairs; rather the professional should have a continuing relationship with the user, and act as its informed *advocate* so as to give the user *expanded choice* such that the preferred set of solutions is arrived at, even if it means a mix of providers who are located beyond the user's immediate vicinity. But essential to the whole personalised endeavour is *partnership provision*: that is, multi-agency and inter-professional partnerships. For example, a secondary school should serve as the 'gateway' to 'learning offers' provided by a network of other schools, colleges and businesses (Leadbeater 2004a: 57–8). Very much of a piece with Leadbeater, the government in England published its *Five Year Strategy for Children and Learners: putting people at the heart of public services* (Department for Education and Skills 2004b). Therein, greater emphasis was placed upon personalisation, choice and partnership among providers, be they state, private, voluntary, community or business (Department for Education and Skills 2004b: 4).

In the UK, the Coalition government which came to power in May 2010 reasserted the principle of individual choice (the term 'customisation' is preferred over 'personalisation') for individual 'personal services' – these being education, skills training, adult social care, childcare, housing support and individual healthcare (Her Majesty's Government 2011):

> Our vision is for public services that revolve around each of us. That means putting people in control, either through direct payments, personal budgets, entitlements or choices.
>
> *Wherever possible, we will increase choice by giving people direct control over the services they use. And where it is not possible to give people direct control, elected representatives should also have more choice about who provides services and how. This is the first principle of open public services.*
>
> (Her Majesty's Government 2011: 8; emphasis in original)

No-one, it declares, 'knows an individual's preferences better than they do'. Individuals 'should be trusted to choose the best services for themselves rather than being forced to accept choices determined by others'. This market-driven vision portends a highly competitive, funding-follows-the-chooser process. This means that funding will go directly to individuals (as 'cash payments, personal budgets, vouchers, tariff payments, loans and entitlements') (ibid.: 14). All this takes much further the personalisation agenda of the outgoing Labour government, and it highlights even more the concerns which had been made about Labour's plans. These plans for personalisation had been most advanced in the field of social care where personal budgets had been proposed in the Darzi Report for those with complex long-term care needs (Lord Darzi of Denham 2008: 43). But a range of 'very big questions' were aired about these plans, all of which preceded the 2008 fiscal crisis. Would large for-profit companies strive and achieve domination of the market? Would they not tend to standardise rather than to personalise provision because it is cheaper to do so? How would the expressed but unforeseen care needs which the personalisation process reveals be funded during a period of fiscal austerity? (Beresford 2008). How would staff be trained (Manthorpe *et al.* 2010), and are staff convinced that the costs of personalisation can be contained within existing, or even reduced, resources? (Ipsos MORI 2010: 22–3). Specifically, too, the politics of knowledge loom large: that is, who decides what shall count as knowledge within hitherto separated epistemic communities, and what shall be the discourse of collaboration? (Lawson 2004: 233).

Even before the Coalition government's 2011 White Paper on the reform of the public services, the MORI polling organisation had provided important evidence on the public's views of choice and personalisation. It revealed that the public's 'key priorities' are that the public services 'should be provided in a way that is fair, but that also meets good quality standards of customer service'. As for 'greater local control, personalisation, choice and accountability', these were not regarded as essential, but as being 'nice to have'; and it was unclear whether the public, unlike the government, saw a necessary causal association between greater choice and higher standards (Ipsos MORI 2010: 13). On the matter of private-sector providers, the public was reported as having mixed feelings: those services which are 'people-focused' (for example, education and health) should not be delivered by private providers; those which are much less so (street cleaning, refuse collection, recycling, leisure centres, parks and traffic management) can reasonably be opened up to the private sector. In sum, the MORI research summarises the public's view thus: 'things are private, people are public' (ibid.: 25).

Personalisation, collaboration and organisational learning

If collaboration for personalisation is deemed to be a 'good thing', and if it is also deemed to be so difficult, then what shall be the theory which informs how this collaboration shall occur, both within organisations and among them? A prominent intellectual strand in this endeavour is informed by the so-called 'social turn', especially within psychology (Gee 2000). By this is meant a shift from focusing upon the individual mind (as in behaviourism and cognitive science) to a focus upon the very interaction between the individual and the situation, whereby it is the interaction which has the ontological status, not the individual or the situation. Gee points to sociocultural psychology and to situated cognition as examples of this social turn. At the pedagogical level, the work on collaborative learning by Slavin (2010) has been referred to. Here we refer to two applications of sociocultural theory: the first as a theoretical basis for inter-agency and inter-professional collaboration; the second, as a theoretical basis for distributed leadership; in that order.

In England, an influential body of empirical research on collaborative inter-professional working has been informed by sociocultural historical activity theory. For example, studies such as the Economic and Social Research Council-funded 'Learning in and for Interagency Working' project (Edwards *et al.* 2009) have drawn on Engeström's theory of expansive learning. Engeström has propounded the theory of 'expansive learning' as a theoretical underpinning of inter-agency and inter-professional working. The process of expansive learning comprises a number of phases, but before considering them it is necessary logically to refer to what Engeström calls an *activity system* (Engeström *et al*. 1995: 320). Specifically, the activity system comprises a number of dimensions: the *subject* of the activity system consists of an individual or a sub-group. This *subject* focuses upon that which it is working on, namely the *object*. Note that the object is not of itself a set and formal goal. The object is that to which the activity is directed and which will be changed. For this change to occur – for these outcomes to be generated – *tools* are needed. *Tools* may be physical or symbolic, external or internal. For example, the *subject* could comprise a group of professionals who are providing services for children; and the *object* in this case would be to achieve inter-agency and inter-professional working. There are three further dimensions of the activity system. The first is *community*, which comprises other individuals and groups who share that same general object. This community itself has a *division of labour*, differentiated by task, power and status. The final dimension of the activity system consists of *rules*, which are both formal and implicit, and which support or limit the actions and interactions within the system (Engeström 1987). It is important to note that an activity system is not necessarily reducible to a formal organisation. It is the activity which counts, not the formal role-structure.

Unlike clearly demarcated bureaucratic structures, there is a certain messiness about collaborative actions. They can variously be described as 'entanglements', 'interplays', 'webs', 'ambiguities' and '*melees*'; they generate 'issues', 'contradictions' and 'tensions'; they bear witness to ephemerality, to shifting alliances and to changing power relations. In short, they comprise an 'horrendously complex picture' (Huxham and Vangen 2005: 251–2). Those with a tidy-minded modern mind-set can feel decidedly unsettled by collaboration, especially by what Engeström calls the 'polycontextuality' of activity systems (Engeström *et al*. 1995: 320). The implication is that activity systems are not bounded by existing formal structures. If an existing activity system does not achieve the object, then a new activity system may need to be formed; a new solution space, no less. This new activity system may comprise a 'mix' of existing ones. It, too, would need a new array of 'dimensions' – tools, rules, community of practice; and so on. Central to Engeström's theory is that the impetus for this new activity system arises from a 'contradiction' which has been brought out into the open. 'Contradictions', it must be stressed, are not the same as problems; they are 'historically accumulating structural tensions within and between activity systems' (Engeström 2001: 137), and they can be surfaced from within and between activity systems.

The contradictions are surfaced as a result of ethnographic research. This is the first stage of expansive developmental research in an activity system. It provides an initial phenomenological insight into the nature of its discourse and problems: that is, insights into the problems, doubts and uncertainties experienced among the participants of the activity. The insights may be acquired by a reading of the internal and public discussions about the activity, by participant on-site observations, and by dialogue with those involved in the activity or with those having expertise in it (Engeström 1987: 269–72). It is from the agreement to resolve the contradiction that the new activity system emerges. Sociocultural activity theory is a prominent theoretical framework for informing the practice of inter-agency and inter-professional working.

A further means of accomplishing personalisation through collaboration is to rethink the leadership style within schools. Distributed leadership, or collaborative leadership, is said to be the solution (Leadbeater 2005; Ritchie and Crick 2008: 42). Like expansive learning, its intellectual roots are in sociocultural activity theory (Gronn 2000; Hartley 2007b). The reasons for the emergence of distributed leadership are as varied as the definition of it (Hartley 2007c). It resonates with a culture where boundary demarcations are becoming open. It relieves the headteacher or principal of an increasing weight of tasks, and seeks solutions from among those with the expertise (though perhaps not with the authority) to provide them. Isomorphically, distributed leadership is of a piece with collaborative learning. Whether or not distributed leadership has a direct causal effect on pupil achievement so far looks to be doubtful (Hallinger and Heck 2010); and nor does there appear to be evidence of a causal association between distributed leadership and personalised learning – or *vice versa* (Ritchie and Crick 2008).

Personalisation (or co-production), expansive learning and distributed leadership have certain affinities to each other. For example, personalisation/co-production and Engeström's expansive learning share some intellectual roots in marketing theory, especially in Victor and Boynton's *Invented Here* which purports to go beyond mere mass customisation (Engeström 2004). Instead, they seek a new understanding of the 'dynamic interactions' among the product, the customer and the firm. This they refer to as 'configuration knowledge' which is accomplished by the process of co-configuration. It occurs

> at the interface of the firm, the customer, and the products or services. It requires constant interaction among the firm, the customer, and the product. [. . .] *The result is that the product continuously adjusts to what the customer wants.*
>
> (Victor and Boynton 1998: 14; emphasis added)

This is, as we argued in Chapter 6, a new form of customisation: it is not just mass customisation, a process which requires at least a one-off product for each customer; rather co-configuration is a 'design process' whereby the company senses, and adapts to, the customer's needs continually in a never-ending, unfinished process (ibid.: 195). Co-configuration necessitates a change in the social relations within the workplace, with much less emphasis upon vertical hierarchical relationships and more on the horizontal ones. It informs Engeström's thinking on the redesign of work (Engeström 2000: 972) as 'knotworking':

> The notion of knot refers to rapidly pulsating, distributed and partially improvised orchestration of collaborative performances between otherwise loosely connected actors and activity systems.
>
> (ibid.: 972)

The 'dark side' of collaboration for personalisation

A new mode of regulation is emerging. It is beginning to suffuse the 'flexible' workplace which is committed to personalised co-production based on co-configuration; and it is seeping slowly into the school through a pedagogy of personalised learning and distributed leadership. In broad terms, a general critique of all of this is that responsibility for the completion of flexible 'boundaryless' work (and any associated underemployment, burnout and stress) falls to the 'actively participating' individuals, not to their managers (Hurd 2011: 20). Specifically, this critique turns on the view that organisational learning (which includes expansive learning, or knotworking) deploys a discourse of humanism in order to enact government policy and economic globalisation as acceptable. This is by no means a recent practice, having occurred in the 1960s when a humanist rhetoric was deployed in order to render post-Fordism acceptable (Boltanski and Chiapello 2005). As then, so now. The term 'learning' has a certain ubiquity about it, being used adjectivally to qualify nouns such as 'organisation' and 'society'. Businesses must continuously 'learn' about their customers, so as to satisfy them, and to co-produce their personalised needs; and all of this 'learning' is 'lifelong', a sign of what Bernstein called the 'totally pedagogised society', a society wherein the education system has only a weak attenuation with the economy, a society within which the commercial purveyors of education seek ever greater 'market share' as the actual providers of education (Bernstein 2001).

There are other concerns and questions about this 'brave new workplace', even among some who had supported it (Victor and Stephens 1994). Will the flatter hierarchies of knotworking and distributed leadership open the way to nepotism and suspicion (Casey 1995: 154); and could incompetence, rather than competence, be 'distributed'? Will it be the case that management retains control and ownership over strategy, while only the tactics will be available for co-production and 'learning'? (Coopey 2004). To be sure, Engeström's collaborative expansive learning does not seem to be set upon brushing the matter of power under the carpet. On the contrary, it is set upon surfacing 'contradictions' as the basis for solution-seeking. But these 'contradictions' are mainly to do with means, not ends; with operations, not strategy; with only 'activity'.

The matter of power relationships in sociocultural activity theory, and especially in Engeström's work, has attracted a sociological critique. Expansive learning tends to be overly concerned with 'contradictions' within 'horizontal' inter-professional divisions of labour, but much less so with the 'vertical contradic-tions' between those who manage or shape these collective and collaborative practices and those who are managed? Put differently: 'what might be the consequences of pointing to contradictions that heads of organisations consider out of bounds for discussion?' (Avis 2007; 2009). Engeström's expansive learning is said not to surface the wider structural contradictions within economic neo-liberalism, and nor is it concerned with radical political movements. It is, in the end, a regulatory practice. To an extent Engeström agrees: 'It is indeed true that studies of expansive learning aim at analysing and generating transformations within and between activity systems that do not necessarily require a large-scale political confrontation' (Engeström and Sannino 2010: 19). The adverb 'necessarily' leaves open the possibility that a wider politics is possible beyond the bounds of the activity systems. In their analysis of home-care provision in Helsinki, for example, Engeström and Sannino report the concerns raised about the 'personal budgets' now being proposed in England as part of the neo-liberal agenda of 'customising' social care. They state: 'In the privatised model, commoditisation of care would take a big leap forward and the contradiction would increasingly be manifested in outright abandonment of old people to the mercy of the market' (ibid.). But this does not deal adequately with the general concern that 'expansive learning' is wholly focused upon matters of managerial and strategic concern. Is the 'expansive learning' of the 'learning worker' to be contained within such narrow work-related horizons? What has become of industrial democracy and adult *education*? In these endeavours, worker education was focused both upon practical skills *and* personal development. Organisational learning has put paid to the latter (Casey 2003: 623). The term 'human resources' conflates the 'human' with the 'resource', as if they are necessarily of a piece? Human resources, like 'learning', are now regarded as an unexceptional and normal concept; and its adoption, ironically, has been quick and widespread even among trade union officials (ibid.).

In order for 'contradictions' to be expressed, trust is a prerequisite; if it is lacking then the expression of contradictions may be held back. Instead of 'voice', there may be silence; or even lies. Trust and reciprocity do not easily emerge in the highly audited, performance-driven companies and public services of neo-liberalism, especially during times of economic downturn when the possibility of lay-offs lingers. There are, too, broader cultural contexts which enable or limit trust. It is, for example, perhaps no coincidence that empowering, 'learning organization' discourses are associated with relatively high-trust cultures, such as Finland. In Finland levels of trust are relative higher than in Britain: in Britain, only 29.8 per cent agreed with the statement 'most people can be trusted'; in Finland, the corresponding figure was 58.0 per cent (Van Schaik 2004). Trust may be confined among workers, not between workers and management. As hoped-for 'communities of practice', workers may be more inclined towards community (an expressive and emotional bonding), whereas managers may dwell upon practice (an instrumental purpose). New flexibilities and organisational configurations are disruptive of these communities. In short, collaboration can have its 'dark side' (Heckscher 2007: 265 *et seq.*).

In capitalist societies, the central contradiction is not contained within the organisation. The object of work is both the creation of useful things (that is, use-value) and the generation of profit (that is, exchange-value). In this endeavour, the individual is not only a creative co-labourer, but is also a disposable, variable-cost budget item under another's control, and can be made redundant. Under these conditions, is trust possible? Is 'owner control' within the private sector, and strong bureaucratic control within the public sector, conducive to trust-based collaborative *community*? Should market forces be the dominant criterion for the allocation of resources? Adler thinks not: even if a high-trust form of hierarchy remained, autocratic governance and owner-control would need to be replaced by participative governance. Furthermore, resource-allocation should not be based on market forces; it should be based primarily – though not wholly – on democratic decision-making (Adler 2007: 76–9).

Summary

This chapter has been to do with the relationship between personalisation and collaboration beyond the classroom. Personalisation emerged as a discourse in the latter phase of the economic upswing between 1973 and 2008. It resonates well with the culture of consumption. As a policy-rhetoric in education and other public services, it meets with ready approval; it strikes a cultural chord. Collaboration also emerges after about 1997 when the then 'macho' and highly rational management discourses began to wane in their powers to elicit the compliance of workers. Just as in the mid-1920s when the emergence of industrial psychology and human relations management theory sought to re-motivate workers, so too after 1997 there emerges a neo-human relations management discourse, a discourse 'soft' in its resonance, and persuasive in its appeals to the social, the collaborative and to the emotional. Collaboration, like personalisation, also has a cultural affinity: at a time when the new flexibilities make light of old boundary practices and demarcations, collaboration fits well with an ICT-enabled capacity for convergence. And collaboration – or the need for it – has been highlighted by widely publicised failures in the coordination of services around vulnerable young children. But the underlying 'drivers' of personalisation – notwithstanding its democratic-sounding avowal of 'choice' and 'freedom' – are marketisation and co-production. Personalisation is a much deeper type of marketisation, one which goes beyond mere 'choice' of structures, and instead purports to bring user and provider together into a continuing and personalised 'co-producer' relationship. And this co-production – this 'prosumption' – may result in a *re*-production in the sense that new configurations and flexibilities among professionals become necessary to meet the personalised needs of the user. What hitherto had been an emphasis on the individual reflective practitioner now gradually gives way to the collective practitioner. Whether or not it actually comes to pass remains an open question.

9 Personalisation and the social order

How might personalisation in education be regarded sociologically: does it contribute to social regulation, or does it enable radical change? Epistemologically, how can personalisation be viewed: is it an agreed construct, or is its meaning contingent upon time and place? In order to explore these questions, we may usefully draw upon Burrell and Morgan's typology of paradigms (Burrell and Morgan 1979). The typology has two dimensions: the horizontal axis marks the epistemological dimension (subjectivist–objectivist); the vertical axis marks the sociological dimension (social regulation–radical change) (Figure 1). In relation to the horizontal axis, do we regard personalisation as a technical matter; and, if yes, then the knowledge sought would be generated by the application of the scientific method. In this case, personalisation would be assumed to be a concept whose definition and operationalisation was agreed upon. If no, then the quest for an understanding or interpretation of personalisation would be derived from a more subjectivist and hermeneutic approach. The vertical axis is concerned with how society coheres or with how it might be changed radically. To elaborate: whereas 'radical change' seeks to replace the status quo, 'social regulation' is concerned with retaining and reforming it; whereas social regulation is concerned with the maintenance of consensus and social order, radical change is set upon exposing contradictions and enabling and/or accomplishing structural conflict

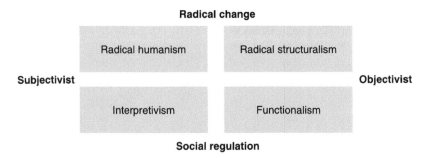

Figure 1 Burrell and Morgan's four sociological paradigms.

Source: Adapted from Burrell and Morgan (1979: 22)

and change; and whereas social regulation is about consensus, radical change is about modes of domination (Burrell and Morgan 1979: 18).

Taken together, these two dimensions – the subjectivist/objectivist, and the radical change/social regulation – comprise Burrell and Morgan's four-fold typology of paradigms: functionalism; interpretivism; radical humanism; and radical structuralism (Figure 1). The paradigms are regarded by Burrell and Morgan as incommensurable; they cannot be mixed because they are philosophically and sociologically distinctive. They are, however, synchronous: that is, they can co-exist; one does not completely supersede another. In that sense, they are competing paradigms. Personalisation may be understood sociologically according to each of these paradigms. We begin with the functionalist analysis of personalisation.

Functionalism

The functionalist approach to social science tends to assume that the social world is composed of relatively concrete empirical artefacts and relationships which can be identified, studied and measured through approaches derived from the natural sciences (Burrell and Morgan 1979: 26). The most advanced theoretical analysis of functionalist theory is arguably Parsons' (1991) *Social System*. Any society – be it a classroom, a family, a factory – has two sets of functional prerequisites: first, the task-related, referred to as 'instrumental' needs; and second, those relating to maintaining social cohesion within and among sub-systems, referred to as 'expressive' needs. Parsons produced a seminal paper 'The school class as a social system' in which he explored the primary functions of the school – the American elementary school in particular – as an agency of both 'socialization' into 'broader social values' (the expressive) and 'allocation' into future 'role performance' (the instrumental) (Parsons 1959). This 'order' broadly accords with what has been termed the Protestant ethic, akin to Parsons' 'central value system'. There is a general assumption that this normative order prevails. It can be tweaked, but not overturned in a radical move. A 'dynamic equilibrium' is sought. The paradigm does not exclude conflict, but it must be manageable and resolvable.

A central concept of functionalist theory is that of 'role'. A role is a set of expectations. Some of them are formally specified (as in a work contract); others are more informal (as in a family). For the most part, these roles are arranged as hierarchies, for efficiency and predictability. An individual's position in the social hierarchy should turn on achievement, not ascription. 'Contest mobility' is preferred to 'sponsored mobility' and nepotism (Turner 1960). For each role, there is a presumed uniformity of the type discussed in Bauman's concept of 'solid modernity'. In schools, some pupils still wear uniforms, a sartorial expression of their shared role; and there are designated spaces, called classrooms, to which they are allocated on the basis of their shared social and intellectual 'characteristics'. These classifications provide the pupil with a sense of purpose and place, an identity no less; and this identity will be clearly demarcated from identities which they may have outside of the school. The expectations of their behaviour will be made explicit, as rules. Transgressions will be defined as abnormal or 'special', and labelled as such, perhaps publicly. Appropriate measures will be taken either to separate or to reintegrate the 'special' pupil. The efforts of the pupil will be assessed according to some universal criterion (an examination), and it will be the pupil's efforts alone which will be recorded. Pupils will not receive a 'group' mark. If this were to occur, then the competitive individualism into which they had been socialised would be undermined, and would doubtless be seen as unfair (Parsons 1991: 163–4).

This education system can be viewed at another level above and beyond the school. In North America, there are school districts and divisions, which – like the corporate structures which they were designed to emulate – ensure that a similar organisational structure based on roles and expectations complements and supports the role of the school. There is an isomorphism of structure both within and among the organisations which comprise the school system. The 'grammar' or code of education systems varies little. That said, within schools, the 'fit' should not be overstated, for there is said to be a certain looseness, or 'loose coupling' (Weick 1976), particularly between those structures which are directly pedagogical (or instructional) and those which are administrative and managerial.

At least, that used to be the case in the 1960s and 1970s, a period when a degree of professional discretion was afforded to classroom teachers: that is, they could shut their classroom door and be trusted to get on with teaching. Today, this is less the case. The standardisers, the quality controllers and the monitors all subscribe to a new 'cult of efficiency' in order to define what shall be acceptable pedagogy, curriculum and assessment in the classroom. In England, this has been a particularly marked trend, with 'national' 'initiatives' in curriculum, pedagogy and assessment continually vying for space in the headteacher's in-tray (or inbox). Even in the US, where education is a state, not federal, responsibility, the funding powers of the federal government limit the state's room for manoeuvre. To acquire federal funds, for example, states must quite literally do the federal government's bidding; and this is especially so in respect of NCLB and President Obama's *Race to the Top* (US Department of Education 2009).

From a functionalist perspective, in what sense would personalisation meet the expressive needs of contemporary society? How would it contribute to the social order? First, it needs to be stressed that the social order to which Parsons referred in the early 1950s is, as argued in Chapter 3, somewhat different from that of the present. In particular, Bell, in the 1970s, revealed a crucial tension: that between, on the one hand, a fractured and uncertain culture which is sustained by a market-driven, consumerist concern with the project of the self; and, on the other, neo-liberal governments which are prone to pruning public expenditure, but which also have a penchant for standardisation and surveillance. The tension is between the centrifugal forces of the former and the centripetal forces of the latter. The equilibrium between the two is not easy to maintain. As for individuals, they are beset by information flows which are unprecedented. The points of reference which used to indicate the way ahead are no longer anchored. Notions of time, space, health, sickness, sex, age, birth, death, reproduction and love are no longer 'data' but 'problems' (Melucci 1996b: 2). From a functionalist perspective, if the market continues to insinuate itself into the realm of education (through 'consumer' choice of school, and through personalised learning), then schools will seek to *socialise* children into a *personalised* mind-set. It will 'fit' a culture which prides itself on the constant makeover; it will 'fit' the emergent tendency to conflate consumption and production.

The capacity of children to 'master' the hidden curriculum of personalised learning may vary according to the socio-economic background of the child. From a functionalist perspective, the family, as a sub-system, should provide anticipatory socialisation for the child before it starts school (and thereafter). The 'hidden curriculum' of the family, so to say, should be such that it 'personalises' the child so that the child can adapt easily to personalised learning. An early exploration of this matter is to be found in Bernstein's (1975, 135) concept of the 'invisible pedagogy', the elements of which are as follows. The teacher retains implicit, not explicit, control; and structures the learning context which the child 're-arranges' and 'explores'. The child, therefore, '*apparently* has wide powers over what he selects, over how he structures, and over the time-scale of his activities'; the child 'apparently regulates his own movements and social relationships'; there is a 'reduced emphasis upon the transmission and acquisition of specific skills'; and the modes of assessment are 'multiple and diffuse' (ibid.: 116; original emphasis).

Families may vary in their capacity to socialise their children in a manner compatible with the invisible pedagogy or with personalised learning. Bernstein posited that in the 'new' middle class family, the mode of regulation would be 'personalised'. Role-demarcations would be less rigid, the structuring of time and space more flexible, and order more likely to be negotiated rather than imposed. All this he distinguished from a mode of regulation which is 'positional': that is, one which appeals to formal hierarchy, and wherein spatial and temporal demarcations were more defined. An ideal-typical and hypothetical example might suffice to explain this. Say that a child, aged about six, were to knock over a glass of milk, causing the milk to fall to the floor. In a positional family, the parent might issue an admonishment to the child; and if the child were to question this then the parent might remind the child that, as its parent, it had the right – even the duty – to admonish the child. That would be the 'end of the matter'. But say, on the other hand, that the child was of a person-centred family. In this case, the parent might well ask the child to wipe the milk from the floor, and politely remind the child to be more careful next time. If the child were to question this, then the child would be advised that someone might slip on the wet floor, perhaps resulting in an injury, which might require attendance at the hospital, which in turn would incur a cost to the health service, thereby possibly resulting in higher taxes for the parent, and less pocket-money for the child.

Person-centred families, which Bernstein called the 'new' middle class, or which (Reich 1992) termed the 'symbolic analysts', may better integrate into those schools whose pedagogy is based on personalised learning. Their children may be more at ease with negotiation than their 'positional' counterparts are. To be sure, both can give 'voice', but its expression may vary in its powers to convince. If it is the case that personalised learning requires of the pupil the ability to co-configure its learning needs with the teacher, then the linguistic and gestural wherewithal to do so becomes crucial. And if, at a 'higher' level, as in the matter of choosing a school, parents seek to make explicit their wishes for a child (assuming they know sufficient about the education system even to be aware of what might be possible), then again the parents' powers of persuasion will vary according to the information which they have, and to the linguistic and cultural wherewithal which they possess. Indeed, even Parsons himself (1959) noted the tendency for more 'progressive' methods (group-work and cooperation; 'indirect' teaching; less competition; projects) to associate more with higher socio-economic catchment-area schools. Elsewhere, the 'traditional' (formal teaching; individualism; competition; 'discrete units of subject matter') prevailed.

Today, unlike in the period of 'solid modernity' inhabited by Parsons, the economy is increasingly globalised, and the media of communication are digital, multiple and inter-connected. No longer does written language mediate the world to the extent that it did; other forms of representation have complemented it (Kress *et al.* 2000: 14). Semantically and practically, therefore, personalisation has been of a piece with ICT. This technology, and the customisation which it allows, portends a new mode of socialisation and regulation. Before digital technologies converged, the young had been socialised partly by broadcast media. Those media (comprising books, television, radio and newsprint) were directed at a passive audience, with little interaction. It was 'received', and it deployed a code, imagery and discourse which in its entirety constituted the means of cultural reproduction; and it was local and national, not global. The digital convergence of ICT altered this, for it portends a *de-* if not a *re-* institutionalisation of education and of leisure. It does not replace what has been termed the 'broadcast socialisation paradigm', but it blurs the boundaries within it. Personalisation, therefore, is inextricably linked to the cyber-world. The cyber-world constitutes an 'environment', and contemporary neuroscience explores how the brain adapts to it, with some good cognitive effects (action video-games can enhance some cognitive tasks), and some deleterious social effects (a tendency to addiction, to distraction and to violence – both physically expressed and privately contemplated) (Bavelier *et al.* 2010). Turkle's seminal study, *Alone Together: why we expect more from technology and less from each other*, warns about the decline of empathy in an age of robotic relationships and digitally mediated 'communication' (Turkle 2011). Internet addiction disorder (IAD) produces abnormalities in the neural pathways (Yuan *et al.* 2011). As adults linger in the analogue world, their children roam the digital universe. They are the challengers to this 'broadcast socialisation' code, and the harbingers of the emergent 'technosocial paradigm' (Holmes 1999: 76–7). Children express this technosocial reality even when these technologies are not actually in use; it is part of their mind-set all of the time.

To draw a 'solid modern' analogy: during the age of mass production and consumption, individuals became drawn into a technocratic mind-set (Berger *et al.* 1974). Even when not at work in the factory, the code of the factory – deference, punctuality, spatial demarcations and neatness – suffused the consciousness, even though it was not necessary that their 'leisure' needed to be structured in this way. For example, an aspect of this consciousness is 'componentiality': that is, assembly-production causes the worker always to see parts (components), not the whole product; the tree, not the woods. Personalised digital technologies – and the mind-sets which they engender – may weaken the traditional normative order of the school which is based upon a 'broadcast socialisation paradigm' (Holmes 1999: 76–7).

So much for the relationship between marketisation, personalisation and the expressive needs of society. What of the instrumental? The US charter school movement, like marketisation in England, had two consequences: an increase in monitoring, specification and the standardisation of curriculum and pedagogy; and a weakening of the public provision of education in favour of for-profit private providers who are themselves subjected to the vagaries of the economic cycle. The first of these consequences has led to a narrowing of the curriculum and a play-safe pedagogy on the part of teachers who are reluctant to go 'off-message' and off course. The path of education is thereby narrowed so that it can be itemised and measured. Neither of these *structural* changes portends a functional fit between schooling and the instrumental needs of the emergent new economy. At a premium in this economy are workers at every level who are creative and innovative, and who are at ease with the abstract as well as the practical. They are workers who will have had 'a very different kind of education than most of us have had' (National Center on Education and the Economy 2008: xxiv).

If the market-driven structural changes are outmoded, then perhaps the *pedagogy* of personalised learning will be functional for the instrumental needs of the new economy. That is, from a functionalist perspective the pupil who has been 'personalised' as a co-producer and a co-configurer of its learning needs will have been readily prepared as a future consumer *and* producer in the sub-system of the 'new' knowledge-based globalised economy. But the near-obsession in education with mistrust, competition, measurement, specification, standards and efficiency does little to provide the context within which the desired trust-based personalised learning can take root. There is a further constraint which is also not structural; it is financial. State-provided education depends upon taxation to a great extent. Bespoke tailoring has always been more expensive than off-the-shelf. Will the presumed expense of personalisation not be dysfunctional at a time of fiscal austerity; at a time when both individuals and corporations might be resistant to calls on their coffers? So the question then becomes a matter of how to proceed with personalisation at a time when standardisation is arguably more financially sustainable. In order to deal with this question, two solutions have been proffered: the technical and the structural. The technical solution is that on-line, Web 2.0 content can personalise learning and reduce the need for costly physical infrastructure. At the same time, it would resonate with a youth culture which is becoming increasingly 'at home' with digital technologies. The structural solution could see more sub-contracting of what hitherto had been publicly funded.

Interpretivism

> They [interpretivist sociologists] are much more orientated towards obtaining
> an understanding of the subjectively created social world 'as it is' in terms of
> an ongoing process.
>
> (Burrell and Morgan 1979: 31)

To adopt the sociological paradigm of interpretivism is to seek to understand the
subjective meanings which actors assign to the world 'out there'. In particular,
phenomenology (a constituent theory of the interpretivist paradigm) argues that
the world does not comprise objects which are fixed and reified in their meaning;
rather it comprises a constellation of meanings which individuals assign to
it. Logically, therefore, there are 'multiple realities', and the number of these
definitions of reality equates to the number of individuals who are able to express
them. On this account, the world of objects has no intrinsic meaning.

This raises a number of issues. First, our predecessors have already made sense
of the world, and they make available to us their 'recipes' for understanding it.
Furthermore, these 'recipes', or taken-for-granted realities, assume the status of
'givens': they are rarely questioned. What hitherto had originally been subjectively
constructed gradually assumes the status of being regarded as objective. Berger
and Luckmann (who adhere to a second theoretical strand within the paradigm
of interpretivism, namely social constructivism) refer to this as the 'objectification
of the subjective' (Berger and Luckmann 1967). Rarely is our definition of
reality called into question; the recipes usually suffice. But not always: occasionally
our definition of the situation does not suffice, and we are no longer able to
'cope'. When these disruptions to our common-sense meanings occur, then
the world out there has to be reinterpreted. What had been 'given' now becomes
problematic. Take an example: a teacher one day enters the classroom dressed in
the costume of a clown. It is not something which the pupils had been expecting.
Their definition of the classroom situation, and of their teacher, has been
disrupted. How will they rebuild meaning out of the 'absurd' situation. It is the
very matters of pointing up the 'slippery' nature of reality, and of observing how
actors rebuild meaning when faced by seemingly 'absurd' situations, which have
been the purpose of ethnomethodology, a constituent theoretical strand within
the paradigm of interpretivism (Lyman and Scott 1970).

The capacity of actors to make sense of what seems at face value to be absurd
will vary. If they are what Schutz (1967) calls 'consociates' (that is, if they share
a time and place, and are in a 'We-relationship') then they can interrogate each
other for an interpretation. If they are 'contemporaries' (that is, they share a time,
but not place) then their capacity for motivational understanding declines
somewhat. And if they are seeking to understanding their predecessors (with
whom they share neither time nor place), then motivational understanding
becomes all the more difficult (ibid.). This last is the historian's problem. There
is a second concern. Although, logically, the number of definitions of reality
equates to the number of individuals who exist, in practice there tend to emerge

shared definitions of reality, or what Berger and Luckmann call social constructions of reality which over time may coalesce into overarching symbolic universes. But which symbolic universe shall prevail? Here enters the matter of power to make a 'symbolic universe' 'stick'.

How does this relate to personalisation? Interpretivism is interested in how personalisation is defined at the level of 'lived' experience. It would raise questions such as: what are the taken-for-granted definitions which are held by those such as pupils, teachers and policy-makers; are these definitions shared; are there emergent categories of shared meanings which might constitute patterned regularities; what are the everyday common-sense 'theories' of personalisation which individuals hold, and why do they adhere to these theories; do definitions of personalisation accord with the actual observations of the symbolisations of personalisation (to do with time, space and social organisation) which are gleaned from ethnographic studies?

All this said, it is difficult to sustain the argument that personalisation-cum-collaboration are wholly at one with interpretivism. In Chapter 8 we argued that the intellectual roots of co-configuration and co-production – both of which are aspects of personalisation – are (after Engeström's activity theory) set within sociocultural theory. Similarly, the same can be said for collaborative learning in the new work order (after Gee *et al.* 1996). So also is it the case that the early theoretical basis for distributed leadership drew heavily on activity theory. Activity theory has an uneasy relationship with interpretivism. It is not the individual agent or the situation/structure which has ontological status in activity theory; it is the conflation of the two. It is the *interaction* between agency and structure which has ontological status, and so it cannot logically fall completely either within Burrell and Morgan's paradigm of interpretivism or of functionalism. There is also the matter of what Engeström calls 'contradictions'. This might suggest that a socioculturally informed personalisation might have a place within the paradigm of radical humanism (see below), but these contradictions are assumed by activity theorists to be either resolvable or ignored, without detriment to the social order (Hartley 2007b). Sociocultural activity theory is regulatory, not radical.

There is an elective affinity between interpretivism and personalisation. The emergence of the interpretive paradigm occurred during the late 1960s, at the very time when 'consumerism' and 'mass customisation' began to take root. Television (especially commercial television) facilitated this. Interpretivism in social theory vied at the time with structural Marxism and functionalism, but since then interpretivism has arguably become the dominant paradigm. Personalisation runs with this trend. Like constructivism, personalisation seems to reject givens. It privileges agency over structure. Just as phenomenology implies the possibilities of individualised realities, so too does personalisation portend the possibility of the makeover. But personalisation does not sit with pessimistic postmodernism and nihilism. Its roots may indeed be in marketing and in consumer theory (and so it trades in the superficial and the provisional), but personalisation requires a *social* relationship based upon an *enduring* co-configuration between consumer and provider. Even so, this social relationship is not an equal one; there is an asymmetry of power between the parties. At root, too, this relationship is calculative and instrumental, not emotional and expressive – even though it may be described as such.

To summarise thus far, functionalism and interpretivism would regard choice and personalisation as functional for the instrumental and expressive needs of society. For the functionalists, policies which promote choice and personalisation set the conditions for the self- and identity-seeking consumption element of a globalised market economy, and also with an emergent pattern of co-production. Producers of goods and services depend upon demand from consumers. Because so many products are cultural products, the producers must persuade consumers continually to refine or to re-make their identities. Style matters; and so, therefore, does personalisation. For the interpretivists, personalisation sits intellectually with a paradigm which speaks of agency, of individual and social constructions of reality, and of subjectivity over objectivity. While functionalism and interpretivism are epistemologically at odds, nevertheless they are both regulatory and seek only to refine the normative order (as in the case of functionalism), or to understand how individuals define it (as with interpretivism). In particular, although inter-pretivists might be concerned with different constructions of choice and personalisation, these are regarded usually as merely preferences and choices of different realities, not as the expression of asymmetries of power. Notwithstanding the *logical* potential of choice and personalisation to undermine the social order, from both functionalist and interpretivist standpoints there is an assumption that a culture of consumption based on choice and personalisation would not result in a breakdown of consensus.

Radical humanism

We have just stated that interpretivism and functionalism are 'regulatory' paradigms. In Habermas' (1987) terms, the functionalist has a *technical* interest in generating *instrumental* knowledge, and the interpretivist has a *practical* interest and seeks *understanding*. But this understanding may be used as a stage for those whose cognitive interest is in *emancipation*. (It may equally be used by those in dominant positions in order to find out – and better to manage – the thoughts of those whom they control.) So regarded, the practical knowledge derived from interpretivism *could* enable radical change. It could come under the gaze of critical theory, and thereby warrant inclusion in the radical humanist paradigm. Central to this paradigm is the notion that consciousness is

> dominated by the ideological superstructures with which he interacts, and that these drive a cognitive wedge between himself and his true consciousness. [. . .] It is a brand of social theorising designed to provide a critique of the status quo.
>
> (Burrell and Morgan 1979: 32)

Critical theorists stress that thought is never free from the effects of power relations; facts do not speak for themselves. And crucially: 'the oppression that characterizes contemporary societies is most forcefully reproduced when subordinates accept their social status as natural, necessary, or inevitable' (Kincheloe and McLaren 2005: 303). A radical humanist analysis of choice and personalisation would seek to make explicit the hidden power relations (at either micro-sociological or macro-sociological levels) which neither interpretivism nor functionalism would 'see'. Indicative of a radical humanist take on personalisation is that by Beach and Dovemark. Personalisation, they argue, is redolent of a calculative self-interest, and is typical of an educational culture which denies an equal and fair distribution of educational resources (Beach and Dovemark 2009: 699).

The radical humanist would ask in whose interests does choice and personalisation reside? Notwithstanding personalisation's appeals to *co*-configuration, to *co*-production and to the free expression of needs and preferences, the intentions of those who invite them should come under a critical gaze. Personalisation and co-production imply a sharing of power, not a willing acceptance of the power of others. But for critical theorists it implies no such thing: it is but a neo-human relations management revival. That is to say, from a critical perspective, personalisation is the co-option of a humanist discourse for an economic neo-liberal purpose. In education, in its quest for legitimacy, personalisation draws upon the nostalgic and humanist appeal of child-centred education. From a critical perspective, the 'voice' of personalisation is a would-be consumer's voice, not that of a citizen-in-the-making (*see also* Fielding 2008). It is also assumed to be an eloquent, persuasive and critical voice, one well able to influence the 'professional' voices. It assumes no asymmetry of power among the interlocutors. But for some – those devoid of either the inclination or the competence to give voice – personalisation may 'co-produce' no more than frustration. For them, personalisation may simply be expressed as silence. From a radical humanist perspective, the legitimatory power of personalisation is that it connects both consumerism and, through its 'child-centred' association, a premodern Romanticism. So 'personalisation' is not just an appeal to consumerism (and therefore is supportive of accumulation); it provides also a safe association with a 'progressive' past whose good times linger in the professional mind of those who knew them (Goodson 2006). Re-labelling contemporary market-driven reforms as 'personalisation' may give the impression that something of the progressive era is being resurrected.

In England, the government has come up with a double-legitimation. As a legitimation of a still highly centralised education system, personalisation appeals both to the market economy and to a consumerist culture wherein the project of the self shows few signs of fading. To be sure, the market and the makeover generate constant instability and unpredictability, and government may well be aware of these centrifugal and potentially disruptive forces on education. The uneasy relationship between economic neo-liberals and One Nation 'Big Society' Conservatives reveals the contemporary tensions between 'economy' and 'society' which Third Way politics has sought to ease. Personalisation and customisation are suitably nebulous terms which themselves can be 'personalised' to suit the self. That is their legitimatory appeal and power.

Sitting a little uneasily within the radical humanist paradigm are some strands of postmodernist theory, especially that informed by Foucault (Anderson and Grinberg 1998). His interest was in how power within modernity is exercised (and less about who exercises it): 'Disciplinary power [. . .] is exercised through its invisibility' (Foucault 1984: 199). In the pre-modern medieval period, power had been visible, ritualised and coercive. In the post-Enlightenment period, the modes of regulation in society altered. The disciplines of the Enlightenment have deployed 'regimes of truth'. They are said to constitute us, frame us and define us. Thus it is that the fields of education, social work and management are all suffused by the disciplinary discourses of psychology, economics and sociology. We are said to be the 'subjects' immersed within them, positioned, caught in their discursive web, entangled: 'Postmodernist epistemology suggests that the world is constituted by our shared language and that we can only "know our world" through the particular form of discourse our language creates' (Hassard 1993: 3). But some postmodernists, heads buried in the text, can slip easily into peddling despair and nihilism, leaving politics to others (Rosenau 2002: 143). The 'seamless web' of discourse has the sense of Weber's iron cage of bureaucratic rationality, offering no hope of escape (Berman 1983: 34). Other postmodernists, the 'affirmative' postmodernists, have no such inclination to opt out of politics, but their 'cause' may not be the 'big issue' causes of the critical theorists. For the latter, the Foucauldian analysis understates the capacity for coercion when disciplinary power does not succeed in producing compliance (Best and Kellner 1991: 55–7). From a Foucauldian perspective, therefore, personalisation is part of a repertoire or discourse which is deployed, or 'distributed', with the purpose of manufacturing consent by appearing to elide the distinction between those who define strategies and those who enact them. It may appeal to the expressive, but its purpose is instrumental: the instrumentalisation of the expressive (Hartley 2003c).

Take some examples. Discourses are not confined to the verbal and to the oral; they can be the very practices and spatial arrangements of an organisation. Open-plan schools, for example, appear to be less hierarchical; similarly, so do desks which are arranged as circles rather than as rows. But circular arrangements are more visible to the teacher, *and* to the gaze of other students. In some personalised learning practices, students work alone, in segregated niches; and rarely might they interact as a class with their teacher. Their sense of the public and of the collective is thereby not developed. Or it might be the case that, during their personalised co-constructions and co-productions with teachers, more of their affects are expressed than would otherwise be the case; in Foucauldian terms, the exercise of pastoral power.

This analysis can be applied to policy pronouncements in education. An analysis of the text which was contained in 17 White Papers on education in England between 1972 and 2005 revealed a subtle appeal to 'soft power' in the rhetoric after the Labour government came to power in 1997. The frequency of the authoritative term 'government' abated rapidly, while that of 'we' rose (Mulderrig 2011: 49). These discursive appeals to 'we' – this apparent 'democratization of discourse' – convey the impression of democratisation, but they are arguably also indicative of the shift in power from producers to consumers in the marketisation project of neo-liberalism (Fairclough 1993: 219). Those soft appeals to the affective, and to the collective, also accord with a more general shift towards normative appeals in management theory after 1997, and with the rise of leaders at the expense of managers. It is a 'democratization of discourse' by government and by corporations. For critical theorists, unlike Foucauldians, what is required is action for emancipation. Overall, from a radical humanist position, it is a question of the radicalisation of *individual* consciousness, giving the lie to the 'naturalized' practices whereby the marginalised consent to their marginality. The agency and action thereafter fall logically within the radical structuralist paradigm.

Radical structuralism

[C]ontemporary society is characterised by fundamental conflicts which generate radical change through political and economic crises. It is through such conflict and change that emancipation of men from the social structures in which they live is seen as coming about.

(Burrell and Morgan 1979: 34)

For radical structuralists, the focus on personalisation and distribution is to misplace the priority: the priority should be on the social relations of production, not on the distribution of consumption. Radical structuralists argue that critical theorists within the radical humanist paradigm have become overly concerned with 'cultural studies': that is, they have shifted the analysis from political economy and the economic infrastructure to the mere 'representation' of race, sexuality, environment, ethnicity, nationality, and identity; that is, to the superstructure, away from the economic base (Zavarzadeh 1994: 93). They ignore the class in culture. They focus only upon the 'ancillary contradictions of capitalism'. These so-called 'differentialists' – whose emphasis is upon giving 'voice' to these interests of race, sexuality, environment, ethnicity, nationality, and identity – effectively set aside the voice of class; and, even more to their discredit, in doing so they claim to offer a subversive critique of capitalism. That is to say, for some left-cultural analyses, consumption itself is regarded as an active social critique and intervention; as a form of resistance whereby 'guilty pleasures' transgress social norms (Ebert 2009: 171). Put differently, the 'differentialists' argue that at a political level one can only radically change society through one's lifestyle, and not by revolution (Ebert and Zavarzadeh 2007: 147). At root, therefore, for the radical structuralists, it is not the mere *identity* (age, gender, ethnicity; and so on) of the labourer which matters for capitalism; it is the cost of labour. What we are left with is the 'culturalization of capitalism' (Zavarzadeh 2003: 18). Radical humanists are accused of being concerned merely with how the 'fruit' of the surplus labour generated by the proletariat is more equitably distributed. Private ownership is assumed; class itself remains unquestioned.

In contrast, the Marxist radical structuralist position reasserts the primacy of class. That position emphasises the matter of whether or not the means of production are collectively owned by the producers, or by private individuals who 'appropriate the products of the producers'. Within capitalism, pedagogy is framed by the social relations of production, and 'must situate its teaching within them and also self-reflexively include the conditions of its own production in its lessons' (Zavarzadeh 2003: 9). Zavarzadeh has no truck even with the likes of Giroux (2000), whose advocacy of radical pedagogy has long endured. But Giroux is said to have missed the point: his 'pedagogy of appearances' borders on a 'class-cleansing' bourgeois pedagogy. For example, in Giroux's analysis, the black and white proletariat are said to be segregated from each other and from other 'racial proletariats'. Giroux's pedagogy is said to carry out 'the political agenda of capital – to pit one segment of the proletariat against the other' (Zavarzadeh 2003: 11–12). Not that this cuts much ice with Giroux who likens this kind of position to 'high-minded puritanism', an 'ideological rigidity' which seems to deride 'difference, cultural politics, and social movements' (Giroux 2000: 6). Even less agreeable to Zavarzadeh are the Foucauldian-inspired discourse theorists and textual analysts who do little to engage in class struggles (Zavarzadeh 2003: 8).

What would personalisation mean for radical structuralists? Insofar as education is concerned, personalised learning would portend a consumerist mentality: that is, 'in order to boost its rate of profit by increasing consumption, capital needs a radically new cultural reality to lure consumers into purchasing the latest commodities as a way of "newing" their identities' (Ebert and Zavarzadeh 2007: 168). Recall the concept of the 'prosumer'. It is said to conflate the processes of consumption and production; it is a co-production, a co-configuration. The pedagogy of personalisation is 'productive' of this prosumer. It anticipates, too, the 'reflexive workplace', one wherein the worker remains a producer of surplus exchange value, but wherein also the worker is freed from some of the 'protocols of labour': that is, from how labour is done, but not from why it is done (Ebert 2009: 139).

It has been stated that the pedagogy of personalised learning has a close affinity to the newly converged digital technologies. The advocates of technology claim that, unto itself, it will enable progressive social change: a technical fix, no less (Robins and Webster 1989). Thus technology-enhanced personalised learning will, like previous technological innovations, accomplish progressive social change, by widening access. History reveals this to be a myth: it did not happen as the result of radio, television or the personal computer; and, from a radical structuralist position, it is unlikely to happen now. Indeed, the fact that corporations are promoting ICT-enhanced personalised learning should not lead us to think otherwise: it is a 'class technology' whereby capitalism is seeking to reproduce the means of its prosumption (Ebert and Zavarzadeh 2000; Ebert and Zavarzadeh 2007: 126–9).

There is within the discourse of personalisation much about co-production. Co-production is always located structurally. In the school, personalisation speaks to a co-production, a 'tailoring' of education to the needs of the pupil. But the 'co-' may be not that between pupil and professional; the 'co-' may be among the young people themselves, whose personalising preferences and processes may not be amenable to the 'nudge' of the school. The school's criteria for conferring status (especially to do with dress code and academic performance) may not be agreed by some pupils. The possibilities for many young people to symbolise their identities turn on their objective class position. But subjectively they may not regard their identities as being class-based, especially if they are lower working class. Instead, they may define themselves by their tastes in music, their digital media and fashion. It is through these means that they seek to express themselves symbolically, if they can afford to. The lack of employment – or even employment in precarious and various low-paid jobs – reduces this possibility. The discourse of personalisation implies a sense of autonomy, but the objective conditions within the labour market serve greatly to limit its realisation. To quote Willis: 'The apparently boundless horizons of consumption have done little to remove the unconscious foot soldiers from their struggles, and have only added another front on which to contend' (Willis 2003: 406). No longer labouring collectively in the now-depleted factories of the industrial era, no longer attracted by the flexible miseries of the low-paid service sector, no longer able to buy into an identity, the contemporary counterparts to Willis' 'lads' assert their status as 'proper' men by ritualised accentuations of their heterosexuality (Kehily and Nayak 1997: 85). Their female counterparts – the new 'at-risk' – face downward mobility and early motherhood. Not so their middle-class 'Others', now the emergent high educational achievers, flexible workers and active consumers of post-industrial neo-liberalism (Kehily 2008).

Summary

Personalisation as a mode of governance and as a pedagogical practice is a sign of the consumerist times. It is a concept which, appropriately, admits much personal interpretation of its meaning. It is neither easy to agree upon its meaning as a concept, nor to operationalise it in empirical studies. It can resonate with a revived Romanticism as easily as it can with the new work order. It can give the harshest practices of overt surveillance a pleasant veneer. When regarded sociologically, it can – depending upon the paradigmatic affiliation of the viewer – be seen as the necessary preparation for life as a producer-cum-consumer (or prosumer) in the new economy (functionalism); or as the very expression of the Vygotskian co-constructed, situated subject (interpretivism); or as a critique whereby the weak come to realise that personalisation's humanist discourse is seeking to persuade them to 'buy into' their very own marginalisation (radical humanism); or as action against personalised prosumption (radical structuralism).

10 Code switch? Education and the personalised society

'Mass' education – primary, secondary and now higher – has had a fairly short history; just over a century in the case of primary education. Without too much stretching of the imagination, the time-traveller of 100 years ago would not feel bewildered by the form and content of the contemporary school and university. Each is more or less of a piece with the so-called modern age, or at least with that form of modernity referred to as 'first modernity' or as 'solid modernity'. This modernity is beginning to show very considerable signs of strain. Its culture and economy seem to be pulling it in different directions.

How can these tensions be understood? Throughout the book, we have explored the insights of a range of educationalists, sociologists, historians and economists. Many of them seem to conclude that something of great moment is occurring, but that its causes and consequences are not well understood. At issue is that the financial crisis brought into very sharp focus some of the discontinuities in contemporary society. There is the conflict of ideologies between, on the one hand, a globalised and integrated market economy, and, on the other, an ideology which furthers the cause of identity, diversity and multi-culturalism (Touraine 2009b: 121). So there exists attenuation between the world of technology (highly rationalised, networked and instrumental) and that of an increasingly differentiated culture (consumer-driven, self-centred, affectual and value-laden). Schools are caught between the two.

If the likes of Bell and Touraine prompt an interest in the cohesion of society, Perez is concerned about the capitalist economy. Informed by Kondratieff's theory of the economic cycles of capitalism, she argued that, first and foremost, it is the profit-motive which drives capitalism. Capitalists will always seek the most productive technology and the optimal form of social organisation in work. The most efficient form of the latter usually lags behind the introduction of the former. During the early phase or 'surge' of a new technology, the financiers hold sway as they invest in what they deem to be a profitable venture. The new technology attracts risk capital, but there is over-investment, and asset values come to exceed their fundamental value. Eventually, the stock-markets collapse, as in 1929 and 2008. Thereafter, a reappraisal occurs, and the role of the state increases as it seeks to put in place new institutional forms which will be more compatible with the new technology which had been 'installed' prior to the collapse – which is what occurred between 1930 and 1945. After this came a long economic upswing during which time there emerged compatibility between the technology and the institutions of society, especially education (Perez 1983: 370). Perez notes, too, that most technological innovations, once deployed after a 'bubble', eventually reach a point when productivity returns level off. It is around this time, as the economic upswing begins to falter, as it did around 1970 (and after 1920), that capitalism turns its attention to the introduction of new 'softer' human-relations-inspired work organisation. The reasoning is that if the technology cannot increase productivity, then instead managers will resort to re-motivate workers by appearing to meet their psychological, social and even spiritual needs.

After 1970, the steady installation of micro-processor technology began to supplant the old mass production techniques. In place of massification, homogenisation and agglomeration would come variety, diversity and dispersion (Perez 1983: 374). The social effects of this technological shift are very considerable: desocialisation, de-institutionalisation and demodernisation (Touraine 2000). The 'surge' and 'installation' of digital technologies has – crucially – occurred at a time when economic neo-liberalism had entrenched itself as dominant in Western capitalism, even though it has been slightly mollified by Third Way politics. Indeed, the market and the micro-processor have marched in tandem. But, by and large, although (neo-liberal) economics and (digital) technology have been in 'sync', the institutional structures of society have remained firmly on a Fordist footing. The great national and public systems of education and health have largely retained their bureaucratic structures. But there has been one exception: parents and patients have come to be defined as customers and consumers. It is they, not the 'providers', who are said to be privileged. The providers, meanwhile, have been prodded into conformity with the ways of the quasi-market, and it has meant increasingly that they mustcompete, not only among themselves, but also with non-profit and for-profit 'stakeholders'. Charter schools, academies and free schools are in the van of this movement. They – and traditional schools – must vie for market share, or suffer the financial consequences. No longer is education to be regarded as a 'prudential' good; it is now more 'visceral', like nearly everything else in a culture which is in thrall to the quick-fix makeover. In much of this marketisation process, political ideology has tended to trounce the evidence. In the first place, it is by no means clear that the public wishes for 'choice' of schools and medical services in the manner presumed by government; on the contrary. Nor is there yet consistent and convincing evidence from the US, England or Sweden that, with social intakes held constant, charter schools, free schools or academies perform better than traditional schools. And there is evidence that they can be socially divisive (Department for Children Schools and Families 2009b: 145–7; *see also* OECD 2011: 1 and 12). In this marketised environment, one way or another, schools and teachers may hesitate to educate those children whose wherewithal cannot be relied upon to produce a good return. The stakes may be too high: some professionals may play the game in order to avoid the shame.

In the age of first modernity, investment in public education was assumed to have a positive causal relationship with economic growth. This was human capital theory; education was a means of *production* in the sense that it anticipated work. It now appears to be less so: since the 1980s, education has also been regarded increasingly as a means of *consumption*. We have argued that there are two strands to education as a means of consumption: the first strand comprised the 'school choice' movement, whereby there was an attempt to enable parents to make a rational choice of (or to express a preference for) a school for their children. In order to provide reliable information about the schools, teachers and pupils were tried and tested, and the results were made public to parents. In order to extend the range of choices, the types of schools on offer could declare a particular curricular specialism, or they could offer a particular ethos which those who sponsored the schools (in England: academies and free schools) adhered to. The second strand, both sequential and complementary to the first, has been an analysis of personalisation in education.

Appropriately for consumer culture, personalisation in education has its intellectual roots in marketing theory. It became prominent as a policy discourse from 2005. Given the increasing emphasis placed on consumerism during the past 20 years it is not surprising that education policy reflects this to some extent. Thus it is that personalisation has emerged in a number of OECD countries as a vision of things to come. Nor has its application applied solely to schooling: social care and healthcare have also come within its purview. The insertion of personalisation and customisation into the discourse of education policy marks also a further stage in the emergence of governance: it is at one with a movement which seeks to steer the responsibility for education towards the individual; it can bypass democratically elected local governments; it can serve to absolve central government; it diminishes collective citizenship (Ranson and Crouch 2009).

Somewhat paradoxically, the prefix of choice in the personalisation of education is '*co-*': that is, the *co*-customisation and the *co*-production of learning. The power of personalisation and customisation is that at one and the same time it can make a range of appeals: to consumer culture (that is, to individual desires and wants); to a new productive work order (that is, to collaborative community and prosumption); and to equal opportunities (that is, each child shall have a tailored education). It is a discourse which both enables accumulation and which deploys a rhetoric of legitimation.

Personalisation has another appeal. It sits well with digital technologies. Indeed, the wide application of the latter is now being regarded as the necessary condition before the former can take root. It occurs at a time when we are moving rapidly from personal computing to hand-held personalised computing. The latter, taken with social networking, raises the possibility – so the argument runs – of more online, personalised curriculum and assessment; whenever and wherever. For some, personalisation (and the collaborations which it spawns) is the social configuration necessary for this new technology to take root. Gee and colleagues (1996) were surely prescient in their alert that sociocultural theory would provide the intellectual supports for personalised/collaborative learning, for distributed leadership and for the inter-agency and inter-professional working which would accomplished personalised needs. The technical solutions for personalisation are said to exist, and companies are extremely keen to exploit this market, and on a global scale.

But personalisation is not just about technical issues. As far as education is concerned, it has implications for curriculum, pedagogy, assessment and organisational structures. A number of typologies of personalisation were explored in Chapter 6, notably those by Leadbeater, by Paludan and by Hargreaves. The optimal type of personalisation approximated to Leadbeater's 'deep', to Paludan's 'total', and to Hargreaves' 'high' conceptualisations. Each of them entrenches the notion of consumer choice, shifting to the individual pupil the responsibility for their own 'learning', *and* for its consequences. It is at one and the same time a privatising endeavour and a 'de-institutionalizing pressure': in sum, 'a gradual yet relentless replacement of the orthodox teacher-student relationship with the supplier-client, or shopping-mall-shopper pattern' (Bauman 2005: 316). Bauman's logic accords with an ICT-driven, just-in-time, on-demand, personalised modularisation (even itemisation) of the curriculum which is delivered by private and for-profit providers. Personalisation in a strong form disturbs the spatial and temporal form of education, and that in turn disturbs the social relations of schooling. All this may be the hoped-for outcome of those with a commercial interest in personalisation, but it must be weighed against those who would say that there is too much at stake to allow strong personalisation (especially of the curriculum) to have free rein.

Personalisation cuts a number of ways. One Nation Conservatives and economic neo-liberals will surely be divided about personalisation (especially about 'deep' personalisation of the curriculum). The former, like Michael Gove, the Secretary of State for Education in England, wish to retain broad control over the curriculum, and to reassert what Young (2011) calls *Future 1* curriculum: highly subject-specific, and given; a 'curriculum for compliance' in Young's words. The economic neo-liberals, on the other hand, may seek a curriculum and pedagogy which admits a personalised (but competence-based and instrumental) approach, typical of which is Scotland's *Curriculum for Excellence,* a curriculum which is constructivist in the extreme, setting great store by individual choice and experience. Here the disciplines dissolve into the realm of personal choice and interest. This is an example of Young's (2011) *Future 2* curriculum. The orientation in British Columbia's *Personalized Learning in BC* (British Columbia Ministry of Education 2011) is towards a compromise between these two curricular types.

The marketisation of education has been most associated with charter and free schools, and with academies. The educational case for these schools, especially charter schools, is unproven. There is mounting evidence that charter schools (which do not especially espouse personalisation) and free schools (some of which do) have yet to reveal consistent academic gains and to allay concerns about increasing social segregation. The interesting case is Sweden which in 1990 made a sudden turn towards the market, with free schools to the fore. Now there are doubts: its national achievement rates are declining quickly, and social segregation is on the rise (Vlachos 2011: 107). The two trends may be correlated. The not-for-profit free schools tend to draw students from more favourable social circumstances when compared to the for-profit schools, but the pupil–teacher ratio in the former is *lower* than that in the latter. If the school system purports to even out social differences, then this resource imbalance is serving to exaggerate them (ibid.: 196).

Education policies are usually framed to manage the inherent tensions between democracy and capitalism. The personalisation of education is such a policy. At root, it is a neo-liberal quest, hatched in the heyday of financialisation and consumerism. It is an add-on to the 'consumer choice' of schools. Whereas consumer choice (or marketisation) was about the offers made by schools, personalisation claims to pay greater heed to the co-produced demands by parents and pupils. Notwithstanding the 'personal' in personalisation, its purpose is not personal development; its purposes are economic and political. Economic, because it purports to prepare the pupil and the student for prosumption, especially in the service and culture sectors of the knowledge economy; it is instrumental and functional. Political, because it strikes a chord with the trend towards governance and away from government. A totally personalised society may be in the offing. Personalisation may be the 'forerunner of 21st-century totalitarianism' (Fielding 2006: 366). Personalisation, like individualisation, may become an obligation; and if personalisation is institutionalised in education, then it will be difficult to intend it away. It may, like individualisation, be rewarding, but equally it may also be penalising (McGuigan 2010: 328). In an identity-obsessed society, personalisation appeals to a Romantic nostalgia and to a technology-enhanced consumerism.

Personalisation, however, is no Romantic ideal: the personalisers are not the New Romantics, though some of them may be de-schoolers. This is little to do with the individualism which states that everyone shall have the right to have rights. To be sure, its rhetoric may be very appealing, even to those who wish no child to be left behind, to those who say that every child matters, and to those who say that one size does not fit all. Such is the persuasive power of aligning education more to the personal that even Touraine, no advocate of the market, appears to come close to endorsing something very close to personalisation. In his analysis of the French education system, he criticises the fact that it is the demands of the state, the society and the economy which prevail over those of the young themselves. It is the young who, argues Touraine, are preoccupied with their 'personalities, their personal lives and projects, and their relationships with their parents and friends' (Touraine 2009b: 268). In order to deal with these preoccupations, Touraine calls for a shift towards a 'demand-led' system, away from the existing 'supply-led' system (ibid.: 269). Here Touraine is referring mainly to the highly centralised system of education in France whose state schools require teachers to ignore matters which are to do with the personality and social origin of the pupil (ibid.: 39). His analysis suggests how easy it is for a market-driven policy of personalisation to appropriate what is a critical humanist position.

Personalisation (more than customisation) strikes a chord with collaboration. It appears not to be solely about the 'me'; it is implicitly about the 'we'. That is to say, the discourse of personalisation leads logically to that of collaboration, hardly a clarion call for me-too consumerism. The logic is that personalisation leads to co-production between customer/pupil and provider, as well as to co-production and distributed leadership among providers who must collaborate in order to meet the personalised needs of the customer/pupil. That is the logic, but so far the limited evidence on the practice is that the 'voices' which must speak their personalised needs look to be very uneven in their capacity to express them. Notwithstanding the attractions of behavioural economics – or so-called 'nudge' approaches – the responsibility for educational needs not being met will not rest with the state; they will be attributed to the failure of the individual to express them. Similarly, the technological means for generating collaborative learning, and for enabling inter-agency and inter-professional solution-spaces, may not easily be realised. The computer firewalls which separate agencies may come down, but the cultural divides may be more enduring. Significantly, in 2015, the OECD PISA assessments intend to incorporate two elements: 'collaborative problem solving' and 'greater use of computer-based testing'. (The contract for developing these was awarded to Pearson (Pearson 2011).)

The path to personalisation and customisation was taken during the credit-boom. That has now ended, and much of Western capitalism faces the prospect not just of personal and bank debts, but also of sovereign debt. It is this last which has triggered the fiscal crisis of the state. And this crisis may now prompt caution about market-driven solutions – including personalisation – to education in general. The evidence that market competition (charter schools, free schools and academies) 'drives up standards' is weak at best if funding and social intakes are held constant. If the excesses of consumerism are deemed to be a prominent cause of the crisis and to be strongly associated with a decline in the well-being of children (in the UK and in the US), then policies which make the same appeals may now be viewed with some circumspection.

The financial crisis has prompted national governments to ponder their policy options in education. Fiscally, they have the option of assigning a higher proportion of national expenditure to education, while reducing it in other activities. If done, that would protect education; if not, some or all of the following directions could be taken. First, governments could standardise the product and process of education, perhaps with 'technical fixes'. Second, they could do more with less by reducing fixed costs and increasing the pupil–teacher ratio. The 'school-day' may give way to more flexible temporal arrangements: perhaps some older pupils will attend only for half a day, thereby allowing for a second 'shift' to attend during the other half. Third, they could reduce their statutory provision in some areas, or – more likely – transfer funds from existing non-statutory areas (like higher education and early education) to statutory commitments. Fourth, they could invite both for-profit and non-profit agencies into the 'market' (philanthro-capitalists are a Victorian example of the latter). Fifth, they could enforce efficiency-mergers of hitherto discrete organisations and call it collaboration. Sixth, they could delay or put aside capital expenditure projects. Finally – and controversially – there is the possibility that school vouchers might reappear, but with the option of allowing parents to purchase personalised add-ons to the basic offer. Notwithstanding the 'mix' of spending adjustments, in England education spending is forecast to fall by 3.5 per cent, per year, between 2010–11 and 2014–15. This would be the largest decline in education spending over a four-year period since the 1950s. Put differently, education spending as a share of national income is set to fall from 6.2 per cent in 2010–11 to 4.6 per cent by 2014–15 (Chowdry and Sabieta 2011: 4).

Few of the foregoing arrangements would establish the structural and pedagogical changes which both new digital technologies and the emergence of prosumption require. These arrangements would be palliative. There may now be parallels to be drawn with the aftermath of the early 1970s when Western capitalism had to confront a perceived economic 'threat' from Asia. At the time, education was said to need a good dose of Darwinism to inject some entrepreneurial spirit into it. For too long it was said to have languished in the lap of the professionals. Thereafter, education was redefined as a 'product' whose providers should compete for market share. But in their pro-market policies both President Reagan and Prime Minister Thatcher were careful to retain some of the 'democratic' discourse which had been entrenched during the post-war period. 'Freedom' was reworked as 'freedom to choose'. Similarly, we may now expect to see a reworking of that same consumerist discourse which has prevailed for the last three decades. The combination of networking technologies, of a restructured time and space, and of collaborative work-regimes are said to be the necessary conditions which will 'co-produce' personalisation. But what of education and democracy? Under the canopy of 'personalisation for all', governments may begin slowly – in Perez's term – to 'deploy' these technologies and collaborations into the realms of pedagogy, curriculum and educational administration. Learning to co-labour may become the mantra of the moment.

References

Abrahamson, E., 1997. The emergence and prevalence of employee management rhetorics: the effects of long waves, labor unions, and turnover, 1875 to 1992. *Academy of Management Journal*, 40(3): 491–533.

Abrahamson, E. and Eisenman, M., 2008. Employee–management techniques: transient fads or trending fashions? *Administrative Science Quarterly*, 53(4): 719–44.

Adler, P. S., 2007. The future of critical management studies: a paleo-Marxist critique of labour process theory. *Organization Studies*, 28(9): 1313–45.

Adler, P. S. and Heckscher, C., 2006. Towards collaborative community. In C. Heckscher and P. S. Adler (eds), *The Firm as a Collaborative Community: reconstructing trust in the knowledge economy*. Oxford: Oxford University Press: 11–105.

Adler, P. S., Kwon, S. W. and Heckscher, C., 2008. Perspective–professional work: The emergence of collaborative community. *Organization Science*, 19(2): 359–76.

Alexander, R., 2001. *Culture and Pedagogy: international comparisons in primary education*, Oxford: Blackwell.

Alexander, R. J., Armstrong, M. and Flutter, J., 2010. *Children, their World, their Education: final report and recommendations of the Cambridge Primary Review*. Abingdon: Routledge.

Allen, R., 2010. Replicating Swedish free school reforms in England. *Research in Public Policy (CMPO Bulletin)*, 10: 4–7.

Allen, R., Burgess, S. and McKenna, L., 2010. *The Early Impact of Brighton and Hove's School Admission Reforms*. Bristol: The Centre for Market and Public Organisation.

Amrein-Beardsley, A., Berliner, D. C. and Rideau, S., 2010. Cheating in the first, second, and third degree: educators' responses to high-stakes testing. *Education Policy Analysis Archives*, 18: 1–36.

Anderson, G. L, and Grinberg, J., 1998. Educational administration as a disciplinary practice: appropriating Foucault's view of power, discourse, and method. *Educational Administration Quarterly*, 34(3): 329–53.

Arreman, I. E. and Holm, A. S., 2011. Privatisation of public education? The emergence of independent upper secondary schools in Sweden. *Journal of Education Policy*, 26(2): 225–43.

Avis, J., 2007. Engeström's version of activity theory: a conservative praxis? *Journal of Education and Work*, 20(3): 161–77.

Avis, J., 2009. Transformation or transformism: Engeström's version of activity theory? *Educational Review*, 61(2): 151–65.

Bagley, W. C., 1910. *Classroom Management: its principles and technique*. New York: The Macmillan Company.

Ball, S. J., 2003. The teacher's soul and the terrors of performativity. *Journal of Education Policy*, 18(2): 215–28.

Ball, S. J., 2006. *Education Policy and Social Class: the selected works of Stephen J. Ball.* Abingdon: Routledge.

Ball, S. J. and Youdell, D., 2007. *Hidden Privatisation in Public Education.* Brussels: Education International.

Barber, M., 2000. The evidence of things not seen: reconceptualising public education. In *OECD Schooling for Tomorrow Conference: 1–3 November.* Available at: http://www.oecd.org/dataoecd/32/18/2669190.pdf (accessed January 21, 2012).

Baudrillard, J., 1993. *America.* London: Verso.

Baudrillard, J., 1998. *The Consumer Society: myths and structures.* London: Sage.

Bauman, Z., 1988. Sociology and postmodernity. *Sociological Review*, 36(4): 790–814.

Bauman, Z., 1998. *Globalization: the human consequences,* New York: Columbia University Press.

Bauman, Z., 2000. *Liquid Modernity,* Oxford: Wiley-Blackwell.

Bauman, Z., 2001. *The Individualized Society,* Oxford: Wiley-Blackwell.

Bauman, Z., 2004. *Work, Consumerism and the New Poor* (2nd edn). Milton Keynes: Open University Press.

Bauman, Z., 2005. Education in liquid modernity. *Review of Education, Pedagogy, and Cultural Studies*, 27(4): 303–17.

Bauman, Z., 2007. Collateral casualties of consumerism. *Journal of Consumer Culture*, 7(1): 25–56.

Bauman, Z., 2011. The London riots – on consumerism coming home to roost. *Social Europe Journal*, (August 9).

Bauman, Z. and Vecchi, B., 2004. *Identity: conversations with Benedetto Vecchi.* Oxford: Wiley-Blackwell.

Bavelier, D., Green, C. S. and Dye, M. W., 2010. Children, wired: for better and for worse. *Neuron*, 67(5): 692–701.

Beach, D. and Dovemark, M., 2009. Making 'right' choices? An ethnographic account of creativity, performativity and personalised learning policy, concepts and practices. *Oxford Review of Education*, 35(6): 689–704.

Beach, D. and Dovemark, M., 2011. Twelve years of upper-secondary education in Sweden: the beginnings of a neo-liberal policy hegemony? *Educational Review*, 63(3): 313–27.

Beck, U., 1992. *Risk Society: towards a new modernity.* London: Sage.

Beck, U., 1997. *The Reinvention of Politics: rethinking modernity in the global social order.* Oxford: Wiley-Blackwell.

Beck, U. and Beck-Gernsheim, E., 2002. *Individualization: institutionalized individualism and its social and political consequences.* London: Sage.

Beck, U. and Grande, E., 2010. Varieties of second modernity: the cosmopolitan turn in social and political theory and research. *British Journal of Sociology*, 61(3): 409–43.

Beck, U. and Lau, C., 2005. Second modernity as a research agenda: theoretical and empirical explorations in the `meta-change' of modern society. *British Journal of Sociology*, 56(4): 525–57.

Beck, U., Bonss, W. and Lau, C., 2003. The theory of reflexive modernization. *Theory, Culture and Society*, 20(2): 1–33.

BECTA, 2008. *Personalising Learning in a Connected World: a guide for school leaders.* Coventry: BECTA.

Bell, D., 1972. The cultural contradictions of capitalism. *Journal of Aesthetic Education*, 6(1/2): 11–38.

Bell, D., 1976. *The Coming of Post-Industrial Society: a venture in social forecasting.* New York: Basic Books.

Bell, D., 1987. The World and the United States in 2013. *Daedalus,* 116(3): 1–31.

Bell, D., 2000. *The End of Ideology: on the exhaustion of political ideas in the fifties: with 'The resumption of history in the new century'.* Cambridge, MA: Harvard University Press.

Bell, D. and Graubard, S. R., 1997. *Toward the Year 2000: work in progress.* Cambridge, MA: MIT Press.

Bentham, J., 1816. *Chrestomathia.* London: Payne and Foss, and R. Hunter.

Bentham, J., 1995 [1787]. *The Panopticon Writings.* London: Verso Books.

Beresford, P., 2008. Whose personalisation? *Soundings,* 40(1): 8–17.

Berger, L. and Luckmann, T., 1967. *The Social Construction of Reality: a treatise in the sociology of knowledge.* Harmondsworth: Penguin.

Berger: L., Berger, B. and Kellner, H., 1974. *The Homeless Mind: modernization and consciousness.* London: Vintage.

Berman, M., 1981. *Re-enchantment of the World.* New York: Cornell University Press.

Berman, M., 1983. *All that is Solid Melts into Air: the experience of modernity.* London: Verso.

Bernstein, B., 1975. Class and pedagogies: visible and invisible. *Educational Studies,* 1(1): 23–41.

Bernstein, B., 2001. From pedagogies to knowledges. In A. Morais, I. Neves, B. Davies and H. Daniels (eds), *Towards a Sociology of Pedagogy: the contribution of Basil Bernstein to research.* New York: Peter Lang: 363–84.

Best, S. and Kellner, D., 1991. *Postmodern Theory: critical interrogations.* Basingstoke: Macmillan.

Bettinger, E. P., 2005. The effect of charter schools on charter students and public schools. *Economics of Education Review,* 24(2): 133–47.

Biggart, N. W. (1989) *Charismatic Capitalism: direct selling organizations in America.* Chicago, IL: University of Chicago Press.

Biggart, N. W. and Castanias, R. P., 1997. *Collateralized Social Relations: the social in economic calculation.* Cambridge: Judge Institute of Management Studies.

Bird, J., 2011. Fashion has become a weapon on the streets of London. *The Independent* (on-line edition), Monday, 15 August.

Birdwell, J., Grist, M. and Margo, J., 2011. *The Forgotten Half.* London: Demos.

Black, P. and Wiliam, D., 2006. *Inside the Black Box: raising standards through classroom assessment.* London: Granada Learning.

Boltanski, L. and Chiapello, E., 2005. The new spirit of capitalism. *International Journal of Politics, Culture, and Society,* 18(3): 161–88.

Bowles, S. and Gintis, H., 1976. *Schooling in Capitalist America.* London: Routledge and Kegan Paul.

British Columbia Ministry of Education, 2011. *Personalized Learning in BC: Interactive discussion guide.* Victoria, BC: British Columbia Ministry of Education.

Bronk, R., 2000. *Which model of capitalism?* Available at: http://eprints.lse.ac.uk/3860/ (accessed November 11, 2011).

Bullen, E., Fahey, J. and Kenway, J., 2006. The knowledge economy and innovation: certain uncertainty and the risk economy. *Discourse: Studies in the Cultural Politics of Education,* 27(1): 53–68.

Burawoy, M., 1988. *Manufacturing Consent: changes in the labor process under monopoly capitalism.* Chicago, IL: University of Chicago Press.

Burrell, G. and Morgan, G., 1979. *Sociological Paradigms and Organisational Analysis: elements of the sociology of corporate life*. London: Heinemann.

Cabinet Office Behavioural Insights Team, 2010. *Applying Behavioural Insight to Health*. London: Cabinet Office.

Cabinet Office Behavioural Insights Team, 2011. *Better Choices: better deals – consumers powering growth*. London: Cabinet Office.

Callahan, R. E., 1962. *Education and the Cult of Efficiency*. Chicago, IL: University of Chicago Press.

Campbell, C., 1989. *The Romantic Ethic and the Spirit of Modern Consumerism*. Oxford: Blackwell.

Campbell, C., 2004. I shop therefore I know that I am: the metaphysical basis of modern consumerism. In K. M. Ekström and H. Brembeck (eds), *Elusive Consumption*. Oxford: Berg Publishers, pp. 27–43.

Campbell, R. J., Robinson, W., Neelands, J., Hewston, R. and Mazzoli, L., 2007. Personalised learning: ambiguities in theory and practice. *British Journal of Educational Studies*, 55(2): 135–54.

Cappelli, P., 1997. *Change at Work*. Oxford: Oxford University Press.

Carnoy, M., 1999. *Globalization and Educational Reform: what planners need to know*. Paris: UNESCO, International Institute for Educational Planning.

Carnoy, M., 2002. *Sustaining the New Economy: work, family, and community in the information age*. Cambridge, MA: Harvard University Press.

Casey, C., 1995. *Work, Self, and Society: after industrialism*. London: Routledge.

Casey, C., 2003. The learning worker, organizations and democracy. *International Journal of Lifelong Education*, 22(6): 620–34.

Castells, M., 2000a. Toward a sociology of the network society. *Contemporary Sociology*, 29(5): 693–9.

Castells, M., 2000b. *End of Millennium*. Oxford: Wiley-Blackwell.

Castells, M., 2008. The new public sphere: global civil society, communication networks, and global governance. *The Annals of the American Academy of Political and Social Science*, 616(1): 78–93.

Center for Research on Education Outcomes, 2009. *Multiple Choice: charter school performance in 16 states*. Stanford, CA: Center for Research on Education Outcomes (CREDO) Stanford University.

Chin, E. M. L. S., 2001. *Purchasing Power: black kids and American consumer culture*. Minneapolis: University of Minnesota Press.

Chowdry, H. and Sabieta, L., 2011. *Trends in Education and Schools Spending*. London: Institute for Fiscal Studies.

Chubb, J. E. and Moe, T. M., 1990. *Politics, Markets, and America's Schools*. Washington, DC: Brookings Institution Press.

Clarke, J., 2010. After neo-liberalism? Markets, states and the reinvention of public welfare. *Cultural Studies*, 24(3): 375–94.

Clarke, J., Newman, J. E., Smith, N., Vidler, E. and Westmarland, L., 2007. *Creating Citizen-Consumers: changing publics and changing public services*. London: Sage.

Clegg, S., 1999. Globalizing the intelligent organization. *Management Learning*, 30(3): 259–80.

Coffield, F., Moseley, D., Hall, E. and Ecclestone, K., 2004. *Should We be Using Learning Styles? What research has to say to practice*. London: National Centre for Vocational Education Research (NCVER).

Coleman, J. S., 1988. Social capital in the creation of human capital. *American Journal of Sociology*, 94(Supplement: Organizations and Institutions: Sociological and Economic Approaches to the Analysis of Social Structure): 95–120.

Coopey, J., 2004. Crucial gaps in 'the Learning Organisation': power, politics and ideology. In K. Starkey, S. Tempest, and A. McKinlay (eds), *How Organizations Learn: managing the search for knowledge*. London: Thomson: 525–42.

Council for the Australian Federation, 2007. *Federalist Paper 2 – The Future of Schooling in Australia: a report by the states and territories* (rev. edn). Melbourne: Department of Premier and Cabinet.

Council of the European Union, 2009. *Official Journal of the European Union: Council conclusions of 12 May 2009 on a strategic framework for European cooperation in education and training ('ET 2020'): (2009/C 119/02)*. Available at: http://eur-lex. europa.eu/LexUriServ/LexUriServ.do?uri=OJ:C:2009:119:0002:0010:EN:PDF (accessed November 11, 2011).

Courpasson, D., 2000. Managerial strategies of domination: power in soft bureaucracies. *Organization Studies*, 21(1): 141–61.

Cresswell, L. and Morrissey, P., 2006. *Personalising the Curriculum at 14–19*. Nottingham: National College for School Leadership.

Crook, C., 2008. Theories of formal and informal learning in the world of Web 2.0. In S. Livingstone (ed.), *Theorising the Benefits of New technology for Youth: controversies of learning and development*. London: ESRC and LSE: 30–4.

Cuban, L., 2004. *The Blackboard and the Bottom Line: why schools can't be businesses*. Cambridge, MA: Harvard University Press.

Curtis, P., 2008. Lottery admissions fallout favours private schools. *The Guardian*. Available at: http://www.guardian.co.uk/education/2008/mar/05/schools.schooladmissions (accessed November 11, 2011).

Czempiel, E.-O., 1992. Governance and democratization. In J. Rosenau and E. O. Czempiel (eds) *Governance without Government: order and change in world politics*. Cambridge: Cambridge University Press, pp. 250–71.

Dale, R., 1979. From endorsement to disintegration: progressive education from the Golden Age to the Green Paper. *British Journal of Educational Studies*, 27(3): 191–209.

Deleuze, G., 1992. Postscript on the Societies of Control. *October*, 59: 3–7.

Department for Children Schools and Families, 2009a. *Number of National Challenge Schools Down*. London: Department for Children Schools and Families.

Department for Children Schools and Families, 2009b. *The Impact of the Commercial World on Children's Wellbeing*. Nottingham: Department for Children Schools and Families.

Department for Children Schools and Families, 2010a. *Space for Personalised Learning Project: Final Report*. Available at: http://issuu.com/davislangdon/docs/s4pl_final_ report (accessed January 21, 2012).

Department for Education and Skills, 2003. *Excellence and Enjoyment: a strategy for primary schools*. Nottingham: Department for Education and Skills.

Department for Education and Skills, 2004a. *Every Child Matters*. London: The Stationery Office.

Department for Education and Skills, 2004b. *Five-Year Strategy for Children and Learners: putting people at the heart of public services*. London: Her Majesty's Stationery Office.

Department for Education and Skills, 2005. *Higher Standards, Better Schools for All: more choice for parents and pupils: Cm 6677*. London: TSO.

Department for Education and Skills, 2006. *Personalising Further Education: developing a vision*. Nottingham: Department for Education and Skills Publications.

Department for Education and Skills, 2007a. *2020 Vision: report of the Teaching and Learning in 2020 review group*. London: Department for Education and Skills.

Department for Education and Skills, 2007b. *Pedagogy and Personalisation*. London: Department for Education and Skills.

Department for Education and Skills, 2007c. School Admissions Code 2007. The Stationery Office. Available at: http://media.education.gov.uk/assets/files/pdf/s/schooladmissionscodeweb060309.pdf (accessed January 21, 2012).

Department for Education and Skills, 2010a. *The Importance of Teaching*. London: Department for Education.

Department for Education and Skills, 2010b. "What Are Academies?" Department for Education. Available at: http://www.education.gov.uk/popularquestions/schools/typesofschools/a005582/what-are-academies (accessed January 21, 2012).

Department of Media Culture and Sport, 1999. All Our Futures: creativity culture and education. In *Report of the National Advisory Committee on Creative and Cultural Education*. London: DMCS.

Dolan, P., Hallsworth, M., Halpern, D., King, D. and Vlaev, I., 2010. *MINDSPACE: influencing behaviour through public policy*. London: Cabinet Office.

Dorling, D. 2009. The age of anxiety: living in fear for our children's mental health. *Journal of Public Mental Health*, 8(4): 4–10.

Dumont, H., Benavides, F. and Istance, D., 2010. *The Nature of Learning: using research to inspire practice*. Paris: OECD.

Duncan, A., 2009. *Remarks of Arne Duncan to the National Education Association – Partners in Reform*. Available at: http://www2.ed.gov/news/speeches/2009/07/07022009.html (accessed November 11, 2011).

Ebert, T., 2009. *The Task of Cultural Critique*. Champaign, IL: University of Illinois Press.

Ebert, T. and Zavarzadeh, M., 2007. *Class in Culture*. Boulder, CO: Paradigm Publishers

Ebert, T. L. and Zavarzadeh, M., 2000. E-Education, the opposite of equality. *Los Angeles Times*, March 23.

Edwards, A., Daniels, H., Gallagher, T., Leadbetter, J. and Warmington, P., 2009. *Improving Inter-professional Collaborations: multi-agency working for children's wellbeing*. London: Routledge.

Eiken, O., 2011. The Kunskapsskolan ('the knowledge school'): a personalised approach to education. *CELE Exchange-OECD*, (2011/1). Available at: http://www.oecd.org/dataoecd/25/47/47211890.pdf (accessed November 11, 2011).

Engeström, Y., 1987. *Learning by Expanding. An activity-theoretical approach to developmental research*. Helsinki, Orienta-Konsultit. Available at: http://lchc.ucsd.edu/MCA/Paper/Engestrom/expanding/toc.htm (accessed November 11, 2011).

Engeström, Y., 2000. Activity theory as a framework for analyzing and redesigning work. *Ergonomics*, 43(7): 960–74.

Engeström, Y., 2001. Expansive learning at work: toward an activity theoretical reconceptualization. *Journal of Education and Work*, 14(1): 133–56.

Engeström, Y., 2004. New forms of learning in co-configuration work. *Journal of Workplace Learning*, 16(1/2): 11–21.

Engeström, Y. and Sannino, A., 2010. Studies of expansive learning: foundations, findings and future challenges. *Educational Research Review*, 5(1): 1–24.

Engeström, Y., Engeström, R. and Kärkkäinen, M., 1995. Polycontextuality and boundary crossing in expert cognition: learning and problem solving in complex work activities. *Learning and Instruction*, 5(4): 319–36.

Equality and Human Rights Commission, 2010. *How Fair is Britain? Equality, human rights and good relations in 2010*. London: Equality and Human Rights Commission.

Esping-Andersen, G., 1990. *The Three Worlds of Welfare Capitalism*. Princeton, NJ: Princeton University Press.

Etzioni, A., 1975. *A Comparative Analysis of Complex Organizations: on power, involvement, and their correlates*. Glencoe: The Free Press.

Fairclough, N., 1993. *Discourse and Social change*. Chichester: Wiley-Blackwell.

Farrell, L., 2004. Workplace education and corporate control in global networks of interaction. *Journal of Education and Work*, 17(4): 479–93.

Fielding, M., 2006. Leadership, personalization and high performance schooling: naming the new totalitarianism. *School Leadership and Management*, 26 (4): 347–69.

Fielding, M., 2008. Personalisation, education and the market. *Soundings*, (38): 56–69.

Foucault, M. 1984. *The Foucault Reader* (P. Rabinow (ed.)). New York: Pantheon.

Fredriksson, A., 2009. On the consequences of the marketisation of public education in Sweden: for-profit charter schools and the emergence of the 'market-oriented teacher'. *European Educational Research Journal*, 8(2): 299–310.

Fukuyama, F., 2006. *The End of History and the Last Man*. Glencoe: Free Press

Galbraith, J. K., 1993. *The Culture of Contentment*. Harmondsworth: Penguin.

Gallie, D., 2007. *Employment Regimes and the Quality of Work*. Oxford: Oxford University Press.

Galton, M., 2007. New Labour and education: an evidence-based analysis. *Forum*, 49(1/2): 157–78.

Gardner, H., 2009. The next big thing: personalized education. *Foreign Policy*, April 15. Available at: http://www.foreignpolicy.com/articles/2009/04/15/the_next_big_thing_personalized_education (accessed 11 November 2011).

Gee, J. P., 2000. The new literacy studies: from 'socially situated' to the work of the social. In D. Barton, M. Hamilton and R. Ivanic (eds), *Situated Literacies: theorising reading and writing in context*. London: Routledge, pp. 180–96.

Gee, J. P., 2004. *Situated Language and Learning: a critique of traditional schooling*. London: Routledge.

Gee, J., Hull, G. and Lankshear, C., 1996. *The New Work Order*. Boulder, CO.: Westview Press.

Gellner, E., 1987. *Culture, Identity and Politics*. Cambridge: Cambridge University Press.

General Secretariat of the Council of the European Union, 2011. Prevention policies to combat early school leaving aimed at children with socioeconomically disadvantaged backgrounds, including Roma. Available at: http://register.consilium.europa.eu/pdf/en/11/st09/st09043.en11.pdf (accessed January 21, 2012).

Gewirtz, S., Ball, S. J. and Bowe, R., 1995. *Markets, Choice, and Equity in Education*. Milton Keynes: Open University Press.

Giddens, A., 1998. *The Third Way: the renewal of social democracy*. Oxford: Wiley-Blackwell.

Gilmore, J. H. and Pine, B. J., 1999. *Markets of One: creating customer-unique value through mass customization*. Cambridge, MA: Harvard Business Press.

Giroux, H. A., 2000. *Impure Acts: the practical politics of cultural studies*. London: Routledge.

Glaeser, E. L., 2005. *Paternalism and Psychology*. Cambridge, MA: National Bureau of Economic Research.

Gleeson, D., 2010. Academies and the myth of evidence-based policy: limits and possibilities. In H. Gunter (ed.), *The State and Education Policy*. London: Continuum International Publishing Group, pp. 199–211.

Goodson, I., 2006. Teacher nostalgia and the sustainability of reform: the generation and degeneration of teachers' missions, memory, and meaning. *Educational Administration Quarterly*, 42(1): 42–61.

Goodwin, M., 2009. Choice in public services: crying 'wolf' in the school choice debate. *The Political Quarterly*, 80(2): 270–81.

Gorard, S., 2005. Academies as the 'future of schooling': is this an evidence-based policy? *Journal of Education Policy*, 20(3): 369–77.

Gorard, S., 2006. Value-added is of little value. *Journal of Education Policy*, 21(2): 235–43.

Gorard, S., 2009a. What are Academies the answer to? *Journal of Education Policy*, 24(1): 101–13.

Gorard, S., 2009b. Does the index of segregation matter? The composition of secondary schools in England since 1996. *British Educational Research Journal*, 35(4): 639–52.

Gorard, S., 2010. Education can compensate for society – a bit. *British Journal of Educational Studies*, 58(1): 47–65.

Gorard, S., Fitz, J. and Taylor, C., 2003. *Schools, Markets and Choice Policies*. London: Routledge.

Grek, S., Lawn, M., Lingard, B., Ozga, J., Rinne, R., Segerholm, and Simola, H., 2009. National policy brokering and the construction of the European Education Space in England, Sweden, Finland and Scotland. *Comparative Education*, 45(1): 5–21.

Gronn, P., 2000. Distributed properties. *Educational Management Administration & Leadership*, 28(3): 317–38.

Grundtvig Project, 2011. *Integrated Model of Personalized Learning: guidelines*, leadlab. euproject.org/. Available at: http://www.leadlab.euproject.org/go.cfm?PageId=6001 (accessed November 11, 2011).

Habermas, J., 1987. *Knowledge and Human Interests*. Cambridge: Polity Press.

Hall, S., 2005. New Labour's double-shuffle. *Review of Education, Pedagogy, and Cultural Studies*, 27(4): 319–35.

Hallinger, P. and Heck, R. H., 2010. Leadership for learning: Does collaborative leadership make a difference in school improvement? *Educational Management Administration and Leadership*, 38(6): 654–78.

Halpern, D., Bates, C., Beales, G., Heathfield, A. and Britain, G., 2004. *Personal Responsibility and Changing Behaviour: the state of knowledge and its implications for public policy*. London: Cabinet Office.

Hansard, 1862. *Education – the Revised Code of Regulations*. – Petitions. HL Deb 04 March 1862, vol. 165, cc. 990–1022. Available at: http://hansard.millbanksystems. com/lords/1862/mar/04/education-the-bevised-code-of#S3V0165P0_18620304_ HOL_8 (accessed November 11, 2011).

Hardman, F., Smith, F. and Wall, K., 2003. 'Interactive Whole Class Teaching' in the National Literacy Strategy. *Cambridge Journal of Education*, 33(2): 197–215.

Hargreaves, A., 2003. *Teaching in the Knowledge Society: education in the age of insecurity*. Milton Keynes: Open University Press.

Hargreaves, A. and Shirley, D., 2009. *The Fourth Way: the inspiring future for educational change/* Thousand Oaks, CA: Corwin Press.

Hargreaves, D., 2004. *Personalising Learning 1: next steps in working laterally*. London: Specialist Schools and Academies Trust.

Hargreaves, D., 2005a. *Personalising Learning 2: student voice and assessment for learning*. London: Specialist Schools and Academies Trust.

Hargreaves, D., 2005b. *Personalising Learning 3: learning to learn and the new technology*. London: Specialist Schools and Academies Trust.

Hargreaves, D., 2005c. *Personalising Learning 4: curriculum and advice and guidance.* London: Specialist Schools and Academies Trust.

Hargreaves, D., 2005d. *Personalising Learning 5: mentoring and coaching and workforce development.* London: Specialist Schools and Academies Trust.

Hargreaves, D., 2006. *Personalising Learning 6: the final gateway – school design and organisation.* London: Specialist Schools and Academies Trust.

Hartley, D., 2003a. Education as a Global Positioning Device: some theoretical considerations. *Comparative Education,* 39(4): 439–50.

Hartley, D., 2003b. New economy, new pedagogy? *Oxford Review of Education,* 29(1): 81–94.

Hartley, D., 2003c. The instrumentalisation of the expressive in education. *British Journal of Educational Studies,* 51(1): 6–19.

Hartley, D., 2007a. Personalisation: the emerging 'revised' code of education? *Oxford Review of Education,* 33(5): 629–42.

Hartley, D., 2007b. Organizational epistemology, education and social theory. *British Journal of Sociology of Education,* 28(2): 195–208.

Hartley, D., 2007c. The emergence of distributed leadership in education: Why now? *British Journal of Educational Studies,* 55(2): 202–14.

Hartley, D., 2008. Education, markets and the pedagogy of personalisation. *British Journal of Educational Studies,* 56(4): 365–81.

Hartley, D., 2009. Personalisation: the nostalgic revival of child-centred education? *Journal of Education Policy,* 24(4): 423–34.

Hartley, D., 2010. Rhetorics of regulation in education after the global economic crisis. *Journal of Education Policy,* 25(6): 785–91.

Harvey, D., 2007. *A Brief History of Neoliberalism.* Oxford: Oxford University Press.

Hassard, J., 1993. Postmodernism and organizational analysis: an overview. In J. Hassard and M. Parker (eds), *Postmodernism and Organizations.* London: Sage Publications, pp. 1–23.

Hastings, S., 2004. Personalised learning. *Times Education Supplement,* 28 March. Available at: http://www.tes.co.uk/article.aspx?storycode=392798 (accessed November 11, 2011).

Hawken, P., Lovins, A. B. and Lovins, L. H., 2011. *Natural Capitalism: the next industrial revolution.* Snowmass, CO: Rocky Mountain Institute.

Heckscher, C., 2007. *The Collaborative Enterprise: managing speed and complexity in knowledge-based businesses.* New Haven, CT: Yale University Press.

Heckscher, C. and Adler, P. S., 2007. *The Firm as a Collaborative Community: reconstructing trust in the knowledge economy.* Oxford: Oxford University Press.

Her Majesty's Government, 2011. *Open Public Services White Paper.* London: Stationery Office Books.

Hirschman, A. O., 1970. Exit, Voice, and Loyalty: responses to decline in firms, organizations, and states, Cambridge, MA: Harvard University Press.

Hochschild, A. R., 2003. *The Managed Heart: commercialization of human feeling.* Berkeley, CA: University of California Press.

Holmes, D., 1999. Adolescent CIT use: paradigm shifts for educational and cultural practices? *British Journal of Sociology of Education,* 20(1): 69–78.

Hood, C., 1991. A public management for all seasons? *Public Administration,* 69(1): 3–19.

Hood, C., 2000. *The Art of the State: culture, rhetoric, and public management.* Oxford: Oxford University Press.

Hood, C., 2006. Gaming in targetworld: the targets approach to managing British public services. *Public Administration Review*, 66(4): 515–21.

Hood, C., Emmerson, C. and Dixon, R., 2009. Public Spending in Hard Times. *ESRC Public Services Programme.* Available at: http://www.christopherhood.net/pdfs/public-spending-in-hard-times.pdf (accessed November 11, 2011).

Hopkins, D., 2006. *Personalised Learning: how can we help every child do even better.* London: Qualifications and Curriculum Authority.

Horne, M., 2005. *Personalised Learning.* London: Department for Education and Skills Publications.

Hounshell, D. A., 1985. *From the American System to Mass production, 1800–1932: the development of manufacturing technology in the United States.* Baltimore, MD: Johns Hopkins University Press.

House of Commons, 2011. Oral answers to questions: education – 7 February 2011. *Hansard* (7 February: Column 18).

House of Commons Children, Schools and Families Committee, 2008. *Testing and Assessment Third Report of Session 2007–08 House of Commons.* HC 169–II: Monday 10 December 2007.

House of Commons Children, Schools and Families Committee, 2009. *National Curriculum: Fourth Report of Session 2008–09, Volume II Oral and written evidence.* London: The Stationery Office.

House of Commons European Scrutiny Committee, 2011. *European Scrutiny Committee – Twenty-Fifth Report Documents considered by the Committee on 5 April 2011: 3 DFE (32482) (32478) Early school leaving.* London: The Stationery Office.

House of Commons Public Administration Select Committee, 2005. *Choice, Voice and Public Services Fourth Report of Session 2004–05 Volume I: HC 49–I.* London: Stationery Office Books.

Humphreys, A. and Grayson, K., 2008. The intersecting roles of consumer and producer: a critical perspective on co-production, co-creation and prosumption. *Sociology Compass*, 2(3): 963–80.

Hurd, F., 2011. HRM and the Development of 'the Organisation': 'Transformations', or tinkering to the (Neo-liberal) facade? In *The Seventh International Critical Management Conference: July 11–13.* Naples. Available at: http://www.organizzazione.unina.it/cms7/proceedings/proceedings_stream_25/Hurd.pdf (accessed November 11, 2011).

Hursh, D., 2007. Assessing 'No Child Left Behind' and the rise of neoliberal education policies. *American Educational Research Journal*, 44(3): 493–518.

Huxham, C. and Vangen, S., 2005. *Managing to Collaborate: the theory and practice of collaborative advantage* (1st edn). London: Routledge.

Inglis, F., 1982. *Radical Earnestness: English social theory, 1880–1980.* Oxford: Martin Robertson.

Ipsos MORI, 2010. *What Do People Want, Need and Expect from Public Services?* London: 2020 Public Services Trust in partnership with RSA Projects.

Ipsos MORI, 2011. *Children's Well-being in UK, Sweden and Spain: the role of inequality and materialism.* London: Ipsos MORI.

Istance, D. and Dumont, H., 2010. Future directions for learning environments in the 21st century. In H. Dumont, F. Benavides, and D. Istance (eds), *The Nature of Learning: using research to inspire practice.* Paris: OECD: 317–38.

Jackson, P. W., 1990. *Life in Classrooms.* New York: Teachers College Press.

Jacques, R. S., 1996. *Manufacturing the Employee: management knowledge from the 19th to 21st centuries.* New York: Sage.

Keamy, R. K., Nicholas, H., Mahar, S. and Herrick, C., 2007. *Personalising Education: from research to policy and practice.* Melbourne: Victoria Department of Education and Early Childhood Development.

Keen, A., 2007. *The Cult of the Amateur: how today's internet is killing our culture.* New York: Doubleday.

Kehily, M. J. 2008. Taking centre stage? Girlhood and the contradictions of femininity across three generations. *Girlhood Studies*, 1(2): 51–71.

Kehily, M. J. and Nayak, A., 1997. 'Lads and laughter': humour and the production of heterosexual hierarchies. *Gender and Education*, 9(1): 69–88.

Kellner, D., 2000. Globalisation and new social movements: lessons for critical theory and pedagogy. In N. Burbules and C. Torres (eds), *Globalisation and Education: critical perspectives.* London: Routledge: 299–322.

Kincheloe, J. L. and McLaren, P., 2005. Rethinking critical theory and qualitative research. In N. K. Denzin and Y. S. Lincoln (eds), *The SAGE Handbook of Qualitative Research.* London: Sage: 303–42.

Kliebard, H. M., 1970. The Tyler Rationale. *The School Review*, 78(2): 259–72.

Kress, G., Jewitt, C. and Tsatsarelis, C., 2000. Knowledge, identity, pedagogy: pedagogic discourse and the representational environments of education in late modernity. *Linguistics and Education*, 11(1): 7–30.

Kumar, A., 2007. From mass customization to mass personalization: a strategic transformation. *International Journal of Flexible Manufacturing Systems*, 19(4): 533–47.

Kumar, A. and Stecke, K. E., 2007. Measuring the effectiveness of a mass customization and personalization strategy: a market-and-organizational-capability-based index. *International Journal of Flexible Manufacturing Systems*, 19(4): 548–69.

Lash, S. and Friedman, J., 1992. *Modernity and Identity.* Oxford: Blackwell.

Lawson, H. A., 2004. The logic of collaboration in education and the human services. *Journal of Interprofessional Care*, 18(3): 225–37.

Le Grand, J., 1991. Quasi-markets and social policy. *The Economic Journal*, 101(408): 1256–67.

Le Grand, J., 2007. *The Other Invisible Hand: delivering public services through choice and competition.* Princeton, NJ: Princeton University Press.

Leadbeater, C., 2004a. *Personalisation through Participation: a new script for public services.* London: Demos.

Leadbeater, C., 2004b. *Learning about Personalisation: how can we put the learner at the heart of the education system?* London: Department for Education and Skills.

Leadbeater, C., 2005. *The Shape of Things to Come: personalised learning through collaboration.* London: Department for Education and Skills.

Leadbeater, C., 2006. The future of public services: personalised learning. In OECD (ed.) *Personalising Education.* Paris: OECD Publishing, pp. 101–14.

Lewis, P., Ball, J. and Taylor, M., 2011. Riot jail sentences in crown courts longer than normal. *The Guardian.* Available at: http://www.guardian.co.uk/uk/2011/sep/05/riot-jail-sentences-crown-courts (accessed November 11, 2011).

Lingard, B., 2003. *Leading Learning: making hope practical in schools.* Maidenhead: McGraw-Hill International.

Lingard, B., 2007. Pedagogies of indifference. *International Journal of Inclusive Education*, 11(3): 245–66.

Lingard, B., 2010. Testing times: The need for new intelligent accountabilities for schooling. *QTU Professional Magazine*, 24(November): 13–19.

Lindsay, C., 2003. A century of labour market change: 1900 to 2000. *Labour Market Trends*, 111(3): 133–44.

Linn, S., 2005. Consuming Kids: protecting our children from the onslaught of marketing and advertising. New York: Anchor Books.

Livingstone, S., 2009. *Children and the Internet: great expectations, challenging realities.* Cambridge: Polity.

Lord Darzi of Denham, 2008. *High Quality Care for All: NHS next stage review final report: CM 7432.* London: The Stationery Office.

Loveless, T. and Field, K., 2009. Perspectives on charter schools. In M. Berends (ed.), *Handbook of Research on School Choice.* London: Routledge: 99–114.

Lubienski, C., 2008. School choice research in the United States and why it doesn't matter: the economy of knowledge production in a contested policy domain. In M. Forsey, S. Davies, and G. Walford (eds), *The Globalisation of School Choice?* Oxford: Symposium Books, pp. 27–54.

Lubienski, C. and Garn, G., 2010. Evidence and ideology on consumer choices in education markets. *Current Issues in Education*, 13(3): 1–31.

Luckin, R., Clark, W., Graber, R., Logan, K., Mee, A. and Oliver, M., 2009. Do Web 2.0 tools really open the door to learning? Practices, perceptions and profiles of 11–16-year-old students. *Learning, Media and Technology*, 34(2): 87–104.

Lyman, S. M. and Scott, M. B., 1970. *A Sociology of the Absurd.* New York: Appleton-Century-Crofts.

Lyotard, J.-F., 1984. *The Postmodern Condition: a report on knowledge.* Minneapolis, MI: University of Minnesota Press.

Mabry, L. and Snow, J.Z., 2006. Laptops for high-risk students: empowerment and personalization in a standards-based learning environment. *Studies in Educational Evaluation*, 32(4): 289–316.

Maccoby, M., 2006. The self in transition: from bureaucratic to interactive social character. In C. Heckscher and P. Adler (eds), *The Firm as a Collaborative Community: reconstructing trust in the knowledge economy.* Oxford: Oxford University Press: 157–76.

McGuigan, J., 2010. Creative labour, cultural work and individualisation. *International Journal of Cultural Policy*, 16(3): 323–35.

MacKenzie, D., 2011. The credit crisis as a problem in the sociology of knowledge 1. *American Journal of Sociology*, 116(6): 1778–841.

McKinsey and Company, 2007. *How The World's Best-performing School Systems Come Out on Top.* Available at: http://www.mckinsey.com/clientservice/social_sector/our_practices/education/knowledge_highlights/best_performing_school.aspx (accessed November 11, 2011).

McNeely, C.L. and Cha, Y.K., 1994. Worldwide educational convergence. *Education Policy Analysis Archives*, 2(14): 1–11.

McNeil, L. and Valenzuela, A., 2001. The harmful impact of the TAAS System of Testing in Texas: beneath the accountability rhetoric. In M. L. Kornhaber and G. Orfield (eds), *Raising Standards or Raising Barriers? Inequality and high-stakes testing in public education.* New York: Century Foundation Press: 127–50.

Maffesoli, M., 1996. *The Time of the Tribes: the decline of individualism in mass society.* London: Sage.

Maguire, M., Perryman, J., Ball, S. and Braun, A., 2011. The ordinary school – what is it? *British Journal of Sociology of Education*, 32(1): 1–16.

Manthorpe, J., Stevens, M., Rapaport, J., Jacobs, S., Challis, D., Wilberforce, M., Netten, A., Knapp, M. and Glendinning, C., 2010. Gearing up for personalisation: training activities commissioned in the English pilot individual budgets sites 2006–2008. *Social Work Education*, 29(3): 319–31.

Marmoy, C. F. A., 1958. The 'auto-icon' of Jeremy Bentham at University College, London. *Medical History*, 2(2): 77–86.

Medina, J., 2009. Laptop? Check. Student Playlist? Check. Classroom of the Future? Check. *The New York Times*, 21st July. Available at: http://www.nytimes.com/2009/07/22/education/22school.html (accessed November 11, 2011).

Medina, J., 2010. Pressed by Charters, Public Schools Try Marketing. *The New York Times*. Available at: http://www.nytimes.com/2010/03/10/education/10marketing.html?pagewanted=2&_r=1 (accessed November 11, 2011).

Melucci, A., 1996a. *Challenging Codes: collective action in the information age*, Cambridge University Press.

Melucci, A., 1996b. *The Playing Self: person and meaning in the planetary society*, Cambridge: Cambridge University Press.

Melucci, A. and Keane, J., 1989. *Nomads of the Present: social movements and individual needs in contemporary society*. Philadelphia, PA: Temple University Press.

Mihm, S., 2008. 'Dr. Doom.' *The New York Times*, August 17, sec. Magazine. Available at: http://www.nytimes.com/2008/08/17/magazine/17pessimist-t.html?_r=1&ref=business (accessed November 11, 2011).

Miliband, D., 2004. *Personalised Learning: building a new relationship with schools*. North of England Education Conference, Belfast, 8th January. London: Department for Education and Skills.

Miliband, D., 2006. Choice and voice in personalised learning. In OECD (ed.), *Personalising Education*. Paris: OECD Publishing, pp. 21–30.

Miller, P. J., 1973. Factories, monitorial schools and Jeremy Bentham: the origins of the 'management syndrome' in popular education. *Journal of Educational Administration and History*, 5(1): 10–20.

Miller, R., 2003. Towards the learning society. In T. Bentley and J. Wilsdon (eds), *The Adaptive State: strategies for personalising the public realm*. London: Demos, pp. 112–23.

Mills, C. W., 1951. *White Collar: the American middle classes*. Oxford: Oxford University Press.

Minc, A., 1993. *Le Nouveau Moyen Age*. Paris: Gallimard.

Molnar, A., 1996. Charter schools: the smiling face of disinvestment. *Educational Leadership*, 54(2): 9–15.

Molnar, A., 2005. *School Commercialism: from democratic ideal to market commodity*. London: Routledge.

Mulderrig, J., 2011. The grammar of governance. *Critical Discourse Studies*, 8(1): 45–68.

Myles, J., 1850. *Chapters in the Life of a Dundee Factory Boy: an autobiography*. Dundee: James Myles.

Nahapiet, J., 2008. There and back again? Organization Studies, 1965–2006. In S. Dopson, M. Earl, and J. Snow (eds), *Mapping the Management Journey: practice, theory and context*. Oxford: Oxford University Press: 80–103.

Nasaw, D., 1981. *Schooled to Order: a social history of public schooling in the United States*. Oxford: Oxford University Press.

National Center on Education and the Economy, 2008. *Tough Choices or Tough Times: the report of the New Commission on the Skills of the American Workforce*. New York: John Wiley and Sons.

National Commission on Excellence, 1984. *A Nation at Risk*. Available at: http://www2.ed.gov/pubs/NatAtRisk/index.html (accessed November 11, 2011).

Neave, G., 1988. On the cultivation of quality, efficiency and enterprise: an overview of recent trends in higher education in Western Europe, 1986–1988. *European Journal of Education*, 23(1): 7–23.

Needham, C., 2009. Interpreting personalization in England's National Health Service: a textual analysis. *Critical Policy Studies*, 3(2): 204–20.

Newman, J. and Clarke, J., 2009. *Publics, Politics and Power: remaking the public in public services*. London: Sage.

New South Wales. Department of Education and Training, 2005. *Report of the Consultation on Future Directions for Public Education and Training : 'one size doesn't fit all'*. Sydney, NSW: Department of Education and Training.

New York City Department of Education, 2010a. *School of One*. New York: New York City Department of Education. Available at: http://schoolofone.org/ (accessed November 11, 2011).

New York City Department of Education, 2010b. *School of One Evaluation – 2010 Spring Afterschool and Short-Term In-School Pilot Programs*. New York: New York City Department of Education. Available at: http://schoolofone.org/resources/so1_final_report_2010.pdf (accessed November 11, 2011).

O'Connor, J., 2001. *The Fiscal Crisis of the State*. Piscataway, NJ: Transaction Publishers.

OECD, 1997. *Issues and Developments in Public Management: survey 1996–1997*, Paris: OECD Publishing.

OECD, 2010a. A family affair: intergenerational social mobility across OECD countries. In OECD (ed.), *Economic Policy Reforms: going for growth*. Paris: OECD Publishing: 181–98.

OECD, 2010b. *PISA 2009 Results: what students know and can do – student performance in reading, mathematics and science (Volume I)*. OECD Publishing. Available at: http://dx.doi.org/10.1787/9789264091450-en. (accessed November 11, 2011).

OECD. 2011. *Viewing the United Kingdom School System through the Prism of Pisa*. Paris: Publications de l'OCDE. Available at: http://www.oecd.org/dataoecd/33/8/46624007.pdf (accessed January 21, 2012).

Offer A., 2003. *Why Has the Public Sector Grown so Large in Market Societies? The political economy of prudence in the UK, c. 1870–2000*. Oxford: Oxford University Press.

Offer, A., 2006. *The Challenge of Affluence: self-control and well-being in the United States and Britain since 1950*. Oxford: Oxford University Press.

Offer, A., 2008. British manual workers: from producers to consumers, c. 1950–2000. *Contemporary British History*, 22(4): 537–71.

Offer, A., Pechey, R. and Ulijaszek, S., 2010. Obesity under affluence varies by welfare regimes: The effect of fast food, insecurity, and inequality. *Economics and Human Biology*, 8(3): 297–308.

Osborne, D. and Gaebler, T., 1993. *Reinventing Government: how the entrepreneurial spirit is transforming the public sector*. New York: Plume.

Osborne, G., 2009. We will lead the economy out of crisis: Speech to the Conservative Party, October 6. Available at: http://www.conservatives.com/News/Speeches/2009/10/George_Osborne_We_will_lead_the_economy_out_of_crisis.aspx (accessed November 11, 2011).

Paludan, J., 2006. Personalised learning 2025. In OECD (ed.), *Personalising Education*. Paris: OECD Publishing: 83–100.

Parsons, T., 1959. The school class as a social system: some of its functions in American society. *Harvard Educational Review*, 29(4): 297–318.

Parsons, T., 1991. *Social System*. London: Routledge.

Paterson, F. M. S., 1988. Measures of schooling: registers, standards and the construction of the subject. *Journal of Historical Sociology*, 1(3): 278–300.

Paton, G., 2007. School places lottery will hit house prices. *The Telegraph*. Available at: http://www.telegraph.co.uk/news/uknews/1544452/School-places-lottery-will-hit-house-prices.html (accessed November 11, 2011).

Pearson, 2011. *Pearson to Develop Frameworks for OECD's PISA Student Assessment for 2015: media note October 7 2011*. Available at: http://www.pearson.com/media-1/announcements/?i=1485 (accessed November 11, 2011).

Perez, C., 1983. Structural change and assimilation of new technologies in the economic and social systems 1. *Futures*, 15(5): 357–75.

Perez, C., 2009a. The double bubble at the turn of the century: technological roots and structural implications. *Cambridge Journal of Economics*, 33(4): 779–805.

Perez, C., 2009b. *Growth after the Financial Meltdown*, mimeo, 25 June 2009. Available at: http://www.opendemocracy.net/files/carlota-3+cp.pdf (accessed November 11, 2011).

Perez, C., 2010. Technological revolutions and techno-economic paradigms. *Cambridge Journal of Economics*, 34(1): 185–202.

Perez, C. and Rutherford, J., 2009. Financial bubbles and economic crises. *Soundings*, 41(1): 30–44.

Perryman, J., 2006. Panoptic performativity and school inspection regimes: disciplinary mechanisms and life under special measures. *Journal of Education Policy*, 21(2): 147–61.

Pietrykowski, B., 2007. Exploring new directions for research in the radical political economy of consumption. *Review of Radical Political Economics*, 39(2): 257–83.

Piore, M. J. and Sabel, C. F., 1984. *The Second Industrial Divide: possibilities for prosperity*. New York: Basic books.

Pollard, A. and James, M., 2004. *Personalised Learning: a commentary by the Teaching and Learning Research Programme*. Swindon: Economic and Social Research Council.

Pollard, S., 1963. Factory discipline in the Industrial Revolution. *The Economic History Review*, 16(2): 254–71.

Power, M., 1997. *The Audit Society: rituals of verification*. Oxford: Oxford University Press.

Priestley, M. and Humes, W., 2010. The development of Scotland's Curriculum for Excellence: amnesia and *déjà vu*. *Oxford Review of Education*, 36(3): 345–61.

Prime Minister's Strategy Unit, 2006. *The UK Government's Approach to Public Service Reform* (Working Document). London: Cabinet Office.

Pugh, A. J., 2009. *Longing and Belonging: parents, children, and consumer culture*. Berkeley, CA: University of California Press.

Putnam, R. D., 2001. *Bowling Alone: the collapse and revival of American community*. New York: Simon & Schuster.

Putnam, R. D., 2007. *E Pluribus Unum*: diversity and community in the twenty-first century. The 2006 Johan Skytte prize lecture. *Scandinavian Political Studies* 30(2): 137–74.

Ranson, S., and Crouch, C., 2009. *Towards a New Governance of Schools in the Remaking of Civil Society*. Reading: CfBT Education Trust.

Ravitch, D., 2007. Get Congress Out of the Classroom. *The New York Times*. Available at: http://www.nytimes.com/2007/10/03/opinion/03ravitch.html (accessed November 11, 2011).

Ravitch, D., 2010. *The Death and Life of the Great American School System: how testing and choice are undermining education*. New York: Basic Books.

Reich, R. B., 1992. *The Work of Nations: preparing ourselves for 21st century capitalism* (1st edn). New York: Vintage Books.

Rhodes, R. A., 1996. The new governance: governing without government. *Political Studies*, 44(4): 652–67.

Riesman, D., Gitlin, T., Glazer, N. and Denney, R., 2001. *The Lonely Crowd: a study of the changing American character*. New Haven, CT: Yale University Press.

Ritchie, R. and Crick, R. D., 2008. *Distributing Leadership for Personalizing Learning*. London: Network Continuum.

Ritzer, G., 2000. *The McDonaldization of Society*. Thousand Oaks, CA: Pine Forge Press.

Ritzer, G., 2010. Focusing on the prosumer: on correcting an error in the history of social theory. In B. Blättel-Mink and K.-U. Hellmann (eds), *Prosumer Revisited: Zur Aktualität einer Debatte*. Wiesbaden: Verlag für Sozialwissenschaften, pp. 61–80.

Ritzer, G. and Jurgenson, N., 2010. Production, consumption, prosumption. *Journal of Consumer Culture*, 10(1): 13–36.

Robins, K. and Webster, F., 1989. *The Technical Fix: education, computers and industry*. New York: St. Martin's Press.

Rosenau, P., 2002. *Post-Modernism and the Social Sciences*. New York: Greenwood Publishing Group.

Rubinson, R. and Browne, I., 1994. Education and the economy. In N. J. Smelser and R. Swedberg (eds), *The Handbook of Economic Sociology*. Princeton, NJ: Princeton University Press, pp. 575–677.

Sahlberg, P., 2011. Paradoxes of educational improvement: The Finnish experience. *Scottish Educational Review*, 43(1): 3–23.

Sassatelli, R., 2006. Virtue, responsibility and consumer choice. framing critical consumerism. In J. Brewer and F. Trentmann (eds), *Consuming Cultures: global perspectives*. Oxford: Berg Publishers, pp. 219–50.

Scase, R. 1999. *Britain Towards 2010: the changing business environment*. London: Department for Trade and Industry.

School of One, 2011. *School of One: one-page overview*. Available at: http://schoolofone. org/resources/sol_onepage_overview.pdf. (accessed November 11, 2011).

Schroeder, R., 1995. Disenchantment and its discontents: Weberian perspectives on science and technology. *Sociological Review*, 43(2): 227–50.

Schutz, A., 1967. *The Phenomenology of the Social World*. Evanston, IL: Northwestern University Press.

Scott, C., James, O., Jones, G. and Travers, T., 1999. From secret garden to reign of terror? The regulation of state schools in England. In C. Hood, O. James, G. Jones, C. Scott, and T. Travers (eds), *Regulation Inside Government: waste-watchers, quality police, and sleazebusters*. Oxford: Open University Press, pp. 139–62.

Scottish Government, 2009. *Curriculum for Excellence: building the curriculum 4 – skills for learning, skills for life and skills for work*. Edinburgh: Scottish Government.

Scottish Government, 2011. *Europe 2020: Scottish national reform programme 2011*. Edinburgh: Scottish Government.

Sebba, J., Brown, N., Steward, S. and Galton, M., 2007. *An Investigation of Personalised Learning Approaches Used by Schools*. Nottingham: Department for Education and Skills/ University of Sussex.

Seldon, A., 2010. *An End to Factory Schools: an education manifesto 2010–2020*. London: Centre for Policy Studies.

Seligman, A. B., 2010. Trust, tolerance and the changing terms of social solidarity. *Balkan Journal of Philosophy*, 2(1): 3–12.

Selwyn, N., 2010. *Schools and Schooling in the Digital Age*. London: Taylor & Francis.

Shenhav, Y., 1995. From chaos to systems: the engineering foundations of organization theory, 1879–1932. *Administrative Science Quarterly*, 40(4): 557–85.

Skolverket (The Swedish National Agency for Education), 2006. *School Choice and its Effects in Sweden* (Offprint of Report 230): a summary. Stockholm: Skolverket.

Slavin, R., 2010. Co-operative learning: what makes group-work work? In H. Dumont, D. Istance, and F. Benavides (eds), *The Nature of Learning: using research to inspire practice*. Paris: OECD Publishing, pp. 161–78.

Sorokin, P. A., 1985. *Social and Cultural Dynamics: a study of change in major systems of art, truth, ethics, law, and social relationships*. New York: American Book Company.

Spring, J. H., 2003. *Educating the Consumer-Citizen: a history of the marriage of schools, advertising, and media*. Mahwah, NJ: Lawrence Erlbaum Associates.

Sterman, J. D., 1986. The economic long wave: theory and evidence. *System Dynamics Review*, 2(2): 87–125.

Stobart, G., 2008. *Testing Times: the uses and abuses of assessment*. London: Routledge.

Stone, P., 2008. What can lotteries do for education? *Theory and Research in Education*, 6(3): 267–82.

Strasser, S., 2003. *Commodifying Everything: relationships of the market*. London: Routledge.

Tapscott, D. and Williams, A. D., 2008. *Wikinomics: how mass collaboration changes everything*. London: Portfolio/Penguin.

Taylor, F. W., 2005. *The Principles of Scientific Management*. Fairfield, IA: 1st World Library Literary Society.

Thaler, R. H. and Sunstein, C. R., 2009. *Nudge: improving decisions about health, wealth and happiness*. New York: Penguin.

The Economist, 2006. The avuncular state. *The Economist*, 378(8472, April 8): 76–9.

The Economist, 2009. Case history: A factory on your desk. *The Economist*. Available at: http://www.economist.com/node/14299512 (accessed November 11, 2011).

The Economist, 2009; 2011. 3D printing: The printed world. *The Economist*. Available at: http://www.economist.com/node/18114221 (accessed November 11, 2011).

Thompson, E. P., 1967. Time, work-discipline, and industrial capitalism. *Past and Present*, 38(1): 56–97.

Thompson, G., 2003. *Between Hierarchies and Markets: the logic and limits of network forms of organization*. Oxford: Oxford University Press.

Thompson, M., 1979. *Rubbish Theory: the creation and destruction of value*. Oxford: Oxford University Press.

Thrift, N., 1999. Capitalism's cultural turn. In L. Ray and A. Sayer (eds), *Culture and Economy after the Cultural Turn*. London: Sage, pp. 135–61.

Thrift, N., 2000. Performing cultures in the new economy. *Annals of the Association of American Geographers*, 90(4): 674–92.

Toffler, A., 1980. *Third Wave*. London: Collins.

Toffler, A. and Toffler, H., 2006. *Revolutionary Wealth*. New York: Knopf.

Touraine, A., 2000. *Can We Live Together? Equality and difference*. Cambridge: Polity Press.

Touraine, A., 2009a. *Thinking Differently*. Cambridge: Polity Press.

Touraine, A., 2009b. The crisis of progress. *European Review*, 1(2): 117–23.

Trentmann, F., 2006. *The Making of the Consumer: knowledge, power and identity in the modern world*. Oxford: Berg Publishers.

Trentmann, F., 2007. Citizenship and consumption. *Journal of Consumer Culture*, 7(2): 147–58.

Tseng, M. M. and Jiao, J., 2005. Mass customisation. In G. Salvendy (ed.), *Handbook of Industrial Engineering: technology and operations management*. New York: Wiley: 684–709.

Turkle, S., 2011. *Alone Together: Why We Expect More from Technology and Less from Each Other*. New York: Basic Books.

Turner, A., 2002. *Just Capital*. London: Pan Books.

Turner, R. H., 1960. Sponsored and contest mobility and the school system. *American Sociological Review*, 25(6): 855–67.

Tyack, D. and Tobin, W., 1994. The 'grammar' of schooling: why has it been so hard to change? *American Educational Research Journal*, 31(3): 453–79.

Underwood, J. and Banyard, P., 2008. Managers', teachers' and learners' perceptions of personalised learning: evidence from Impact 2007. *Technology, Pedagogy and Education*, 17(3): 233–46.

US Department of Education, 2009. *Race to the Top Program: executive summary*. Available at: http://www2.ed.gov/programs/racetothetop/executive-summary.pdf (accessed November 11, 2011).

US Department of Education, Office of Educational Technology, 2010. *Transforming American Education: learning powered by technology*. Washington, DC: US Department of Education.

UNICEF Innocenti Research Centre, 2007. *An Overview of Child Well-Being in Rich Countries*. Florence: UNICEF Innocenti Research Centre.

Van Schaik, T., 2004. Social capital in the European Values Study surveys. In *OECD-ONS International Conference on Social Capital Measurement, September 25–27*. London. Available at: http://www.afsp.msh-paris.fr/publi/banques/evssocialcapital2002.pdf (accessed November 11, 2011).

Varney, D. S., 2006. *Service Transformation: a better service for citizens and businesses, a better deal for the taxpayer*. London: Stationery Office Books.

Victor, B. and Boynton, A. C., 1998. *Invented Here: maximizing your organization's internal growth and profitability*. Cambridge, MA: Harvard Business Press.

Victor, B. and Stephens, C., 1994. The dark side of the new organizational forms: an editorial essay. *Organization Science*, 5(4): 479–82.

Vlachos, J., 2011. Friskolor i förändring. In L. Hartman (ed.), *Konkurrensens konsekvenser Vad händer med svensk välfärd?* Stockholm: SNS Förlag: 66–110.

Waller, W., 1932. *The Sociology of Teaching*. New York: Wiley.

Webb, R. and Vulliamy, G., 2007. Changing classroom practice at Key Stage 2: the impact of New Labour's national strategies. *Oxford Review of Education*, 33(5): 561–80.

Weber, M., 2003. *The Protestant Ethic and the Spirit of Capitalism*. New York: Courier Dover Publications.

Weick, K. E., 1976. Educational organizations as loosely coupled systems. *Administrative Science Quarterly*, 21(1): 1–19.

Wexler, P., 1992. *Becoming Somebody: toward a social psychology of school*. London: Routledge.

Whitty, G., 2008. Twenty years of progress? English education policy 1988 to the present. *Educational Management Administration and Leadership*, 36(2): 165–84.

Wilby, P., 2008. A year when the personal became political. *New Statesman*, 136(4875–7): 14–15.

Wilcox, B., 2007. *Hansard: House of Lords*. November 14, 696(6), Column 561.

Williams, S. J., 2001. *Emotion and Social Theory: corporeal reflections on the (ir)rational.* London: SAGE.

Willis, P., 2003. Foot soldiers of modernity: The dialectics of cultural consumption and the 21st-century school. *Harvard Educational Review*, 73(3): 390–415.

Young, M., 2011. The return to subjects: a sociological perspective on the UK Coalition government's approach to the 14–19 curriculum. *Curriculum Journal*, 22(2): 265–78.

Yuan, K., Qin, W., Wang, G., Zeng, F., Zhao, L., Yang, X. and Liu, P., 2011. Microstructure abnormalities in adolescents with internet addiction disorder. *PLoS ONE*, 6(6): e20708.

Zavarzadeh, M., 1994. The stupidity that consumption is just as productive as production: In the Shopping Mall of the Post-al Left. *College Literature*, 21(3): 92–114.

Zavarzadeh, M., 2003. The pedagogy of totality. *Journal of Advanced Composition*, 23(1): 1–54.

Zimmer, R., Gill, B., Booker, K., Lavertu, S., Sass, T. R. and Witte, J., 2009. *Charter Schools in Eight States: effects on achievement, attainment, integration, and competition.* Santa Monica, CA: RAND Corporation.

Zuboff, S., 1989. *In the Age of the Smart Machine: the future of work and power.* New York: Basic Books.

Index